FILM MUSIC

VISUAL & PERFORMING ARTS

Film Music

Peter Larsen

REAKTION BOOKS

Published by Reaktion Books Ltd
33 Great Sutton Street
London EC1V 0DX
www.reaktionbooks.co.uk

First published 2005

Printed and bound in Great Britain by CPI Antony Rowe, Chippenham, Wiltshire

British Library Cataloguing in Publication Data
Larsen, Peter
    Film music
    1. Motion picture music – History and criticism
    I. Title
    781.5´42´09
    ISBN-13: 978 1 86189 341 3

Contents

At any rate, music in the theatre is an unsolved problem – for anyone
who happens to regard it as a problem at all.

Béla Balázs, *Der Sichtbare Mensch*, 1924

Introduction

We talk about seeing a film, which is slightly misleading. For we also *hear* a film. There is dialogue on the soundtrack. There are various forms of noise. And there is music. Sometimes we notice the music. At other times we completely forget it because the events and the characters on the screen take up all our attention. Occasionally, the music lingers in our ears after we have returned home from the cinema. In certain cases, we are so enthusiastic about the music that we go out and buy the soundtrack CD.

Film music is part of the film, part of the film experience and part of the cultural context surrounding the film. As simple as that. If, however, we start to think more carefully about what film music is, what it is actually used for, how it functions within the context of the film, and why there is any music in films at all, we quickly notice that things are not quite so simple. Immediately, a whole range of questions arises. These are the subject of this book.

Questions

The first questions have to do with the history of film music. The music we hear in today's cinemas is the latest phase of a long, complicated history. Things used to be very different. There was live music in the cinemas of the silent films; today, the music is part of the film soundtrack. The music for silent films in the 1920s differed from that played at film performances in the late 1890s. After the breakthrough of the sound film, film music was for a long time synonymous with symphonic orchestral music; today, film music can be everything under the sun – orchestral music, electronica, pop, rock – and much more besides.

If one asks about the *when* of film music, this immediately involves questions related to musical functions: *what* was the music used for back then? What is it used for today? What did – and does – music do to the film? Specialist literature has many answers to such questions. What is lacking, however, is a more detailed answer to the question as to *how* film music solved – and solves – its tasks in practice. If one tries to answer this question, a new one immediately poses itself: how does one set about describing and analysing film music? Here there are no standard answers, no established tradition to build on. Analyses of the role of music in specific, individual films are in short supply.

And finally: *why* is there music in films at all? Is there any special reason? Is music necessary for us to gain an optimum film experience – or could one just as well do without it?

Overview

In the following chapters, I discuss such questions, as well as some of the answers available in the literature. My point of departure is the historical questions: I outline the changing roles music has played from the very first films up to the present day, and present a number of analyses of music for specific films. The analyses are meant to illustrate and exemplify the historical presentation: they outline how film music was typically constructed during certain periods of film history. The analyses also have a wider purpose: to demonstrate certain general points of view regarding film music as well as practical procedures that can be the starting point for further analyses.

Film music challenges many commonly held views, about both music and films. And it raises a number of basic questions, for example, about the meaning and significance of music and the relationship between music and emotion – questions that have been on the agenda of music theory since Antiquity. Film music also leads inevitably to questions about the narrative potential of music, a theme that has been a key issue over the past 15–20 years within so-called *new musicology*. Music also forces film researchers and narratologists to take up fundamental concepts for discussion and revision: It problematizes the very idea of what a 'film' is. Where does the boundary go between film as textual *object* and film as *performance*? What is a film narrative? Who is the narrator? What does music narrate? And who 'narrates' the music?

In the historical and analytical chapters, One–Eight, I discuss these and similar theoretical issues. In the two concluding chapters I return to some of the earlier questions, giving them a more overall treatment as well as summarizing the discussions of the functions of film music from the previous chapters.

The music of mainstream films

My ambition has not been to write a world history of film music. What interests me here is the role music plays in the Western world in the average film. For this reason, developments within American films must be centre stage in the presentation, especially in the four chapters that deal with the role of music in sound films. The musical solutions that were established in Hollywood in the early 1930s quickly became the predominant industrial standard throughout our part of the world, and have been so since. And over the past fifty years Hollywood has also been the place where the most important alternatives to this very standard have been developed.

So this is a history of the development of mainstream film music in the Western world and will not deal with distinctive national characteristics – even though a discussion of, for example, certain parts of European film history would probably have introduced more light and shade into the discussion. Nor do I intend to deal with the role of music in earlier or contemporary art films or various kinds of experimental avant-garde films. Nor will I include Sergei Prokofiev, Dimitri Shostakovich, Benjamin Britten and all the many other famous composers who have occasionally written film music. Precisely this type of music, on the other hand, is often dealt with in specialist literature.[1]

Film music, film sound

Film music is part of the film sound, and it is always dependent on the available sound technology. That was true when sound films had their breakthrough in the late 1920s. It is still true today. Over the last few decades rapid developments have taken place within this field. The introduction of the Dolby system in 1977, the subsequent generations of Dolby stereo and surround sound, the possibility of multitrack recording, etc. – all these things have improved the quality of sound in the cinema. And the new technological possibilities have been tried out by the film avant-garde, by directors of mainstream films and by sound-designers and composers alike.

In the course of the book, I will discuss various issues related to the development of sound technology. But film sound is something else and something more – much more – than music. For this reason, it is perhaps necessary to emphasize at this early stage that this is a book about *film music*, not about film sound in general. The study of film sound has been one of the absolute growth industries of film research since the early 1980s. The literature is comprehensive, but I rarely include it in my discussion, mainly because sound researchers do not usually deal with issues related to film music, but also because some of this literature is somewhat proselytizing in nature, presenting sound as the 'last frontier' of film research, which is often done by toning down the importance of music in both the history of film and in the general film soundscape.

Problematics of film music

People who write about film music often claim that precisely this subject is overlooked and neglected in film research.[2] I do not do so, for the claim is incorrect. One only has to take a quick look at Claudia Gorbman's useful annotated bibliography from 1987 to realise that.[3] Even though she has made a critical selection of the existing specialist literature, the list is surprisingly long. It contains approximately a hundred European and American books and articles from the 1930s onwards, and furthermore has references to technical manuals and various reference works. Other bibliographies – both before and after this one – paint the same picture.[4] Film music has been a central theme in film literature ever since the earliest theoretical writings. In addition, since the 1980s, as cinematography increasingly became institutionalized as a university discipline, there has been an explosive growth in academic dissertations and articles in journals about film music.[5] Before one begins to talk about a visual hegemony in film research, one should recall that there actually is considerably more literature about film music than, for example, about the visual aspects of film.

In writing this book, I have relied on many different scholarly works, both old and new. I have learned something from all of them, but this will not prevent me from making critical comments on some of them during the following chapters. In contemporary specialist literature there is a tendency to criticize one's predecessors and to present the history of research as a movement from dark ignorance to radiant revelation.[6] I do not do that. For that is also incorrect. If one penetrates the academic jargon in the more recent presentations, one immediately realizes that there is quite a large amount of continuity in the specialist literature. From the old practical manuals on how to write film music up to the theoretically informed texts of the past few years, there is a basic consensus about what the main issues in the field comprise and how they are to be dealt with.[7]

Film music is an unsolved problem – if one is able at all to see it as such, the old Hungarian film theorist Béla Balázs wrote in 1924.[8] That was then. Much has changed in the course of the eighty or so years that have passed since then. Whether or not film music is still an unsolved problem is open to discussion. But there is at least a problematics of film music, a cohesive set of historical, analytical and theoretical issues that have been – and continue to be – discussed in an ever-increasing specialist literature. My book is conceived as an introduction to this problematics, and as a contribution to the discussion.

I

Silent Films, Talking Music

In every book on the history of films one can read: the silents were never silent. From the very outset, live music was played to moving pictures. Music was always an integral part of showing a film. Film historians never tire of emphasizing this.[1] Here, however, agreement ends. What kind of music was played? How was it played? And why? And how did the audience react?

When it comes to the earliest days of film music, many of these basic questions remain unanswered. First and foremost because the source material is limited. This applies in particular to information about the initial establishment phase of 1895–1910. Even though it is no more than a century ago since the first strips of film were shown, much has been lost, much consigned to oblivion, and much is impossible to reconstruct. The source material of the early history of film music consists of scattered recollections, imaginative anecdotes, cinema programmes, advertisements and newspaper articles. And, as the historian Martin Miller Marks observes: 'What is wanting in all these instances is specific information about actual music – something that will shine in front of the dim backdrop.'[2]

The dim backdrop

From the very outset, music was played – is what they write. But when did this 'outset' begin? And was music actually played? Take, for example, the famous presentation at the Grand Café in Paris on 28 December 1895, when the Lumière brothers showed their films to a wider audience. In a textbook on the history of film music and techniques, Roger Manvell and John Huntley write that the showing of the small strips of

film was accompanied by a piano.[3] But on what do they base this asser-
tion? Contemporary newspapers write practically nothing about the
event and the few articles available do not mention music. In a retrospective account from 1965 the French film historian René Jeanne does mention something about a piano playing a cheerful melody.[4] But if one
reads the text more closely, it is clear that this is something he imagines:
he was not himself present at the Grand Café on that famous December
day in 1895. His own first encounter with the Lumière films took place
a couple of weeks later, in January 1896. In the section of his recollections dealing with this, however, he mentions neither piano nor music.[5]

Other contemporary eye-witnesses react in the same way. In interviews many years later, they talk enthusiastically about the sight of moving pictures, but never mention music. For a while, the rumour circulat-
ed among film historians that someone had found the programme from
the first showing at the Grand Café, and that it mentioned a *pianiste-com-
positeur* by the name of Emile Maraval, who played on a Gaveau piano.[6]
This turned out to be a false trail: in 1991, Italian film historian Gianni
Rondolino demonstrated that the mysterious programme was in actual
fact a poster for a later showing, probably from 1896, maybe even later.
His conclusion was that it is 'highly unlikely that the Lumière brothers'
first showings can have been accompanied by some sort of musical performance in the hall'.[7]

The circumstances surrounding the first Lumière showing in
England on February 1896 are similarly dim. A second-hand account
implies that music – perhaps – was played on the harmonium.[8] When,
a couple of months later, the films were shown in two music halls in
London, they were – perhaps – accompanied by orchestral music.[9] And
in America? The Lumières' projectionist, Félix Mesguish, states in his
memoirs that music was played at the first showings. But it is clear from
the context that the musicians did not start playing until after the performance was over, playing the 'Marseillaise' as a tribute to the French
projectionist.[10]

The Lumière brothers were not the only ones to experiment with
moving pictures at that time. As early as 1893 Edison and his associ-
ates made films that they showed in small peep-shows. In 1896 Edison
bought the rights to the projection system Vitascope, which was
demonstrated in April of the same year in a music hall in New York.
Programmes from the event state that there was an orchestra present
and that overtures, intermission music and a concluding concert were

played, but it is not clear whether the musicians also played during the actual showing of the film.[11]

Spectacular theatre and optical entertainment

In other words, it is difficult to determine whether film historians are correct when claiming that music was played to moving pictures from the very outset. On the other hand, it can be objected that it would be strange for the first films *not* to have been accompanied by music: Edison, Lumière and the other film pioneers chose revue theatres and music halls for their showings, i.e. establishments where songs and music were already on the programme. Films were also shown in penny arcades, where they were accompanied by music played on various forms of mechanical apparatus. And the source material does at least state that musical accompaniment was usual in the years after 1895, when the film strips were shown as spectacular features in mixed programmes at variety theatres, music halls and vaudevilles.

The early film was part of contemporary popular entertainment. It was especially connected to spectacular nineteenth-century forms of theatre. The Swedish film historian Rune Waldekranz points out that the emergence of the film must be understood as part of a general optical orientation that characterized the entertainment industry throughout the century.[12] The 'optical melodrama', a commercial theatre form designed for an urban mass audience, 'functioned in most respects as a cinema film prior to the arrival of the film', as he writes.[13] In the melodrama theatres, the scenic effects were enhanced with the aid of lantern slides, and the action was dramatized by spectacular lighting effects. Music played a pivotal role in these performances. The orchestra 'introduced the main character and his most important fellow actors, illustrated emotions and thoughts at crucial moments, accentuated every change in the action and the play'.[14] In many instances, the dramatic climax of the plays was marked by tableaux or mimed scenes, supported by suitable music.

Alongside this type of spectacular theatre and other popular forms of entertainment based on live performances, many kinds of optical entertainment emerged in the course of the nineteenth century based on the showing of images: shadow plays, diorama, magic lantern shows and, after the invention of photography, shows including photographic devices. In such contexts too, music played an important role. One example is the Frenchman Emile Reynaud's *théâtre optique*, which opened in 1892. Reynaud had, among other things, constructed a device that could project drawings onto a screen and produce relatively complicated movements. These performances, which he called light pantomimes, were a kind of early animated film. The musician Gaston Paulin had composed music for the individual films which, it is said, followed the varying rhythms of the pictures extremely closely.[15]

Many other examples can be given of the connection between music and optical entertainment in the latter half of the nineteenth century, and some that illustrate that films could easily fit into such a context. The English film pioneer Cecil Hepworth, for instance, states in his memoirs that in 1897 he bought a basket of discarded film strips. He had a large collection of slides that he organized into small series with a narrative content. He added some suitable strips of film and toured the provinces with a combined slide and film strip show, accompanied by talks and music. 'Never in my life, either before or since, have I experienced more intense enthusiasm than that produced by these short, primitive films in an audience seeing the film for the first time,' he writes. One of the series that always met with great enthusiasm was 'The Tempest'. It consisted of half a dozen slides and a short film. The first slide showed a calm sea; this was followed by slides of an increasingly stormy sea, culminating in the showing of the film: 'splashing, crashing waves at the entrance to a cave'. Hepworth's sister accompanied all of this on the pianoforte: 'soft, gentle music' to start with, ending in 'wild music'.[16]

From music halls to palaces of distraction

Films began by being short, exotic features in the mixed programmes of the theatres and variety theatres. Gradually, however, the film strips became longer and longer. Films broke out of their traditional framework and eventually became an independent form of entertainment, which gradually became too big for the traditional entertainment venues. The first real cinemas appeared in Europe at the end of the nineteenth century and in the United States at the turn of the twentieth. Many were housed in shop premises and converted theatres, but the first major wave of newly built cinemas started around 1905. Musicians from the traditional entertainment establishments followed the film

across to the new premises, taking with them many of their old musical habits. For example, community singing was normally included in
the performances, just as in the old vaudeville theatres. The lyrics of
the songs were shown as slides on the screen.[17]

To begin with the music was played by a pianist or a small group
of musicians but, as films grew increasingly popular and the audiences
more numerous, the musical framework was also expanded. In the
years after 1910 the cinemas grew larger and larger, and music became
an important stock-in-trade of their marketing.[18] When all the cinemas
in the same town were showing the same films, the individual cinema
manager could use the music to distinguish himself from his competitors. Music was also more generally used to bolster the cinemas' social
reputation. In the early twentieth century a change took place in the
accompaniment towards the lighter end of the classical repertoire.
From then on only the smallest cinemas could get by with a single
pianist. Elsewhere the pianist was accompanied by a violinist and a
drummer, possibly by a small string or wind ensemble. The most
important cinemas established their own large orchestras.

In the 1920s the real expansion took place. Everywhere in the
major cities of Europe and the United States monumental cinemas
were built, and it became obvious that the film had its roots in revues
and vaudevilles, or rather that the film is the modern successor of
nineteenth-century popular entertainment. In the new cinemas films
were mainly part of a larger, mixed performance.[19] A typical performance in a major American city cinema lasted about two and a half
hours. A third of the time went on an opulent stage show. The performance began with the orchestra playing an overture. Works by
Wagner, Liszt, Tchaikovsky, Verdi, etc. were always enthusiastically
received, as long as they were played well enough, said the leading cinema manager of the time, Hungarian-born Erno Rapée. Every cinema
orchestra of a certain size naturally had movements of Tchaikovsky's
symphonies and excerpts from Wagner's operas – 'The Ride of the
Valkyries' and 'Wotan's Farewell', for example – on their repertoire.[20]
After the 'classical' overture there was a stage show lasting anything
up to 30 minutes, with various singers, dancers and artistes. Then the
cinema newsreel, a couple of short films and finally the main film – a
fiction film lasting up to 80 minutes.

The performances in the largest cinemas were lavish shows, with
music as an integral part. 'In this country we are supreme in utilizing

music in the motion picture theatre,' writes the American cinema manager and composer Hugo Riesenfeld in 1926.[21] But he adds that European cinemas are eager to learn. 'They are engaging our conductors to go over and take charge of presentations in their theatres.' Erno Rapée is an example of this: after his success as manager of New York's most important cinema orchestras, he travelled to Europe, where he spent the years 1924–6 as guest conductor.

And the Europeans were eager to learn. Cinemas were built and music was played, inspired by the American models. The many new cinemas in Berlin in the 1920s were a recurrent theme in heated discussions about the 'Americanization' of Germany. To call all these new 'optical fairylands' cinemas would be disrespectful, Siegfried Kracauer writes in a contemporary article. They are palaces of distraction. And the sumptuous buildings are a fitting setting for the large, complex performances: 'Gone is the time when films were allowed to run one after another each with a corresponding musical accompaniment.' Out of the pupa of the cinema 'a glittering, revue-like creature' has crawled: the '*Gesamtkunstwerk of effects*'.[22]

In the film palaces people of the modern metropolis cultivate 'the cult of distraction', Kracauer writes. And the film theoretician Rudolf Arnheim says that it was music in particular that was treated 'as a kind of cult' during the last years of the silent film. The conductors at the large cinema theatres 'were just as famous as the directors of the films which they "illustrated"', and the newspapers employed music critics 'who examined pan-faced whether the accompaniment had fitted the film or not'.[23]

Music was an important part of the total performance as well as an important contribution to the film experience. This applied not only to the major cities and not only to the largest cinemas. 'Wherever there is a cinema of any size, there is now a good orchestra', Hugo Riesenfeld writes in 1926. He estimates that there are at that time 18,000 cinemas in America, and concludes by saying that the cinema musician has become 'a commercial asset'.

The sound of films before sound films

In one of the first theoretically inclined books about film music, the German author Kurt London writes: 'the beginnings of the film were at the same time the beginnings of the soundfilm.'[24] This is not so paradoxical as it might seem at first glance. For in a certain sense the earliest silent films had at their disposal all the sound sources we normally associate with modern sound films.

The silent film 'talked'. In many instances the lines of the characters in the film were read out by people behind the screen. There were troupes of actors who specialized in synchronized recitation, and the demand was sufficient for a drama academy to be established in New York that trained actors for this particular function.[25] It was more usual, however, for there to be a 'narrator' in front of the screen who regularly explained what was going on.[26] In many cases the narrator also 'acted' the characters in the film and said their lines with a distorted voice. In Japan this function was developed into an independent art form: the *benshi* interpreted the films and said the dialogue, accompanied by traditional music. Intertitles were kept to a minimum to allow the *benshi* an opportunity to display his skills. The *benshi*s were often more popular than the film actors, and their strong position explains why the silent film survived in Japan many years after other countries had switched to sound.[27]

The silent film also had other types of sound. In many cinemas *bruiteurs*, 'noisemen', were employed, people who provided the film with sound-effects from an arsenal of apparatus and instruments of the same kind as was later used for radio drama. In the largest cinemas sound machines were installed. The English Allefex from 1912 could produce 50 different sound-effects – the sound of running water, for example, bird song, storms, dog barks. And in addition to all this there was the music. In some cases, various mechanical devices were played – gramophone, pianola, mechanical piano, steam organ or the Orchestrion, the jukebox of the time. First and foremost, though, there was live music in every conceivable shape or form, from the lone pianist and the few musicians of the earliest years of the silent film to the large symphony orchestras of the 1920s.

In 1925 Erno Rapée tells contemporary cinema owners how to compose an orchestra to match the available finances: piano, violin and cello are a minimum. If more musicians can be afforded, one ought to start with an extra violin and then add a flute, cornet, drums, trombone, clarinet and another violin – in that order. The orchestra can subsequently be expanded in two directions, with the addition of either strings or brass and wind instruments, depending on what type of music the cinema wishes to emphasize, although 'the strings can be used in a more diversified way and will always constitute the nucleus of any orchestra', Rapée writes.[28] Like many of the cinema conductors of his time, he had a solid foundation in classical music. After having worked as an opera conductor in Europe he settled in the United States and in 1917 was appointed conductor at the Rialto Theater, the first American cinema to have its own symphony orchestra. He later worked at the Rivoli and Capitol as well as the Fox Theater in Philadelphia. In his advice to the cinema owners he mentions that he had 39 musicians at his disposal at the Rivoli and 70 at the Capitol. At the opening of the new Roxy Theater in 1927 he conducted an orchestra of 110 musicians.

Appearances of popular singers were a regular feature of the cinema programme, but singing was also occasionally used as an accompaniment to the actual film, for example in connection with screen versions of operas and operettas. Singer and chorus from two of Berlin's opera houses were used at the premiere of a version of Wagner's *Lohengrin* in 1916.[29] Erno Rapée recalls that he once allowed a mixed choir to sing the funeral march from *Madame Sans Gêne* during a highly emotional death scene. 'The effect was almost uncanny,' he remarks.[30]

Two types of sound, two types of music

So the silent film had speech, 'natural sound' and music at its disposal. But the reason why the term sound film is never used in this context is of course that these sounds were 'external' to 'the film itself'. They were produced on the spot, inside the cinema, while the film was a series of 'preserved' moving pictures, possibly supplemented by intertitles. The music was played *live* there and then; the images were 'recorded' – the characters and events shown were 'registered' in another space and time. And while the conserved images did not change from one showing to the next, the music was always variable. Even if the musicians played the same music at each performance, there were always slight differences from the previous performances. It was not until the late 1920s that the technological breakthrough came that made it possible to conserve music and all other sounds on the same material as the images. With the introduction of sound films, all film sounds became 'internal' phenomena.

If we are to describe the relation between live sounds and conserved images on the screen, the term *diegesis* ought perhaps to be introduced. It is used in modern film theory as a term for the film's *story world* – the 'world' in which the fictive events are enacted. The crucial question then is how we as spectators imagine the positioning of the sounds in relation to this world, whether they are a part of it or outside it, commenting on it. In the former case we speak of *diegetic* sound, in the latter of *non-diegetic* sound.[31]

One could perhaps think that the sound of the silent film was non-diegetic: the various sounds were quite literally produced outside the world of the film narrative. But the 'external' nature of the sounds is a matter of a practical and technical nature, something that does not have any consequences for how they actually function and are experienced by the spectator in the context of the film narrative. When the films were shown in the cinema the sounds had the same basic functions as later in sound films. The silent film, for example, had both diegetic speech (actors who stood behind the screen and said the lines of the fictive characters) and non-diegetic speech (the 'narrator' who stood in front of the screen and interpreted the events). The sound-effects of the noisemen created an illusion of diegetic sound. And even if the film music mainly functioned as a non-diegetic commentary on the screen events, it could also be used for diegetic purposes, as when the pictures showed a scene from a ball and the cinema orchestra accompanied with a waltz that 'fitted' the characters dancing.

The old pianist

Although the silent film had many types of sound at its disposal, it was always live music that was the central source of sound during the performances. But what sort of music? And how was it played? In his *Theory of Film* (1960), Siegfried Kracauer tells a melancholy little story about the cinema of his youth where the music 'followed an unpredictable course of its own'. It was played by an alcoholic pianist who sat there lost in his own thoughts, never looking up at the screen.

> Sometimes, perhaps under the spell of a pleasant intoxication, he improvised freely, as if prompted by a desire to express the vague memories and ever-changing moods which the alcohol stirred in him; on other occasions he was in such a stupor that he played a few popular melodies over and over again, mechanically adorning them with glittering runs and quavers. So it was by no means

uncommon that gay tunes would sound when, in a film I watched, the indignant Count turned his adulterous wife out of the house, and that a funeral march would accompany the blue-tinted scene of their ultimate reconciliation.[32]

The cinema pianist who plays what he feels like, without a thought for what is happening on the screen, is a recurring theme in literature about the music of the silent film.[33] But can it really be true that there was no connection between music and film? We know that the music of the spectacular melodramas and the various forms of optical entertainment were carefully coordinated with the screen images. Is it not more reasonable to expect that musicians who had been trained to follow a scenic sequence with 'suitable music' would continue to do so when they eventually left the theatre and took jobs in the cinemas?

Because of the nature of the source material, it is difficult to answer that question. But Martin Miller Marks has pointed out that the oldest preserved sheet music would suggest that the early films were accompanied by 'suitable music'.[34] His first example is a collection of pieces of music that were played in connection with showings of small strips of film shot with the German Max Skladanowsky's Bioscope camera. The films showed fragments of variety numbers and were used as a feature of the entertainment programme at the Wintergarten in Berlin, from 1 November 1895 until the end of the year, i.e. almost two months before the Lumière showing in Paris. The following year Max Skladanowsky toured with his pictures in the Netherlands and Scandinavia.[35] The music used on these occasions was written for strings plus eight woodwind and eight brass. It consisted of an introduction, fifteen numbered pieces and a finale. About half of the numbers had been specially written for the occasion by an unknown composer. There are many unresolved issues relating to this music and how it was used, but probably each of Skladanowsky's small strips of film was accompanied by a 'suitable' piece, e.g. *Kamarinskaya*, Glinka's fantasy based on two Russian songs, was presumably played as an accompaniment to a 'Russian dance' performed by 'the three Tcherpanov brothers'. And if this is correct we can confirm that the film historians – despite all uncertainty and misunderstandings – are right: there is at least one example of music having been played to moving pictures 'from the very outset'.

Miller Marks's second example is *L'Assassinat du Duc de Guise* from 1908, a French film that was to convince the pillars of society that the new medium could be used for something else and more than mere popular entertainment. In accordance with the high ambitions of the promoter Henri Lavédan this first *film d'art* was accompanied by music written by the well-known French composer Camille Saint-Saëns. While Skladanowsky's music is a series of small, independent pieces intended for accompanying a sequence of independent variety numbers, Saint-Saëns's music is a more traditional composition, a thematically coherent suite comprising an introduction and five movements that corresponds to the division of the film into acts or tableaux. The music in the individual sections is closely coordinated with the events on the screen.

Unsuitable music

The music of Skladanowsky and Saint-Saëns demonstrates, according to Marks, 'that film music of the earliest years encompassed the same broad range of possibilities encountered in dramatic music before and after'.[36] But it is an open question whether it is possible to draw such far-reaching conclusions. Two examples with an interval of thirteen years between them are hardly a sufficient point of departure for gen-eralizations. Furthermore, these two examples were probably quite atypical, compared to the music that was usually played at cinemas during the establishment period: the Skladanowsky music was written for a major promotion campaign – it was to be played at one of the very first presentations of moving pictures ever, and Saint-Saëns's music was a commissioned piece of work, written for a highbrow prestige project.

It is difficult, moreover, to ignore the fact that a number of con-temporary sources support the prevalent idea of a lack of coordination between film and music. As late as 1909, a time when musicians and cinema owners had had fifteen years to get used to the situation, a journalist for the New York *Daily Mirror* writes: 'Bad judgment in the selection of music may ruin an exhibition as much as a good pro-gramme may help it.' He has recently witnessed a touching scene with a grieving widower performed to the tune of 'No Wedding Bells For Me', a popular song about the joys of a bachelor life with the refrain: 'Gee whiz! I'm glad I'm free! No wedding bells for me!'[37]

The American trade journal *Moving Picture World*, published from 1907 onwards, started a special column about film music in 1909, 'Music for the Picture', conducting among other things a campaign for better film music. On 3 July 1909 the leader writer urges cinema owners of the time to take more notice of the music. In his opinion half the pianists he has heard over the past six months ought to have been given the sack.[38] On 28 February 1910 an experienced film musician praises the journal for its efforts, adding that if the pianists actually tried to 'conform their music to the picture', the cinemas would be able to count on much larger audiences.[39]

Rick Altman, who has analysed a number of American trade journals from the period 1905–29, argues that a gradual shift takes place as regards the relation between film and music around 1907. Early in the century, 'film' is very much a heterogeneous phenomenon, and there is not one but many kinds of musical practice, depending on what kind of film one is dealing with. It is not until after 1907 that a common professional standard develops as to how films are to be accompanied musically. According to Altman, this system is up and running in 1912.[40] But when Hugo Riesenfeld takes stock of the American film music situation in 1926, he mentions that ten to twelve years earlier it was perfectly possible to hear a lone pianist who 'drummed mechanically on a tuneless instrument', playing the same worn-out tunes 'whether the screen showed a tender romance or the villain getting his just reward'. Erno Rapée recalls once having heard Dvořák's *Largo* played 'with frightful tuning and wrong tempo' as an accompaniment to a cinema newsreel showing 'dancing cannibals, Italian Army, Streets of New York, etc.' And European writers can report similar experiences. The German film pioneer Oskar Messter, for example, writes that film music as late as 1913 was quite mediocre, even in major cinemas; the cinema orchestras played 'pieces of music and fantasies that on the whole did not reflect the content of the film'.[41]

These and many similar examples seem to indicate that Marks is optimistic when he wishes to use Skladanowsky's music and the Saint-Saëns composition as 'strong evidence' that many films from the very outset were accompanied by 'suitable music'.[42] The many counter-examples would seem to indicate that when it comes to the relation between film and music the establishment phase was an unresolved period where different tendencies clashed. It is probably more reasonable to imagine the situation as a kind of scale, with major prestige projects and well-integrated music at the one end and more amateur, uncoordinated accompaniments at the other.

Compilation, composition and narrative integration

No matter how one interprets Marks's examples, they do at least show that efforts were being made to coordinate music and film in the early period of the silent film, and that these efforts – something he himself points out – both relied on older traditions of stage music and pointed forwards to what were going to be the main tendencies in the consolidation phase of the silent film.

When it comes to the relation to older traditions, the Skladanowsky music is clearly based on the pattern from nineteenth-century varieties and music halls, while the Saint-Saëns music is a thematically coherent composition, related to stage music of the type that could be heard in theatres as an accompaniment to ballets, pantomimes or melodramas.[43] Prospectively the two examples of music illustrate a division that will characterize music in the second phase of the silent film: the Skladanowsky music is a *compilation*, a musical collage of material that has been collected together from various sources, while the Saint-Saëns music is an *original composition*, written for one particular film.

Film historians have for many years used the terms *attraction* and *narrative integration* to mark the difference between the two main phases of the silent film period. During the establishment phase the actual showing of the moving pictures was the attraction of the performance, and the films that were shown themselves consisted of attractions. They were constructed according to the pattern of varieties and vaudevilles as series of spectacular, independent 'numbers' and optical tricks. In the years after 1910 films become increasingly organized, with the aim of telling stories; the individual sections are integrated into the fiction; the films close in around themselves and become self-sufficient narrative wholes.[44]

Marks suggests that his two musical examples also illustrate this difference: the Skladanowsky music has the nature of an attraction and the Saint-Saëns composition can be seen as an early example of music that is intended to be part of the narrative integration strategy. But no matter how far the music is subordinate to the narrative in the course of the second phase of the silent film period, it nevertheless retains its independent nature. The large glamorous orchestras of the cinema palaces naturally accompanied and supported the narratives of the films but that they could become the object of cult-like worship, as

Arnheim remarks,[45] was because they were *an attraction in themselves* – in the same way as the pianist and the community singing in the little provincial cinema was. The German sociologist Emilie Altenloh, who carried out the world's first film-sociological study, writes in her report from 1914 that it is not the film but the music that is the 'main attraction' for the female spectators.[46]

The music of the silent films is not film music in the modern sense – it is *cinema music*: an external addition to the moving pictures, part of the total *performance* more than part of the film and its narrative.[47] The independence of the music in the performance and its 'external nature' in relation to the film is also evident at the practical level, in that the film producers and distributors did not have control over what music was played in the various cinemas. In some cases attempts were made to control the choice of music by, for example, sending gramophone records along with the films. But throughout the silent film period it was mainly the cinema owners who were responsible for the choice of music. In other words it was in principle the local cinema musicians who decided what type of music was to be played with the individual film, and how. In the years around 1910 and subsequently this clearly becomes a problem. When the film develops into a narrative medium, the music must contribute to the narrative integration. This is no simple matter.

Musical guidance

Even if attempts are made to avoid cheerful music during burial scenes, etc., the musical material and coordination with the picture must of necessity differ from one cinema to the next. The individual conductor's interpretation of the film narrative is usually highly personal, Emilie Altenloh writes in 1914: 'One conductor will announce an amorous scene with a flourish, the next conductor will prepare for this climax using gentle melodies.'[48] And when the author of an American manual of 1913 advises pianists at provincial cinemas to change their repertoire from one week to the next so that the audience does not get bored, this is a direct indication that the music followed the cinemas, not the films – that, in other words, the music was an independent attraction intended to entertain the audience rather than to support the film narrative.[49] That this is how it was becomes even clearer during the heyday of the cinema orchestras in the 1920s. It will be 'the leader's discretion as to the requirements of the theatre if it needs stringy or brassy type of music', Erno Rapée writes.[50] It is not the nature of the film but of the theatre that determines the nature of the music.

Under the technical conditions it was practically impossible to shift responsibility for the selection of music back onto the film producers themselves. But an attempt could at least be made to control the cinema musicians, to try and influence their choice of music. In 1909 the Edison company began to print *musical suggestion sheets* that were distributed along with the films. From 1910 these were referred to as *cue sheets* – their 'cues' marked where in the film a particular piece of music is to be played. Gradually it became normal for all major film companies to send cue sheets along with their films, and this practice continued throughout the rest of the silent film period.

Initially it was presumably so-so when it came to narrative coordination. Bert Ennis, who wrote cue sheets for the Edison company during the first years, mentions that he normally did not see the films at all, just read the press agents' summary of the plot and then wrote cues with the aid of a good memory plus catalogues from the major music publishing companies in New York's Tin Pan Alley.[51] Ennis had a background in this part of the music industry, so it was mainly popular tunes of the time that he suggested to accompany the films. From time to time, however, he also indicated various well-known pieces from the classical repertoire, such chestnuts as *Träumerei* or the Pilgrims' chorus from *Tannhäuser*, for example – just to show a little 'class', as he put it.

An early cue sheet

The suggestion by the Edison company for the *Frankenstein* film of 1910 can serve as an example of the cue sheets of the first years.[52] This short film was a free adaptation of Mary Shelley's famous novel. According to the press material, 'all the really rather repellent situations' had been removed and the film had concentrated on 'the mysterious and psychological problems to be found in this strange account'.[53] On the sheet there are fourteen cues with corresponding musical suggestions. The cues refer to obvious changes in the action. The basic pattern is *until–afterwards*: when the film commences, 'Then You'll Remember Me' is to be played *andante*. This continues *until* the scene in Frankenstein's laboratory; *afterwards*, 'Melody in F' is to be played – first *moderato* until the monster is created, afterwards *increasingly agitato*, etc.

The music suggestions are barely outlined – the pianist himself must improvise the transition from '*moderato*' to 'increasingly *agitato*' after Frankenstein has created the monster. This is typical of the cue sheets of the early period: in many instances, it was thought sufficient to indicate a *tempo* (*agitato, moderato*, etc.) or a mood (gloomy, cheerful, etc.) and the musicians could either improvise from then on or themselves find some piece of music that could 'fit'. The actual music suggestions on the Frankenstein sheet include nineteenth-century opera with the Brides' chorus from Wagner's *Lohengrin* – to be played when the 'wedding guests leave' – and Carl Maria von Weber's *Der Freischütz*. Weber's music apparently functions as a sort of leitmotif: the pianist is requested to play 'dramatic music' from *Der Freischütz* every time the monster appears in the film. The fact that the suggestions are unspecified implies that the opera was considered so well known that a pianist would immediately understand what 'dramatic music' was involved. The rest of the musical references have mainly been taken from lighter contemporary repertoires. The English folk song 'Annie Laurie' is played when 'the maid enters with the tea pot'. The introduction's 'Then You'll Remember Me' comes from Michael Balfe's popular opera *The Bohemian Girl* (1843) and, like Anton Rubinstein's 'Melody in F', was a standard salon piece around 1900.

Cue sheets gradually become an important element in film company marketing to cinema owners. When it comes to the choice of music the basic pattern is the same as in the first examples: known themes from the classical nineteenth-century repertoires are mixed with salon pieces and contemporary popular tunes. The sheets themselves, however, gradually become more sophisticated and the music suggested increasingly differentiated. A cue sheet for the film *The Cat and the Canary* (1927) is a 'sumptuous eight-page brochure with coloured front cover', writes Martin Miller Marks, mentioning that the brochure contains 66 cues, and that the pieces of music have been taken from works by 20 composers. The brochure also contains detailed descriptions of recurring themes and suggestions as to how the music ought to be played.[54] In the later part of the silent film period cue sheets also contained suggestions to the operators concerning the performance speed of the film. The picture rhythm could change from sequence to sequence – a love scene could be slowed down to 14 pictures a second, while an action scene could be speeded up to over 24 pictures a second.[55]

Anthologies and manuals

The film companies tried to control and coordinate the music via increasingly detailed cue sheets, but there was of course no guarantee that their advice would be taken. It could be that the musicians did not know the music that was suggested, that they did not have it, or that the pieces were too difficult. Some of these problems were gradually resolved by the publication of *anthologies*, collections of pieces of music that could fit typical situations in films of the time. The anthologies followed the main tendencies of the early cue sheets. The repertoire consisted of popular melodies mixed with diverse classical favourites, but newly composed *mood music* was also printed, often composed on the basis of easily recognizable templates, sometimes obvious plagiarisms of classical models. The pieces were classified and organized according to how they could function in relation to typical film scenes, mainly according to *mood* and *tempo*, as in the cue sheets.

One of the earliest American examples of this is the *Sam Fox Moving Picture Music* series.[56] The first volume was published in 1913 and comprised 25 pieces of piano music. The composer's name was John Stepan Zamecnik, a qualified violinist, who had studied under Anton Dvorák in Prague and had been conductor of the Pittsburgh Symphony Orchestra before accepting a post as musical leader of a vaudeville theatre that later became a cinema. The pieces he wrote for the Fox series are short and simple, designed so that they can be played by untrained pianists. The titles indicate in cue-like style what type of film scenes they could be used for:

Festival March	Cowboy Music
Indian Music	Grotesque or Clown Music
Oriental Veil Dance	Mysterioso-Burglar Music
Chinese Music	Hurry Music (for struggles)
Oriental Music	Hurry Music (for duels)
Mexican or Spanish Music	Hurry Music
Funeral March	Hurry Music (for mob or fire scenes)
Death Scene	Storm Scene
Church Music	Sailor Music

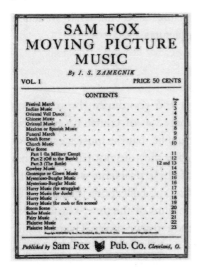 

1.1 The first volume of *Sam Fox Moving Picture Music* (1913)

War Scene   Fairy Music
   Part 1 (In Military Camp)   Plaintive Music
   Part 2 (Off to the Battle) Plaintive Music
   Part 3 (The Battle)

The following year, the Remick Press published a collection of piano pieces: *Remick Folio of Moving Picture Music*, 'over 100 Dramatic, Descriptive, and Characteristic Numbers Suitable For Any Theatrical Performance or Exhibition Requiring Incidental Music', composed by J. Bodewalt Lampe. In the years that followed three new volumes of the *Sam Fox* series appeared, and Zamecnik also wrote more advanced music for such series as *Sam Fox Photoplay Music* and *Sam Fox Cinema Impressions*.

The most important of the American anthologies is Erno Rapée's *Motion Picture Moods for Pianists and Organists* from 1924.[57] It contains about 700 pieces of music, arranged according to 52 mood categories. In the margin of each page there is a list of page references to the 52 main sections, so that the pianist could quickly find the next piece when the action of the film called for it. The anthology mainly contained music by classical composers, but also had a number of newly composed pieces specially written for films. The following year Erno Rapée published his *Encyclopaedia of Music for Pictures*, with cues arranged in alphabetical order.[58] Under each cue are the titles of a number of suitable pieces of music, with references to composers and publishers. The encyclopaedia also contained an article on how one can operate a cinema and conduct a cinema orchestra. Rapée has simple, practical solutions to most problems: if the film breaks, keep on playing; if a fire breaks out in the machine room, turn on the lights in the auditorium and play a popular tune everyone can sing to, etc.

The European counterpart to Rapée's *Motion Picture Moods* was the German anthology *Kinobibliothek*, a ten-volume series published by the Italian composer Giuseppe Becce from 1919 to 1929. Some of the pieces were available on gramophone records for musicians who were unable to read music. The series had a wide circulation. *Kinobibliothek* was shortened in common parlance to *Kinothek* – a word that in the European context eventually came to be used for the film music anthology genre of the time. Becce also published *Allgemeines Handbuch der Film-Musik* (1927), a two-volume work in collaboration with the composer and film-writer Hans Erdmann.[59] In this manual the authors summarize the musical experiences of the silent film period and in volume two include a thematic register of mood music. This register was highly systematized, based on an intricate classification system, with detailed subdivisions and cross-references. 'Dramatic expression', for example, was divided into 'Tension' and 'Climax'; 'Tension' was then divided into 'Misterioso' and 'Agitato', etc. Under 'Tension – Agitato' one could find references to music that suited 'Pursuit, flight, making haste. Fight. Heroic battle. Confusion, unrest, horror. Restless crowds: tumult. Restless nature: storms, fire'.[60]

During the 1920s a comprehensive array of manuals on film music was thus built up, ranging from large, thematically organized collections of music, such as Rapée's *Moods*, to more modest instruction books on how to accompany films. In addition many cinemas built up their own collections of music. An orchestra leader employed by a major cinema with a well-equipped library would have thousands of pieces of music at his disposal and would be able to find functional music for every occasion. The music collections of cinemas in major cities were enormous; some had orchestral parts for over 25,000 pieces of music.[61]

Custom-made compilations

Hugo Riesenfeld, who had experience both of composing and compiling music for film performances, writes in the overview from 1926 that a musical leader who is to compile a new programme of music every week has to have an almost unlimited supply of music. In the same context he explains how an orchestra leader typically works in planning the music for a film showing:

> In preparing the music for a film, the director first has the picture run off while he makes notes. He then consults his library for selections which he believes will produce the proper atmosphere. With these before him he again calls for a running off of the film, and working at a piano, he tries out the music he has selected. Now and then he presses a button which notifies the projectionist to stop the machine while he looks for a different number or makes further notes. After the music is assembled and timed to the film, it is turned over to copyists who prepare a complete score for the musicians. Usually three or four days are devoted to rehearsals.
>
> Very often, if the arranger cannot find satisfactory music for a certain bit of action, he is obliged to compose some himself.[62]

Riesenfeld concludes that this work calls for such great musical skills that only the major theatres can afford it. 'It cannot be expected that the musical head of a theatre in a small town will be able to write as good a score as an expert employed by a metropolitan theatre.' This points directly at what was the main problem of film music: that it was not a common institutional practice, that the music altered according to the size and geographical location of the theatre and, of course, that the music was dependent on chance variation as regards the talent and skills of the musicians. If one wished to control the music it was not enough to send out cue sheets or to rely on the music library and musical imaginativeness of the music director.

A solution to some of these problems could be for the film companies themselves to hire professional people to do the work – to collect suitable pieces of music and/or compose new music – and that a score could be published to follow the individual film. But considering the fact that most productions of the period were entertainment films with a relatively short distribution time, this was no obvious economic solution, and it was only used in connection with major productions. The typical example is the music for *The Birth of a Nation* (1915), D. W. Griffith's epic about the American Civil War. It has been claimed that Griffith took part in the musical planning and that he himself wrote some of the music. It is difficult to judge how much of this is true, but it is clear at any rate that he had a strong wish for the music to be an integral part of the film narrative. It was composer and conductor Joseph Carl Breil who had the responsibility for realizing Griffith's musical expectations.

For a film of this vast scope correspondingly magnificent music had to be played: orchestral music, symphonic music. Breil solved this by using a mixture of compilation and composition. He borrowed and adapted a number of pieces from the central orchestral repertoire of the nineteenth century, including excerpts from Weber's *Der Freischütz* and Bellini's *Norma*, from Beethoven's 'Pastoral' symphony, Tchaikovsky's *1812 Overture* and Grieg's *Peer Gynt Suite*. He mixed these fragments with traditional popular melodies. Wagner's 'Ride of the Valkyries', for example, is played when the Ku Klux Klan ride out, replaced by 'Dixie' when the victory over the black rebels is celebrated. Breil furthermore wrote a whole series of new themes that were used as leitmotifs. This resulted in a long, coherent orchestral score that is coordinated with the action of the film with the aid of more than 200 cues. At the premiere of the film and during the following tour the music was played by orchestras of more than 70 musicians. At later performances copies of the score were distributed, along with selections of orchestral parts designed for various types of orchestra.

Custom-made compositions

Most of Griffith's films after *Birth of a Nation* are provided with scores. But this practice did not become widespread. Scores with music compiled for particular films continued to be something mainly done in connection with large prestige productions.

Camille Saint-Saëns was early in the field with the music for *L'Assassinat du Duc de Guise* (1908). In the last part of the silent film period more films are produced that have all the music specially composed for the occasion, but when Hugo Riesenfeld writes his overview in 1926 the American examples can be counted on one hand. The field is too limited to have any appeal for composers, he writes. Once again it is the short life-span of the films that set the limits – for the composers as well as for the film companies. Specially composed music, like specially compiled film music, is mainly reserved for major productions or productions for very special occasions. Early American examples are Mortimer Wheeler's music for three spectacular adventure films with the popular Douglas Fairbanks in the title role: *The Thief of Bagdad* (1924), *Don Q, Son of Zorro* (1925) and *The Black Pirate* (1926). Zamecnik, Rapée and Riesenfeld all composed music for Hollywood productions. During his stay in Europe Rapée also wrote music for some of the period's most important German silent films: Ewald Dupont's *Varieté* (1925) and Friedrich Murnau's *Faust* (1926).

Many of the most interesting examples of specially composed music come from Europe. Saint-Saëns was not the only well-known composer of the time who was ensnared by films. His fellow-countrymen Arthur Honegger and Darius Milhaud both wrote film music – Honegger for Abel Gance's *La roue* (1922) and *Napoléon* (1927), Milhaud for Marcel L'Herbier's *L'inhumaine* (1924). In Germany Paul Hindemith wrote music for Arnold Fanck's documentary *Im Kampf mit dem Berg* (1921). Richard Strauss adapted his own music when *Der Rosenkavalier* was made into a film in 1925. He also wrote some new music, and himself conducted the orchestra during the premiere performance in the Dresden Opera House, for part of the time, at any rate. According to Kurt London he was unable to get the orchestra to follow the film and finally had to hand over the baton to a 'proper' film conductor.[63]

Becce and Erdmann, authors of the German *Handbuch*, not only wrote compilations but also original scores, including scores for two of Murnau's films, Erdmann for *Nosferatu* (1921–2), Becce for *Der letzte Mann* (1924). The main example from Soviet films is *The Battleship Potemkin* (1925), which Sergei Eisenstein made at the request of the Soviet Government in memory of the unsuccessful Russian revolution of 1905. At showings abroad *Potemkin* was accompanied by specially composed music by the German composer Edmund Meisel. Eisenstein continued his collaboration with Meisel in *October* (1927), another commissioned film, this time in memory of the October revolution in 1917. Towards the end of the period Dimitri Shostakovich wrote music for Kozintsev and Trauberg's *The New Babylon* (1929).

Music was also organized for contemporary experimental films. Showings of Luis Buñuel's *Un chien andalou* (1928), for example, were accompanied by tango music and excerpts from Wagner operas on gramophone records, while two other important French avant-garde films, René Clair's *Entr'acte* and Ferdinand Léger's *Ballet mécanique*, both 1924, were shown to specially composed music by Erik Satie and George Antheil respectively. In Germany Hindemith composed music for a mechanical organ to accompany a trick film and Meisel provided the music for Walter Ruttman's experimental urban documentary *Berlin – Die Sinfonie der Großstadt* (1927). The score stated that musicians equipped with sirens, rattles and the like were to be spread out around the cinema so as to give the spectators a sound experience that corresponded to the pictures of the metropolis on the screen.

Gottfried Huppertz, who wrote the music for Fritz Lang's national-romantic epic *Die Niebelungen* (1924), was later given the assignment of composing the music for Lang's science fiction film *Metropolis* (1927), the most expensive and most ambitious European film of the entire silent film period.

In chapter Three I will discuss the music for *Metropolis* and use it to demonstrate a number of the characteristic features of music for silent films. But first a few more general considerations in the analysis of film music must be discussed.

2

Analysing Film Music

Analysing films is something that requires learning by doing: by watching and writing about films for oneself, and, equally important, by reading and learning from analyses that other people have written. However, when it comes to the analysis of the role of music, little help is at hand in the available literature. Books and articles have been written about the history of film music and its theory. But actual, thorough, analyses of the function of the music in particular films are rare. Most of the examples take the form of brief, illustrative features in presentations that are theoretical or historical in their orientation. However, even though no real tradition has been developed within this field, one is not left completely high and dry when seeking to describe and analyse the music of a given film. It is possible, for example, to consider how analysis is carried out more generally – in film studies as well as in musicology.

Form and meaning

Towards the end of David Bordwell and Kristin Thompson's textbook *Film Art* is a chapter with examples of various analyses of films. The authors begin by outlining how Howard Hawks's classic screwball comedy *His Girl Friday* (1940) could be analysed. The most striking impression gained from this film is *speed*, they write, suggesting a reduction in tempo, in terms of analysis: 'By breaking the film into parts and seeing how the parts relate to one another logically, temporally, and spatially, we can suggest how classical narrative form and specific film techniques are used to create this whirlwind experience.'[1] There are a number of important points concerning the analysis of films in this brief remark:

• A film analysis always has a particular *interest* as its point of departure: one analyses because one wants to know something – for example, what creates the impression of 'speed' in *His Girl Friday*. In other words there are many kinds of film analysis, depending on the analyst's point of departure.

• The basic interest will in many cases have to do with understanding, explaining and exploring a particular experience of the film. In Bordwell and Thompson's example it has to do with understanding how we as spectators get to *experience His Girl Friday* as a tremendously 'fast' film.

• Even though film analyses must of necessity differ from each other, since they are trying to answer issues that are essentially different, they will very often adopt the same procedure. Most begin with some form of subdivision – or *segmentation* – of the film. The film is broken down into sections and then their relation to the totality is examined.

To analyse is, then, to ask questions and to attempt to find answers, and the answers are normally found by segmenting what is being analysed. This segmentation can, for example, simply consist in taking an overview of the course of events; in other cases it may prove necessary to account for each individual shot in a film sequence. How the segmentation is carried out in practice depends on what the underlying interest of the analysis is. For the same reason it is difficult to say anything general about the results of the analyses. It can, however, be pointed out that an analytical segmentation often demonstrates that the narrative progression of the film is based on underlying *formal* patterns of *similarities and differences*.

'Repetition is basic to our understanding any film,' Bordwell and Thompson write.[2] Characters and places turn up again and again, bits of dialogue are repeated, images and camera positions are repeated. In certain cases we may be dealing with exact repetitions, though normally it is a question of more general similarities and parallels, of major or minor alterations – for *difference* and *variation* are also basic principles in the construction of a film. Usually there is a certain logic or pattern in the way in which the interaction between similarities and differences develops in the course of the film. The underlying logic of development is most obvious if one considers the macro-level of the narrative and compares the beginning with the ending.[3] Seen from a very general point of view most films tell a story about an initially negative situation which, by virtue of a succession of events, gradually changes until a positive final situation is attained.

On the basis of a knowledge of genre, etc., we as spectators will expect the film we are watching to follow a particular logic of development. So while we are watching the film we will always have *expectations* as to how it will *continue*. Films require 'that the audience participate actively in the ongoing process by making hypotheses about "what will happen next" and readjusting expectations accordingly and by adapting their expectations in accordance with this', Bordwell and Thompson write, emphasizing that our involvement in works of art depends to a great extent on such expectations.[4] The point of course is that films and other works of fiction never take a direct route to their goal; they constantly refute our expectations and force us to change our hypotheses as to 'what will happen next', and often it is not the goal at all but the detour that is the most important thing. Film analysis can help us understand how these changes and detours come about, and how they function.

When we analyse a film in this way, we are, as is apparent, mainly interested in formal and structural relations. We investigate how a given film is constructed so as, ultimately, to understand why it is experienced in a particular way. In many connections, however, we do not only discuss formal and structural issues; we cannot avoid looking at questions of *meaning* and *significance*. What is the point of this? What is this supposed to mean? we ask, and try to understand how a scene, an image, a camera angle, a line, a facial expression, functions in the context of the film. It is normally relatively simple to answer that kind of question on the basis of everyday experiences or knowledge of the genre, but there is always an element of interpretation involved, and the importance of the interpretation increases as soon as we begin to raise more general and comprehensive questions about the meaning or significance of the film. An analysis of Griffith's *Birth of a Nation* can uncover the basic structure of the narrative; it can demonstrate how the conflict between whites and blacks during the Civil War is presented; and it can present the underlying system of values. But if we ask why the conflict is presented in precisely this way, or for the basis for the film's system of values, the answer has to be sought outside the film itself via an interpretation of the social context of the film.[5]

Experience and expectation

There are many kinds of musical analysis, writes musicologist Nicholas Cook.[6] Superficially they might seem to differ a lot from each other, but on closer inspection it transpires that most of them actually function in roughly the same way. And, it could be added, in roughly the same way as film analyses. They ask, at any rate, the same kinds of question:

> They ask whether it is possible to chop up a piece of music into a series of more-or-less independent sections. They ask how components of the music relate to each other, and which relationships are more important than others. More specifically, they ask how far these components derive their effect from the context they are in.[7]

In other words music analysis – like film analysis – is based on segmentation, on dividing up a piece into larger or smaller sections. Segmentation makes it possible to investigate the relations between the individual sections and determine how they function within the totality. Furthermore, and probably just as important, music analysis – again just like film analysis – is an interest-controlled activity. If we are trying to work out what music analysis can really tell us, we ought to start by asking what makes one analysis good and another one bad, Cook writes, 'because this immediately raises the question: good in what sense? Good for what?'[8] Ideally we always analyse with a specific purpose, to solve actual problems, to understand how actual works are constructed and function. And the interests normally emerge from questions to do with experience: 'we normally expect an analysis to tell us something about the way we experience music,' Cook writes,[9] emphasizing that objections to many of the old techniques of music analysis had to do with the fact that they were not faithful to musical experience.[10]

Initially, then, music analysis addresses the same basic issues as film analysis. There are also, however, a number of important similarities at the more concrete, analytical level: 'Expectation pervades our experience of art,' film analysts Bordwell and Thompson write. 'In listening to a piece of music, we expect repetition of a melody or a motif'.[11] And analysts of music investigating a piece of music will be interested in the repetitions and all the other formal patterns, in the same way as when film analysts investigate a film. They will study similarities and differences, variations, developments, etc., and the musical elements that create and run counter to our expectations. The interaction, for example, between 'open' and 'closed' forms: what in the music causes us to believe that the work will necessarily continue? And continue in a particular way? How do we know when the piece of music is over, that it can no longer continue?[12]

Music analysis also has the same limits as film analysis. When we analyse the first movement of Haydn's Symphony No. 83, we can present a kind of x-ray of the music, point to how the individual sections of the movements balance each other, show how things develop from beginning to end. But if we says that the movement contains a deep philosophical thesis, that it expresses the Enlightenment ideal of 'tolerance', we have moved outside the field of analysis.[13] The analysis cannot 'prove' that this is how things are, but it can at least establish an internal, musical basis which, combined with other observations and relevant historical material, can form a point of departure for interpretations that arrive at statements to do with the social or philosophical 'content' of the symphony.

This relationship between work-based analysis and generalizing interpretation is sometimes thought of as a conflict. While a music theorist such as Cook assumes a relatively pragmatic position, there are others who feel that a music analysis ought to be based on more comprehensive theories of interpretation if it is to be anything more than a mere description. Descriptive accounts do not have any explanatory force in themselves, according to music theorist Alan Walker: 'You do not solve problems by describing them.'[14] But, Cook objects, 'everyday experience show that it is precisely in this way that one is all the time solving problems'. Without a description it is normally difficult to see what the problem really is or whether there is any problem at all.

> So in analyzing music: reading the score several times, describing the details of the music in ordinary language, perhaps parsing the more complex chords – these simple procedures are usually more productive than immediately launching into some complex, theory-laden analysis. And in any case the difficulty two analysts can have in even agreeing what the facts of the matter are shows that the simplest description is not really neutral, but already involves interpretative criteria of some sort.[15]

Cook concludes that despite all theoretical shortcomings, a simple description of the musical experience would be a practical point of departure for an analysis.[16]

Music in context

With these brief remarks about the analysis of films and music I have indicated certain frameworks for the analyses I will undertake in the following chapters. The analyses are determined by a specific interest: the aim is not to present a 'total', 'exhaustive' analysis of the actual music but to describe and understand the role of the music in the film, and subsequently to use points from the analysis to say something more general about the functions of film music within the given historical period. In the next chapter the task will be to shed light on the music of the silent film era with the aid of Gottfried Huppertz's music for Fritz Lang's *Metropolis*. This analysis, like the subsequent ones, will be based on the segmentation of the composition; it will concentrate on the mutual relations between the individual elements and on the function of the elements in the totality.

But, it could be asked, what totality are we dealing with here? The methods of music analysis have been developed to describe autonomous, cohesive and often highly complex works. When musicologists analyse a movement of a Beethoven symphony and examine the relation of the musical elements to the totality, it is the movement itself, or possibly the entire symphony, that is the totality. When we are dealing with film music, it is not the whole musical composition but the film that is the totality. Film music is functional music – music whose structure has been determined by factors that lie outside the music itself. For that reason film music will often be made up out of fragments, of snatches of music that do not immediately have any musical connection. A traditional music analysis would therefore ignore what is special about film music: that it functions as part of a larger, extra-musical whole.

The potential for grasping the functions of film music with the aid of the methods of film analysis ought at first glance to be greater, since film scholars are used to taking many different elements into consideration in their analyses, mise-en-scène, lighting, picture composition, cutting, etc. However, as noted above, they seldom deal with music. There are of course exceptions, but the main rule is that if music is mentioned at all, it is in the form of brief remarks in passing, and normally it is described as a simple repetition of what the pictures are showing. One of the most important tasks of film music is to function as a 'parallel' commentary on the film, Siegfried Kracauer writes in *Theory of Film*. Music 'restates, in a language of its own, certain tendencies, or meanings of the pictures it accompanies'.[17] This is a good summary of the role music plays not in films but in the average film analysis. Kracauer enlarges on the idea of music's parallel commentary with a couple of examples: 'a gallop illustrates a chase, while a powerful *rinforzando* reflects the climax, as it unfolds on the screen'.[18] These sorts of linkages are frequent in the literature of film analysis, and when reading them, we often have the suspicion that it is the images in the film that have determined the description and thus the choice of descriptive adjectives; that, for example, it is the 'chase' and 'climax' of the film narrative that cause Kracauer to hear – and describe – the music as 'quick' and 'powerful'. We begin to wonder if the spontaneous – and unavoidable – experience of film music 'fitting' the entirety of the film and 'fitting' the content of the images may cause us to ignore other dimensions in the music, dimensions that can be just as important for the overall film experience.

If we are to avoid the narrative force of the images coercing us to hear only the elements in the music that repeat what the pictures say, we must also try to hear what the music itself says 'in its own language', to use Kracauer's formulation. The most practical procedure is to divide the analysis into two phases, beginning by concentrating on 'the music itself', attempting to maintain a certain distance from the overall film narrative, and then to change perspective and allow the film to be the overall context of the analysis. In the first phase, we adopt a music-analytical approach, segment the musical course of events, compare the individual segments, describe their position in the local musical context, etc. During this first description we can mark with cues how the elements are positioned in relation to the larger cinematic sequence and its segments. In the second phase we choose the film-analytical approach and discuss how the music interacts with the sequence of images and other elements in the totality of the film.

Modes of presentation

A simple verbal description of the music is a good starting point, Cook writes, but there is no avoiding the fact that there is a difference between describing music and describing images or dialogue or action in a film. When, for example, Bordwell and Thompson remark that the first scene in *His Girl Friday* ends with the main character inviting two other people to lunch, and that the next scene starts with all three arriving at the restaurant, it is immediately clear what they mean.[19] Most readers will understand what cinematic segments are being talked about, and how the sequence has been divided up. Even readers unfamiliar with the film will, on the basis of this description, be able to identify what they ought to pay special attention to if they one day were to see it. One cannot count on a corresponding level of understanding when writing about film music.

Anyone can see what a photograph, a film image or a figurative painting represents and describe it in words. Anyone can retell what is written in a text. It is, however, much more difficult to say what a piece of music 'means' or 'deals with'. Music, like a series of images or a text, is an organized sequence of elements. But unlike images and texts this sequence does not produce a precise content. While images and texts are *signs*, i.e. complexes of *signifiers* that convey *signifieds*, music is first and foremost structured sound, sounding *form*, sequences of notes organized in relation to underlying syntactic codes. Images and texts are signs that *refer* to and *represent* something outside the signs themselves. Literature, drama, film are representational art forms. Music is not.

The difficulties involved in providing a verbal description of music have to do with this fact. Music does not 'represent' anything; it does not convey a different 'content' that one can refer to and use as a point of reference in the description. So one is forced to describe 'the music itself'. But there is no generally comprehensible way of doing this. Most precise verbal descriptions will need the reader to have mastered a certain amount of music terminology. And even readers with a certain level of musical competence know from experience that in many instances it is much easier to see – and realize – an analytical point by looking at music notation or some other kind of graphical representation than to read a verbal description. On the other hand reading music is not a generally widespread proficiency.

There is no simple solution to such problems of presentation (and, it should be noted, this could well be a reason why the role of music is seldom dealt with in the literature of film analysis). In the following analyses I attempt to facilitate reading by using a combination of modes of presentation. I give a simple verbal description of the musical sequences. In the description I point to how the sequences can be segmented, to mutual relations between the elements, etc. Readers who have access to the actual films – on video or DVD – can 'listen along' to this description with the aid of my cue-like indications of how the music is positioned in relation to the sequence of images. In most cases I also demonstrate my points with the aid of music notation examples.

Terminology

Even though the intention is to avoid 'technical' descriptions, it is necessary to use certain musical terms. Most of them are explained in the course of the analyses. It is, however, perhaps a good idea to discuss a couple of the most important of them at this juncture.

Motif

When it comes to terminology, too, there is an interesting coincidence between film analysis and music analysis. In *Film Art* Bordwell and Thompson emphasize the importance of repetition for the understanding of a film. They continue:

> It is useful to have a term to help describe formal repetitions, and the most common term is *motif*. We shall call any *significant repeated element in a film* a *motif*. A motif may be an object, a color, a place, a person, a sound, or even a character trait. We may call a pattern of lighting or camera position a motif if it is repeated through the course of a film.[20]

As is evident, there are really two terms here – *element* and *motif*. Element is the 'unmarked' term, motif the 'marked' one. Everything in a film can be considered to be elements, parts of the cinematic totality; but in an analytical context, an element only becomes a motif if it is *repeated* – and *recognized* as a repetition. Defined thus, a motif is the basic term of film analysis. It is the term used when one wishes to draw attention to similarities and repetitions during the course of events, and the motif is also the background against which one measures differences, changes and variations.

In precisely the same way motif is the central term of music analysis. A motif is '[a] short musical idea, melodic, harmonic, rhythmic, or any combination of these three', William Drabkin writes.[21] As is clear from this definition, motif is just as comprehensive a term in music analysis as in film analysis: All aspects of the musical whole can become motifs. And what creates the motif is also in this case repetition: a motif is 'most commonly regarded as the shortest subdivision of a theme or phrase that still maintains its identity as an idea'.[22] A musical element becomes a motif if it retains its identity, i.e. if it is repeated and recognized as a repetition.

The musical motif – again like that of the film – is an element that is used as a point of departure for the construction of larger structures. The actual transformation of an element into a motif creates such a structure: At the instant one hears the motif for the second time and understands that one has heard it earlier, it retrospectively places some important markers in the musical time sequence, while also creating expectations regarding new repetitions or variations.

Theme

In music analysis a distinction is normally made between motif and *theme*. A motif, as mentioned, can be melodic, rhythmic or harmonic, or any combination of these three; a theme on the other hand is usually based on a *melody*, a series of notes arranged in a temporal sequence. In addition a motif is a short, incomplete, musical idea, while a theme, which can be made up of two or more different melodic motifs, forms an independent, complete and enclosed unit. Drabkin points out that the relation between motif and theme corresponds to that between a theme and a whole movement or a composition. In each case, the smaller unit is experienced as being incomplete, 'yet it has a special identity with important consequences for the shape and structure of the larger'.[23] The theme, then, functions, as does the motif, as a building block in the construction of larger structures. Some of the most durable musical forms are based on themes that are repeated (*rondo*) or developed and transformed (the classical *sonata form*) or varied (*theme with variations*).

Sequence

Music analysis operates with many other terms in the description of basis elements in a composition, e.g. phrase, figure, period. These will not be dealt with further in this context. But there is good reason for mentioning the phenomenon *sequence*, since it plays an important role in many of the analyses to come. In music analysis the term 'sequence' is used about a short, melodic motif that is repeated several times after each other, but at a higher or lower level on the actual scale.[24] In some cases the melody is simply moved up and down the scale, but retaining the same intervals between the notes; in others the intervals are adapted to meet the requirements of the scale.

An example

Mozart's 12 Variations in c major, K. 265, are based on 'Ah, vous dirai-je Maman', an old popular song that parents of Suzuki pupils have learned to dread under the name 'Twinkle, Twinkle, Little Star'.

2.1: 'Ah, vous dirai-je Maman' ('Twinkle, Twinkle, Little Star')

The *melody* has a simple structure: a section of four bars (A), followed by a different section (B), also four bars; finally, the first section (A) is repeated. The sections of the ABA structure are made up of short two-bar *motifs* (marked in the music as a, b and c). Motif a is an introduction to something, b is the conclusion: Together a+b form a rounded whole, a *theme*. The deviating B section placed between the two A themes, starts with c, which is then repeated. But, as the music makes clear, c is really a repeat of b, or rather a *sequencing*: c is arrived at by moving b a tone up.

The entire melody can be described as a play between similarities and differences. The A sections are based on the difference between a and b. The overall structure is based on the repetition of A and the difference between A and B, while B at the same time is based on a kind of repetition of b. The melody can therefore be described in a number of different ways – (1) as ABA, (2) as a+b | c+c | a+b or (3) as a+b | b_x+b_x | a+b.

3

Back to the Future: *Metropolis*, 1927

Fritz Lang's science-fiction film *Metropolis* was the UFA film company's most ambitious project to date, and the most expensive film until then in the history of film-making. The shooting took eighteen months. Colossal sets were built; futuristic cars and machines were produced; experiments were made with the most advanced film techniques of the time; and thousands of extras took part,[1] and the music naturally had to live up to all these exertions. When *Metropolis* had its premiere in Berlin on 10 January 1927 it was accompanied by grandiose symphonic music written by the composer Gottfried Huppertz.

Huppertz was born in 1887. He studied music in Cologne and worked as a singer and actor at the Hoftheater in Coburg, where he eventually advanced to the position of 'Hofsänger' (an honorary title). In the early 1920s he came into contact with Fritz Lang and his wife, the author and scriptwriter Thea von Harbou. He had a number of minor roles in some of Lang's films, *Kämpfende Herzen* (1921) and *Dr Mabuse, der Spieler I–II* (1922), and composed the music for Lang's great national epic *Niebelungen* (1924) and Arthur von Gerlach's *Zur Chronik von Grieshuus* (1925). *Metropolis* was his last silent film project. After the Nazi takeover he wrote music for a number of sound films, including two directed by Thea von Harbou. He died in 1937.

Huppertz's music for *Metropolis* is interesting for several reasons. First, it is one of the relatively few pieces of specially composed music from the silent film period. Second, from the very outset the music was planned to be an integral part of the film, and was written in close collaboration with Lang and von Harbou. And, third, Huppertz's music came to play a highly important role in how posterity later understood the film.

In search of the lost film

Metropolis is a film historian's nightmare, a film that was smashed into a thousand pieces that no one has ever managed to reassemble, and a textbook example of the fact that the distinction between original and copy is difficult to maintain when dealing with modern visual media: *Metropolis* exists in a dizzying number of versions. But when film historians try to reconstruct the original film, they are met with the ironic problem of there actually never having been one original but three, all of which have disappeared.[2] Over the years all three 'originals' have been shortened and reorganized by directly cutting the negatives. The result, the film historian Martin Koerber writes, is 'that a quarter of the film, including the very core of the story as conceived by von Harbou and Lang, must be considered irrevocably lost'.[3] This has not prevented film historians from trying to reconstruct this irrevocably lost film.

In the late 1980s film historian Enno Patalas made a working copy by joining together material from a number of existing versions. Patalas's work, which was based on a close reading of the original shooting script and other material, has since been continued in an attempt at actually reconstructing the film. One of the surviving negatives has been taken as the point of departure. Every single frame has been scanned and stored on a computer in HD format and then cleaned with the aid of digital technology. In this reconstruction work Gottfried Huppertz's music has been an important aid.

At the German premiere the music was performed by a symphony orchestra comprising 66 musicians. When a shortened version premiered in autumn 1927, Huppertz was still listed as the composer but, according to the critic Roland Schacht, there were only a couple of motifs left of the original score. 'As far as the rest is concerned, a well-tried potpourri of Chopin, *Der Freischütz* and a few popular songs from the Kinothek have been resorted to.'[4] Huppertz's music suffered the same fate as the film itself – it was cut to pieces, and, for many decades, it was other composers' music that was used when the various versions were shown in the cinema.[5] However, unlike the excised sections of the film, Huppertz's music did not disappear. Even when dealing with the music it is difficult to speak of an 'original version', for there were many. In accordance with the practice of the time Huppertz ensured that the music could be played by several different constellations of musicians – by a single pianist, by a large symphony orchestra and by a smaller salon orchestra of about 30 musicians.

Huppertz's manuscript of the score and of a piano version have been preserved,[6] as have a number of orchestral parts. But the most important source is a printed piano part, intended for distribution with the film. This is actually a piano version of the score with an indication of how the music had been orchestrated for a salon orchestra. The idea was that this piano part could be used by the cinema pianists, but that it could also – and perhaps primarily – function as a score for conductors of salon orchestras.

It is this piano version which, combined with the film script and censorship information, has been the basis for the most recent attempt at reconstruction. The piano part includes, to begin with, more than a thousand cues that indicate where and how the music is to be positioned in relation to the action of the film. Furthermore, there are tempo indications, changes in time, changes of key, etc. that refer to what is happening on the screen and can suggest what the content and length of the missing scenes may have been.[7] The result was presented on a DVD in 2003.[8] I use this as my point of departure and make use of the first ten minutes of the film as an analysis example.[9] First, a brief description of what we see on the screen during these ten minutes (illus. 3.1).

Metropolis starts with white opening credits on a black background. After a while, the credits begin to roll upwards. The music starts, indicating that now the *film* has begun. But it takes a while before the *narrative* gets underway. After the credits one first sees the film's high-flown *Sinnspruch*, its motto: 'The mediator between brain and hands must be the heart.' This is followed by a short title sequence where 'abstract' forms shape the word 'Metropolis' and fade over into an animated drawing of skyscrapers. The title sequence dissolves into a picture of three pistons. This marks the start of a montage sequence, which consists of shots of machine parts in rapid motion. The sequence ends with a picture of two clocks. The face of the large one has only ten hours marked on it. When the second hand reaches ten, there is a cut to a factory siren at the bottom of a dark skyscraper landscape. Then an intertitle appears: 'Shift Change'. A line of workers is moving along a long corridor on their way out of the factory, while a new shift comes moving in the opposite direction.

In the following sequence, we first go down into the workers' underground city, then up to 'The Club of the Sons', where young men

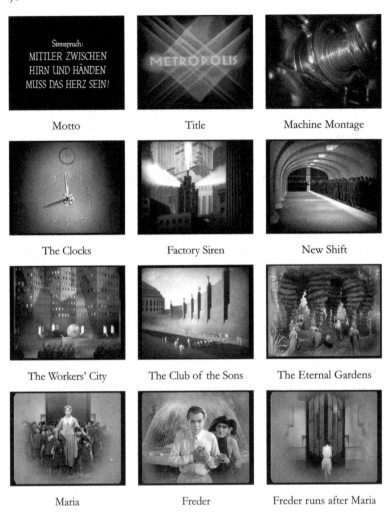

Motto   Title   Machine Montage

The Clocks   Factory Siren   New Shift

The Workers' City   The Club of the Sons   The Eternal Gardens

Maria   Freder   Freder runs after Maria

3.1: *Metropolis:* The opening

from rich families amuse themselves at a stadium. Finally, we are taken to 'The Eternal Gardens', where young women parade the latest fashions. Here we meet one of the 'sons', Freder, who is running around with one of the women. Their game stops when a young woman, Maria, comes in through the garden gate together with a group of ragged workers' children. Freder remains standing there, struck by lightning. And when Maria and the children are ejected from Paradise, he runs after her to find them again. 'But this is what happened to

Freder – son of Joh. Fredersen, master of Metropolis – when he went in search of the girl:' the intertitle says, indicating by means of the colon that only now does the real story begin.

Music for the film 'of the same name'

As described, the opening is quite complex. The film starts, the pictures of machinery introduce us to the theme of the film, we are introduced to three different environments – The Workers' City, the Stadium, The Eternal Gardens – and meet Freder and Maria, the two main characters of the film. Finally, the narrative project is indicated: Freder has to find and solve the mystery of the mysterious woman. Musically, too, one can speak of a complex opening and, as in the visual narrative, the music ends with a strong indication of the fact that a section has come to an end. What happens in this section? Let us listen to the music, and take a look at the score for *Metropolis. Musik zum Gleichnamigen Ufa-Film* – Huppertz's 'music for the UFA film of the same name'.[10]

The opening credits

The music begins during the opening credits with a slow, pompous fanfare played by trumpets against a background of strings. The point of departure for the fanfare is a short, rhythmic motif – an upward leap of a fifth in C major – which is then sequenced in the following bars.

3.2: *Metropolis*. Fanfare

Motto and title sequence

Powerful drumbeats then mark the transition to a new section. The whole orchestra strikes up, moving through the next three bars towards the basic key of C major, while the motto of the film is shown on the screen. C major is reached precisely when the animated title sequence starts. Supported by powerful drumbeats, the orchestra plays a strictly marked motif of quavers (illus. 3.3). This figure is repeated with a slight variation and the music then comes to rest. The opening is over. The film is underway.

3.3: *Metropolis*: Title music

Machine montage

When the pictures of the machines appear on the screen, a new musical section begins. The first thing we notice is the difference in tempo. After the solemn fanfare, the music moves at a considerably faster tempo, which seems to follow the rhythm of the pistons. In the course of a comparatively short space of time, the rhythm changes abruptly from 4/4 to 6/8 to 2/4. In each of these three sub-sections simple, short brass motifs are introduced and repeated, accompanied by hectic, rhythmic figures in the strings. In terms of style, the music echoes the 'machine music' of the 1920s, the modernistic experiments of the time that celebrated the age of the machine and industrial urbanity with dissonant, dynamic music.[11]

During the final section, we hear increasingly clearly that above the orchestra there is a rhythmic accenting by glockenspiel and woodwind and, when the pictures of the two clocks are cut to, we see that this level of the music indicates the rhythm of the second hand. When the hand reaches ten, this slows down the music, which concludes with a series of dissonant chords that imitate the sound of a factory siren. A new section starts.

The workers

Two rows of workers move in opposite directions along a long corridor. The tempo of the music is 4/4 and relatively slow (*andante moderato*), keeping pace with the movement of the rows. The strings play a two-bar motif, the key of which is initially hard to define: The first note, G, is supported by an ambiguous whole-tone chord (A-B-D$^{\#}$). Only on the third beat does it emerge that the key is actually G$^{\#}$ minor, but the whole-tone feel is maintained in the motif, which in the next bar gradually moves upwards with the notes B-C$^{\#}$-D$^{\#}$.

Andante moderato

3.4: *Metropolis*: The workers, first motif

The motif is repeated with a minimum of variation. A new two-bar motif is then introduced: a falling minor scale from G#, played directly on the beat, supported by chords.

3.5: *Metropolis*: The workers, second motif

The falling figure is then sequenced, i.e. repeated and transposed without any mediating transition from the key of G# minor to E minor.

The Workers' City

The dissonant chords are heard once again, together with a new picture of the factory siren. After this, while the workers enter a lift and descend into the depths, a new motif in the minor begins, still in 4/4, but now at a slightly brisker pace (illus. 3.6).

The new motif takes the form of a simple, gradual movement up and down the first three notes of the E minor scale: E-F#-G-F#-E. The phrase is played like a round by deep and high strings with an interval of two beats. The motif is then sequenced – and the round structure repeated – without leaving the E minor scale, first from G, then from B. The section concludes with a falling melodic line which is repeated (illus. 3.7).

The segment concludes with a repetition of the third motif, transposed one octave up. Then, without a transition, a repetition of the first worker motif starts, while the first shot of the underground workers' city appears on the screen. The motif – which has now been transposed from the original key of G# to C minor – is repeated while the descending lift movement halts. The final chord is held for a brief moment – then the motif is repeated a third time, followed by the second worker motif, first in C minor and then in G$^\sharp$ minor, while the workers enter The Workers' City.

3.6: *Metropolis*. The workers, third motif

3.7: *Metropolis*. The workers, fourth motif

Stadium

After this last indication of the worker's theme, we hear the sound of a harp in A$^\flat$ major as a transition to the next section. The scene with the young men at the stadium is announced by a fanfare motif. Then follows a brief piece of music that is clearly divided into two: after an introductory section, a melody in A$^\flat$ major follows – adapted to the fast tempo of the runners – that ends with a clear indication of the tonic as the winner breaks the tape.[12] Change of scene to The Eternal Gardens.

The Eternal Gardens

During the first part of this scene, the orchestra plays a waltz: after a 32-bar intricate introduction that seems to be compiled out of many different waltz clichés, a tuneful motif emerges that is played three times – first in A$^\flat$ major, then in G$^\flat$ major and finally in B major – alternating with more loosely structured interludes. The first part of the motif is shown in illus. 3.8.

3.8: *Metropolis*: Waltz

A tremolo in the violins warns of something important in the offing. Maria and the children enter the garden, accompanied by a short four-bar motif, played on the oboe with a string accompaniment).

3.9: *Metropolis*: Maria

The key is E^b major. The theme is clearly divided into a rising (bars 1–2) and a falling motif (bars 3–4). The melody is simple, singable, but takes a strange turn in the second half. One would instinctively have expected it to return to its point of departure and come to rest in E^b major. Instead it is transposed without any transition to G major at the bar preceding the final section.

The theme is repeated immediately afterwards, played this time as a violin solo with strings in the background. The key is now B major. The melody ends in E^b major and continues without any transition into the melody played when the young men raced against each other in the stadium (illus. 3.10). In the following, this melody is linked to Freder.

3.10 *Metropolis*: Freder theme

3.11 *Metropolis*: Freder motif

It is an eight-bar winding line, constructed as a series of sequences derived from a small, rhythmic upbeat motif (illus. 3.11).

The many incidences of this motif are marked with an x in illus. 3.10. The accompaniment moves quite conventionally from the point of departure in E^b major via F minor and B^b major back to E^b major, but there is a surprising effect in bar 6. Instead of the expected F minor chord under the A^b of the melody, there is an E major chord. Even though A^b/G$^{\#}$ is the major third of the scale of E major, this harmonization sounds quite strange, because the E major chord is alien to the key of E^b. This deviation is resolved immediately afterwards when the melody returns to E^b major.

While the orchestra repeats the waltz theme, Maria points to the people in the garden and says to the children: 'Look, these are your brothers.' The Maria theme is then heard three times, each time in a new key, while the officials try to hustle her out of the garden. She looks entreatingly into the camera. Cut to Freder, who holds his hand to his heart. And while Maria and the children leave the garden the orchestra plays a melody in B major.

3.12: *Metropolis*. The heart melody

The form is A–A'. The melody is extremely simple. It sounds rather like a hymn or a folk song and has a correspondingly simple harmonic foundation, apart from the fact that the second time round it does not end as expected in B major but in D major.

The end

When Maria has left the garden Freder looks around in pensive mood, while the waltz motif is played by a solo cello. Pause – and then he rushes off to find Maria, while the orchestra plays a powerful ending.

Musical idiom, artistic idiom

Even though we have only looked at about ten minutes of the film, we have already encountered examples of most of the features that characterize Huppertz's music.

Musical idiom

The music has a certain late-Romantic feel to it, but there are many deviating features as well. Here is constructivist-expressionistic 'machine music' with dissonances and hard, unintegrated clashes of various rhythms. Here are imitations of contemporary popular music: the waltz in The Eternal Gardens is an example of this, and later on one hears a jerky, syncopated foxtrot.[13] Here are short musical effects – the factory siren, for example, the sound of a harp, the violin tremolo – which are not characteristic of any particular musical idiom but which signal the utility function of the music. These are effects that are typically used in various forms of incidental music written for stage productions.

Harmonics

The music has a tonal feel to it, although sometimes the harmonic basis is challenged: the introductory fanfare has been constructed as a kind of musical montage where the basic motif shifts from c major to distant keys before returning once more and finishing with an emphatic c major chord; the workers' theme starts with an indefinable whole-tone chord that points in various directions; the Maria and Freder themes are accompanied by chords alien to the keys in question, etc. We are not dealing with a severely challenged tonality, more with brief, discreet deviations that are used as isolated musical effects to colour a melodic phrase or theme.

Formal idiom

The formal idiom of the music is announced by the short fanfare motif in the very first bars of the score: the *Metropolis* music is a constructivist montage made up of short, striking motifs. It admittedly includes a couple of longer themes, but generally speaking all the themes, even the winding Freder theme, are composed of short, motif-like phrases presented in regular, clearly defined patterns. And when these themes return later in the film, it is usually only the basic motif or the introductory bars that are played. The fact that the music is constructed in this way means that one seldom finds a traditional musical 'development' of the material. The larger sections are made up of chains of motifs and themes, mainly with the aid of three techniques: *repetition, sequencing* and *unmediated montage*. Naturally, it is considerations related to the narrative of the film that determine this constructional principle. The way the music is constructed it can be interrupted and change direction in the space of a few bars or beats without making a detour using fairly long intermediary transitions. The joining together of the major sections of the music is adjusted in certain cases via the underlying chord progressions, for example, by a new theme continuing in the same key as the previous one, although often the sections are simply assembled without any intermediary transitions.

Continuity

Even though the movement is constructed as a series of short motifs, it does not fall apart; it forms a long, cohesive composition. The music follows and 'covers' the whole film from beginning to end. There are admittedly a couple of general pauses en route, but they are used first and foremost as special effects. They prepare or emphasize particularly important events.

Diegetic music

During the original showing of *Metropolis* the music and narrative took place, quite literally, in two separate worlds, in two different spaces. As discussed in chapter One, music for the silent film was usually an 'external' accompaniment, a kind of supplement or comment on the events in the diegesis.[14] But even if the live music was performed in the cinema auditorium in front of the screen, it was nevertheless sometimes to be understood as if it was in the film, in the diegesis. In these instances it represents the sounds in the fictional universe that the silent film is not itself capable of reproducing.

In the course of the first ten minutes of *Metropolis*, for example, we hear the rhythmical accentuation by the music of the movement of the second hand and the dissonant sound of the factory siren, examples of noises in the diegesis being imitated and represented by musical means. Later on in the film the music simulates the sound of a big explosion in a machine hall and Maria's warning blows on a large gong in The Workers' City. Music is also used to represent speech: on his tour of the factory halls, Freder experiences a work accident and sees in a vision one of the large machines being transformed into a Moloch that devours the workers. This vision is accompanied by a striking, primitive-exotic theme, and when he later visits his father, 'The Master of Metropolis', the theme is heard once more, while the pictures show Freder talking agitatedly and intensely. In this case the music represents both the sound of Freder talking and what he says. In addition, the 'talking' of the music does not only refer to an event in the diegesis but also to how one of the fictional characters has experienced this event. The music represents the accident filtered through Freder's subjective consciousness.[15]

Later on in the film, a mad inventor, Rotwang, constructs a robot with the features of Maria. When he presents the false Maria to the guests at a night club, she dances a suggestive dance while the cinema orchestra plays Huppertz's stylized 'variety music'. Here, the music has what is perhaps its most obviously diegetic function. It represents *music* – a piece of music that is played in the fictional world and that the characters in the fiction are thus able to hear. This, however, only lasts for a brief moment. While the music continues, we cut to a shot of Freder, who is lying ill in some other part of the city. And we understand that the music has now switched to a different narrative mode – it no longer alludes to the music of the fictional space but functions as a non-diegetic accompaniment. And this is how the music functions for most of the film. There are, however, several kinds of non-diegetic music, both in this film and in films in general.

Non-diegetic music

Reading instructions

In many cases the music for *Metropolis* functions as a kind of reading instruction, as an external clarification or underlining of the basic narrative structure. The sections of the music follow those of the film narrative. The music 'scans' the narrative, marks the major transitions in the action with the aid of changes of melody, rhythm and tempo. Within the individual sections the rhythm of the music is furthermore often used to underline a movement in the pictures – as, for example, when the music follows the machines, the second hand, the rows of workers, etc. We are not dealing with close 'synchronization' here, rather with an approximate rhythmical 'agreement' between music and image.

Signal

There are also examples of a change of mood or action in the narrative being given an extra emphasis with the aid of an isolated musical effect – the arpeggio, for example, when we ascend from the The Workers'

City; the violin tremolo when Maria enters the garden; the general pause followed by the strongly accented final cadence when Freder runs out of the garden. In such instances, the music is used as a kind of pointer. It is a warning signal that prepares the viewer for an important moment in the narrative.

Commentary

In most cases, however, the music does not only have formal functions; it provides a sort of commentary on the course of events. For example, one hears a distorted version of the 'Marseillaise' in the last part of the film when the workers rise up in revolt and shout: 'Death to the machines!' And while the workers destroy the machines, the skewed quotation is repeated. Clearly, it is 'insurrection', 'rebellion', 'revolution', that is referred to in such instances and with the aid of the distortion the music gives the impression of distancing itself from the events.

Leitmotif

Most cinema-goers will presumably recognise the 'Marseillaise' quotation and understand what it means. On the other hand, only very few will notice that the orchestra on many occasions during the film plays variations on the medieval funeral hymn 'Dies Irae' ('Day of Wrath'), normally used in connection with warnings of death and calamity. In this case the musical quotation is a kind of coded comment that can only be 'read' by the initiated. This, of course, is not practical when one considers that the film is meant to appeal to a large audience. Therefore Huppertz also uses other kinds of musical commentary. His most important effect is the use of leitmotifs.

A leitmotif is a theme or some other cohesive musical idea that is used in a musical-dramatic work 'to represent or symbolize a person, object, place, idea, state of mind, supernatural force or any other ingredient', writes Arnold Whittall.[16] Practically all the themes I have mentioned in my description of the first ten minutes of the music for *Metropolis* are leitmotifs in this sense of the word. On its first appearance the motif is linked to a specific person (Freder, Maria), an environment (The Workers' City, The Eternal Gardens), an emotion (Freder's love of Maria), and when it later reappears the intention is for the viewer to be reminded of the first occurrence and to 'hear' the reference to this person, this environment, etc.

Figure and ground

A couple of Huppertz's leitmotifs have a completely local function. The waltz that signals The Eternal Gardens, for example, is only heard three times at the beginning of the film. The rest of the leitmotifs I have mentioned above, however, recur again and again during the rest of the film, while new themes continue to be introduced.

All the main characters have leitmotifs connected to them as they enter the action: Freder's father, the father's secretary, the father's henchmen, the inventor Rotwang, the robot woman, etc. The revolt of the workers and Freder's function as a mediator between the workers and the capitalists is also signalled by a leitmotif. In a number of cases, as Rainer Fabich has pointed out, there are musical similarities between groups of leitmotifs, for example between the Rotwang and the Moloch leitmotif, or between the robot and the Revolt leitmotif – similarities that suggest and emphasize underlying narrative connections.[17]

Classical music is usually based on a fairly limited thematic material. The supreme example is the sonata form, which normally builds on only two melodically and harmonically contrasting themes. They are presented at the beginning of the movement, subsequently 'developed' via a series of variations, modulations, etc., and finally recapitulated, while their mutual harmonic contrast is resolved and the movement concludes. This is not the case with music built up around leitmotifs. Because the music is going to be used as an accompaniment for a narrative, it can in principle have new thematic material added to it as long as the exposition of the narrative has not yet been concluded. In *Metropolis* this phase lasts a very long time. The main characters of the story and the basic conflicts have not been established before Rotwang has created the robot, and even after the exposition is really over, new leitmotifs emerge. At the beginning of the last part of the film, 'Furioso', Huppertz introduces a theme which is then used as an accompaniment for scenes where Maria and Freder save the workers' children from a catastrophe.

Even so, it is clear that the composition has reached a saturation point at this stage or, more correctly, the narrative has entered its concluding phase. During the first parts of the film, in which the characters are introduced and the action is constantly making new, unexpected turns, the music is divided into short, clearly marked sections that follow the narrative development quite closely. In the concluding part of the film, where the action concentrates on the revolt of the workers and the rescue operation in the workers' city, series of leitmotifs related in terms of 'content' are linked together to form fairly long cohesive segments, as when the destruction of the machines is accompanied by a potpourri-like movement, where the *Marseillaise* quotation is interwoven with fragments of the robot and revolt motifs.

We can now state more precisely what is characteristic of Huppertz's music. At the local level it is constructed as a series of short motifs that, by means of repetition or sequencing, form more extended themes or melodies. At the level of the total composition these themes and melodies occur again and again, in constantly new combinations and variations, according to the development of narrative. At this level the music can be described as a montage of leitmotifs.

In stage music based on leitmotifs there will normally be a musical tension between 'figure' and 'ground'. The leitmotifs are integral parts of the overall movement, but at the same time can be distinguished as independent elements, and when they are experienced in this way as 'figures', the rest of the music functions as a kind of more neutral, unmarked 'background'. The characteristic thing about Huppertz's composition, however, is that the tension between figure and ground is neutralized or, rather, there is no ground, there are only figures. The music consists almost entirely of leitmotifs.

A musical ideal model

Huppertz's music for *Metropolis* is an exception. First, we are dealing with an original composition, a form of film music that was extremely rare at the time. Second – and very much connected to this – it was written for one of the most ambitious and experimental film projects of the age. Even so, this is 'typical' silent-film music, at least in the sense that it follows the international norm established from 1910 onwards, via the recipes in cue sheets, anthologies, manuals, trade magazines, etc. Huppertz's music fulfils the three standard requirements: it is *continuous*; there is a *correspondence between images and music* and it is based on *leitmotifs*.[18]

Continuous accompaniment

The demand for continuous accompaniment is underlined time after time in contemporary literature. The continuity of the music is to create or support the narrative continuity. It is not thought that the image alone can bear the narrative. The opening and conclusion of the narrative are considered to be particularly critical phases, and so are transitions between scenes that are separate in terms of geography or chronology, and transitions between images in a crosscut. In such instances it is absolutely necessary for the music to be heard without any pauses, 'eliding fissures by offering its own continuity in place of the images', as Kathryn Kalinak puts it.[19]

Short pauses are permitted, for example when turning over sheets of music, at points where the action cannot be misunderstood or when the intertitles convey important information. But as we have seen in connection with the music for *Metropolis* a pause can also function as an anticipation or underlining of a dramatic situation. In his *Encyclopaedia*, Erno Rapée remarks that when an unexpected person appears in the action, or when someone commits a crime, silence is an extremely powerful effect. He concludes that all unexpected events ought really to be accompanied by silence.[20]

That a pause can have such a dramatic effect at all is precisely because the rest of the music is cohesive and follows the narrative of the film. The pause is part of the music but represents at the same time a deviation from the norm, marking because of this break that a corresponding break is taking place in the narrative. In other words the pause is an example of the second requirement: that the music is to 'fit' the content of the pictures.

Correspondence between image and music

The correspondence is established at different levels. The various sections of the music are to correspond formally to the sections of the film, 'cover' them, i.e. be precisely as long as they are. This often means that the conductor has to 'stretch' the music to make it fill out the timeframe at his disposal. If one is forced to play the same piece of music four or five times, the instrumentation ought to be varied, Rapée writes. If the actual point in the film is very dramatic, the music can be transposed a semitone up or down. 'As long as you vary your instrumentation or your tonality it will not get tiresome', he remarks. How the music is to stop when the action takes a new direction is another, related, problem. Rapée relates that formerly the music simply broke off when the film had reached the next section, but that in his opinion this was an antiquated way of doing things. The conclusion of the individual numbers ought not to seem to be breaks but rather fade-outs. 'The more segues you can arrange between your numbers the more symphonic the accompaniment will sound.'[21]

The music must also correspond in terms of content to the images. In chapter One I mentioned the early discussions about a lack of agreement between music and image, and how gradually a kind of code was established as to what sort of music ought to be played with what. The anthologies were particularly important in this connection. The short pieces of music in *Sam Fox Moving Picture Music* or in Becce's *Kinothek* were not just of practical help to conductors of cinema orchestras. They also functioned in a broader sense as models, examples that demonstrated what music for a funeral, a death scene, etc. ought to sound like.

Leitmotifs

In chapter One I mentioned the *Frankenstein* cue sheet from 1909, where the pianist was requested to play a theme from Weber's *Der Freischütz* every time the monster appeared. That musical themes can be linked to characters in the action and function as leitmotifs is 'a natural law which must on no account be broken', a writer remarks in *Moving Picture News* in 1910.[22] In a manual from the same year the authors provide a simple, down-to-earth recipe for how one ought to proceed. The theme 'should be announced in the introduction, it should be emphasized at the first appearance of the person with whom it is linked, and it should receive its ultimate glorification, by means of tonal volume, etc., in the finale of the film'.[23] And when in 1925 Rapée gives cinema conductors good advice about how to organize music for a feature film, leitmotifs are just as important an element as mood music:

> Firstly, determine the geographic and national atmosphere of your picture; Secondly, embody everyone of your important characters with a theme. Undoubtedly there will be a Love Theme and most likely there will be a theme for the Villain. If there is a humorous character who makes repeated appearances he will also have to be characterized by a theme of his own.[24]

With these two techniques, most of the work has already been done, according to Rapée. If, for example, the action takes place in China, one uses 'Chinese' music both to underline the general atmosphere of the film and as a basis for the leitmotifs for the characters. And if there are two Chinese characters and one English character, the Englishman must of course be provided with 'English' music, so as to create a strong contrast.

Huppertz's music for *Metropolis* fulfils the three standard requirements, but at the same time it problematizes the simple parameters of the ideal model. For, as the above analysis has shown, the concepts 'correspondence' and 'leitmotif' actually cover a whole range of very different things. In the following chapter, I summarize some of the main points of the analysis and use them as a basis for an initial overview of the functions of film music.

4
Musical Meanings

The capacity of music to convey meaning is a recurring and controversial subject in the literature of music theory. What does music mean? What does a melody say? What does a sonata narrate? There is no simple answer to such questions.

Music, as discussed earlier, is not a representational art form, but under special circumstances it can be used to convey meaning. Melodies, types of music, genres, styles, etc. can in certain instances function as signs and refer to something other than themselves. There are a number of different possibilities, but most of them can be traced back to two basic sign-functions: music can represent non-musical phenomena by virtue of *structural resemblance*, and music can evoke *associations with other music*.

Structural resemblances

In the introduction to *Metropolis* there is a chord that sounds like a factory siren. At the beginning of one of Vivaldi's violin concertos, the soloist plays certain figures that sound like bird song.[1] Something in the music resembles, and is used as an imitation of, familiar non-musical sounds.

Such musical signs are reminiscent of onomatopoeia in language, the 'bow-wow' of a dog, the 'oink-oink' of a pig. Onomatopoeic sounds imitate other sounds but, because they are *language sounds*, they are always adapted to the phonetic structure of the language in question. In Norwegian a cat says 'mjau', in English it says 'miaow'. In a similar way musical imitations of sounds are adapted to the musical idiom involved. They refer to extra-musical phenomena but are first and foremost music. If we heard the piece with the dissonant chord from the beginning of *Metropolis* on its own, without images, it is uncertain whether we would realize that this was meant to imitate the sound of a factory siren. In the same way the violin figures in the Vivaldi concerto are first and foremost a musical effect, a virtuoso introduction to a virtuoso piece of music. Perhaps we only think of these figures as birdsong because we have read in the concert programme that the piece is called *Il Cucù* (The Cuckoo). In these two examples the musical reference is supported and emphasized by the context: the film image and the programme note control our experience and draw our attention to the fact that the music can also be listened to in a different way – as *something other than music*.

The context also plays an important role when the rhythm of the music is used to represent extra-musical phenomena. We describe musical rhythm by means of such adjectives as 'quick', 'slow', relativizing expressions that always assume a comparison. A given rhythm is, or is experienced as, 'quicker' or 'slower' than some other rhythm. We do not normally consider the fact that a basic musical rhythm or the rhythm of a musical phrase also resembles phenomena outside music itself. We only realize this if someone demonstrates it for us, as, for example, when the rows of workers in *Metropolis* move along the corridor in time to Huppertz's music. Because the music and the images are coordinated, a *perceptual equivalence* is created. It is as if the rhythm of the music *matches* the movement in the images, and vice versa. One sees the movement and sees the rhythm of the music in the movement; one hears the music and hears the movement of the images in the rhythm.

Connotations and associations

The music that accompanies the introductory machine sequence in *Metropolis* is an example of such coordination and equivalence. The rhythm of the music seems to follow the motion of the machines. But at the same time the music says 'machines', 'avant-garde', 'modernity', etc. because it resembles and is therefore reminiscent of the music used by the avant-garde composers in the 1920s when they wanted to express their fascination with the technology of the modern world. These meanings do not need help from the images to be audible. If one knows the period of music history, one catches the reference immediately.

Huppertz's 'machine music' is an example of music referring to other music, and by virtue of these references acquiring broader cultural meanings. These meanings are related to the phenomenon that linguists and semioticians refer to as *connotations*, the type of 'co-meanings' or 'extra content' produced in a text on the basis of style, choice of vocabulary, etc. Every ordinary Norwegian sentence has an immediate 'denotative' meaning, but at the same time something else and more is expressed. Because of the construction and choice of vocabulary, it carries a secondary content: 'Norwegian' or, better perhaps, 'Norwegianness'.[2] Similarly, the improvisation by a jazz musician on a standard melody, no matter the nature of the actual melody and the actual improvisation, will always mean 'jazz', and awaken a number of associations connected to the culturally and socially defined ideas the listener has about what 'jazz' is.[3]

Stereotypes

No music is completely new and original, it all reminds one in some way or another of other music. All music conveys culturally established connotations. By virtue of style, musical idiom, instrumentation, etc. music refers to music of the same type and thereby to particular historical periods, particular countries, particular social environments. One does not have to be a music expert to be able to hear that baroque music is 'old' 'classical' music, or that Dexter Gordon plays 'jazz'. Most people can recognize 'music from the Tyrol' and 'Chinese', 'Spanish' and 'Greek' music. We know that music played on the bagpipes means 'Scotland', that pretty tunes played on the accordion and mandolin mean 'Italy' and that the sound of an untuned piano means 'silent film'.

Many such connotations are of course cultural stereotypes. It is uncertain if what we spontaneously recognise as typical 'gipsy music' actually is so. The main thing is that we get these associations, no matter whether they are 'correct' or not in terms of music history. The film composers know that we have considerable knowledge of musical styles and their cultural references. Therefore they use styles as signs when, for example, they wish to indicate the time and place of the film narrative. In *Sam Fox Moving Picture Music* Zamecnik provided the cinema pianists with examples of typical 'Chinese music', 'oriental music', etc. In *Metropolis* Huppertz accompanies the machine montage with typical 'machine music' of the age. 'Western music' is played with Western films, and when we hear deep, rhythmic beats on kettledrums and a melody with 'strange' intervals, we know that Red Indians are on the warpath.

Formulas and quotations

It is not only the general style of a piece of music that can evoke cultural associations. Within a given style, certain motifs, phrases, rhythms, etc. can convey quite precise meanings, because they are similar to those normally used in particular social contexts.

When, for example, we hear the trumpets leap a fifth upwards in the first bar of the music for *Metropolis*, one immediately knows that this is a *fanfare*, with all the associations this has with a solemn, ceremonial opening. When the orchestra later plays music dominated by the brass section, with a strongly marked drum accompaniment, we realize – without thinking consciously about it – that this is a march, and we know that marches are linked to the military and to war. The waltz that introduces The Eternal Gardens has associations with Vienna and dancing and festive occasions; the syncopated foxtrot played by saxophones and percussion gives the scenes in the nightclub connotations of hectic modern night life.

Local meanings

The musical connotations mentioned so far are global: all bagpipe music means 'Scotland'; all fanfares mean 'solemn ceremony'. But there are also examples of meanings connected to a single piece of music. 'La Marseillaise' means 'France'. 'Auld Lang Syne' means 'New Year's Eve'. Gounod's 'Marche funèbre d'une marionette' means 'Alfred Hitchcock'. Certain pieces of music are linked to precise, particular meanings, either because the music arose in particular historical contexts or because it has been used in particular situations.

Such meanings are evoked every time the actual piece of music is played. That is why the *Frankenstein* cue sheet recommends the cinema pianist to play 'The Bride's Chorus' from *Lohengrin* when the images show scenes from a wedding. And in *Metropolis* Huppertz demonstrates with the aid of his 'Marseillaise' reference that such meanings can be evoked simply by using a brief quotation.

Leitmotifs

The dissonant chord at the beginning of *Metropolis* represents a factory siren because the music at this point sounds like a factory siren. The 'Marseillaise' quotation makes us think of revolt and revolution because this particular melody is linked historically to the French Revolution. Both when it comes to structural similarities and when it comes to musical connotations in a broad sense, the meaning of the signs is, as the semioticians say, *motivated*, i.e. the meaning is determined by external factors. In verbal language words such as 'miaow' and 'oink-oink' are motivated signs, but these are special cases. Language is primarily based on arbitrary signs, i.e. there is no direct relationship between the sign and its reference. There is, for example, no justification in terms of content for Norwegians to call a cat 'katt', or a pig 'gris'. It is, however, more doubtful if music can display arbitrary signs. It is not my intention to open this discussion here, merely to point to the leitmotif phenomenon.

A leitmotif is a short piece of music that, for particular contextual reasons, has acquired the function of a sign and has come to mean something else than itself within a particular context. Certain theorists are of the opinion that most leitmotifs are initially arbitrary: they do not convey meaning themselves when introduced into the movement; they are assigned meaning. But it can be argued that this assignment is not arbitrary. The point of leitmotifs is precisely that they acquire meaning because they are introduced at the same time as one sees particular persons, etc. in the opera or the film. This means that leitmotifs are quite as motivated as, for example, the 'Marseillaise', which came to mean 'France', because it was sung during the French Revolution and became France's national anthem. If a leitmotif functions as it is meant to, this is because the musical theme refers to its first appearance and evokes the meaning it was assigned in that particular situation. The only thing that distinguishes a leitmotif from, for example, the 'Marseillaise', is its 'local' nature, i.e. that the meaning is only comprehensible within the limited context of the individual music drama or the individual film.

Music and emotion

Often it can be unclear what a leitmotif is really referring to. Similarly there can be often disagreement as to what leitmotifs 'say' about the

referent. Some theorists believe that the musical phrase and its reference are linked completely mechanically via the first shared appearance
in the music drama, and that the leitmotif after that only functions as
a kind of musical signal. But is it correct that leitmotifs do not say anything at all? Is the joining of motif and reference in a film such as
Metropolis completely accidental?

Take, for example, the first workers' theme. It is introduced along
with images of sad, tired workers returning home after a long working
day. But it is not simply because of the rhythmic coordination of
images and music that this theme sounds sad and tired. It is as if the
music itself is sad and tired, which has probably to do with the fact that
we are dealing with a slow theme, that it is in the minor, and that it
starts with a chord that is harmonically ambiguous. Or take the melody
that accompanies Freder throughout the film. Rainer Fabich writes:
'The triad-based melodics in the major characterise Freder as a cheerful person.'[4] Perhaps he is right. There is, at any rate, a long musical
tradition for associating the various keys with emotional qualities. So it
is at least not unlikely that Huppertz chose to write a simple melody in
E^b major precisely so as to characterize Freder's cheerfulness. And it is
not unlikely either that when we listen to the music we experience it as
cheerful, glad, carefree or the like.

The workers' theme is sad; Freder's theme is cheerful – we say.
And it is not only leitmotifs that we talk about in this way. In our everyday lives we are always describing music and musical experiences with
adjectives that refer to basic human emotions. We talk about 'happy'
and 'gloomy' music, about 'mournful' and 'melancholy' melodies. But
what do we really mean by such formulations? The relationship
between music and emotions is one of the most hotly debated themes
in the literature of music theory, and has been ever since Antiquity.
Some theorists believe that the expression of emotion is the most
important form of musical meaning; others that music is incapable of
expressing emotions.[5]

Today there is increasing agreement that music is able to express
emotions, at any rate very basic emotions such as happiness, fear,
hope. And there is usually also agreement that a distinction ought to
be made between music itself and the experiencing of it. If modern
music theorists, for example, talk about a piece of music as mournful
or fearful, they do not – unlike their colleagues in the Renaissance and
the Baroque – usually mean that the piece is capable of causing

mournfulness or fearfulness in the listener; they are talking about a quality of the music itself. The emotions lie in the music as a quality one hears and recognizes in the same way as one hears and recognizes major and minor, dissonances and consonances, etc., music philosopher Peter Kivy writes.[6] But how is it possible for one to hear emotions in music? Kivy – and many other modern music theorists – emphasize that since music is not a representational art form, it cannot 'imitate' or in some other way 'represent' emotions. Something else is taking place: we experience the emotional qualities of the music directly, without having to make a detour via a representation. We do not hear a 'representation' of happiness or of a happy person; we hear 'happy music' or, rather, we hear music that sounds happy. This clarification does not, however, solve the basic problem. For the problem still is: how does it happen? Why does the music sound happy, mournful or sad?

The literature in the field provides a number of different answers. The music semioticians claim that there is not initially any 'natural' connection between the music and its emotional content. Admittedly, many people throughout history have experienced that particular musical features give them associations with particular emotions, and they have been able to agree on what emotions are involved. But, the semioticians object, these patterns of associations are historical–cultural constructs. This, for example, is how the Canadian music semiotician Jean-Jacques Nattiez explains that the Western keys are connected with particular emotions: the association was established in practice at a particular historical point in time, by composers and musicians, and has afterwards been transmitted via general musical culture, via teaching, etc.[7] That people in general experience major keys as cheerful and minor keys as mournful is, from this point of view, no different than bagpipes eventually coming to mean 'Scotland', or that a particular musical theme in the course of the film *Metropolis* comes to mean 'Freder'.

Music psychologists give a similar answer. John Sloboda discusses historical material that would indicate that texts with a particular emotional content have been accompanied by melodies based on particular combinations of intervals during a very long period of music history.[8] Sloboda's explanation is that the musical intervals did not initially have any content, but because certain combinations were regularly associated with certain texts, they were gradually assigned the same emotional content as the texts themselves.[9] From a different theoretical stand-point Leonard B. Meyer arrives at a similar understanding: when certain musical aspects are experienced time and time again in connection with texts and the like that either indicate an emotional mood directly or hint at it, this gradually creates an association by virtue of prox-imity. Meyer also indicates an alternative possibility, that music and emotion are associated on the basis of some experienced similarity.[10] This is a possibility Sloboda considers, based on cognitivist psycho-logy: the similarity does not necessarily have to do with the music actually 'resembling' the emotional expression. It is possible to imagine that the music opens up analogies with the semantic system we use when talking about our emotions, and that because of these analogies a shifting of musical relations onto emotions takes place.[11] Sloboda himself uses the cognitivist term *mapping* about this relation: we use, so to speak, the 'map' of the emotions to describe how we experience the musical landscape.

Other writers believe there must be more 'natural' reasons for our experiencing connections between music and emotion. Peter Kivy, for example, sees a kind of analogy between music and other forms of human expression: when we experience a piece of music as being 'happy music', this is because the music reminds us of how happy people talk and move. The experience is based on an analogy between two 'con-tours', between the acoustic form of the music and 'the heard and seen manifestations of human emotive expression.'[12] Though Kivy tries to express himself very precisely and is very cautious about his formula-tions, it is obvious that the 'contour theory' is open to the same objections that he himself has made against theories that presuppose that music is a representational art form. In addition the contour theory finds it difficult to explain why most Westerners experience major keys as cheer-ful and minor keys as mournful. There is nothing in the 'configuration' of major and minor scales that can be said to imitate human expressions of emotion. Kivy himself is clearly not satisfied with the contour theory. But, as he remarks, its attraction is apparently indestructible. 'It simply refuses to die, in spite of its numerous difficulties.'[13]

Kivy finally abandons the contour theory, and also abandons the problem. Instead he chooses to consider the musical experience as a *black box*. Certain musical features are sent into the black box, and out come certain expressive qualities. But 'what causes what goes in to pro-duce what comes out – of that we are ignorant'.[14] Naturally, this is not an acceptable solution for a philosopher or a music theorist, but it is at least a practical solution. And it is a practical solution that can be acceptable in our film music context. Even though there is disagreement between music philosophers and music theorists about what actually happens, we have to accept as a historical fact that in Western culture there is a tendency to associate particular musical features with particular emotions, and that these associations can be utilized in a film music context.

It admittedly took quite a while for the musicians in the cinemas of the silent film to understand this. As we saw in chapter One the early film audiences complained that 'suitable music' was not being played to the films. The criticism in particular applied to the lack of coordination between music and image as regards the emotional atmosphere. With the aid of cue sheets, anthologies and manuals, musicians gradually became able to solve these problems. And from the end of the silent film period onwards it was generally accepted that one of the tasks of the music is to indicate and support the atmosphere of the film narrative, to establish its emotional mood. There was also a certain amount of agreement as to how this was to be done.

It ought to be emphasized, however, that only a fairly restricted emotional code was established in the final phase of the silent film and continuing into the period of the sound film, a code based on very simple, basic emotional categories that people generally agree about hearing in music: sorrow, happiness, fear, dread, etc. The more complex emotions and moods one seems at times to hear in film music are usually determined relationally, they arise because of the relation between the music to other music and to the general cinematic context. An example from *Metropolis* illustrates this.

When we hear Freder's theme for the first time, as an accompaniment to the events in The Eternal Gardens, it sounds 'happy' and 'cheerful', but also – and perhaps in particular – 'rushing', 'swelling', 'energetic' or 'powerful'. According to Rainer Fabich, it is the triad-based melodic style in the major that creates this impression. But there are in fact many similar melodies that do not produce such associations. Maria's theme, which has immediately preceded it, is just one example. That the Freder theme is experienced as being 'cheerful' and full of youthful exuberance at this point, has not only something to do with the key, but just as much with the fact that the tempo changes from 4/4 to 3/4, that the theme is played by the whole orchestra, and that it replaces the rather static Maria theme, which was played by a solo violin. Moreover, the Freder theme is formed as a relatively long-drawn-out melodic line, in marked contrast to most of the other themes we have so far been presented with.

As this example suggests, the experiencing of the emotional content is not determined by a single musical feature but by many parameters – by tempo, melodics, harmonics, timbre, etc., and not least by the total cinematic context. There is without doubt a certain 'cheerfulness' in the Freder theme, but this basic mood is differentiated and modified by the context, partly via similarities and differences in relation to the music that has immediately preceded it, and partly via the interaction with the images.

Interaction

As has been shown, musical meanings exist on a scale that ranges from extremely simple structural similarities via complex, cultural connotations to the locally produced references of leitmotifs, to which can be added various expressions of emotions that can be linked to certain sections of the music. It is, however, important to emphasize that these semantic functions are not mutually exclusive. One and the same piece of music can convey many kinds of meaning simultaneously. An example of this is in the last section of *Metropolis*, where Huppertz with virtuosity activates large parts of the semantic scale.

The robot woman has stirred up the workers. They set about attacking the machines. When the revolt starts, the orchestra first plays a roll on the drums, followed – as a kind of prelude – by the skewed quotation from the 'Marseillaise'. While the workers pour from The Workers' City up into the factory halls, we hear a rather long piece of music in which many sections are closely coordinated with the movements on the screen. The music is a strict march dominated by percussion and marked trumpet signals, and it is constructed as a chain of leitmotifs: the section starts with part of the robot theme, followed by the revolt theme. In this instance, then, one and the same piece of music has three different functions: the march matches both the rhythm of movements shown in the images and produces connotations with struggle and war, and the connotations are supported by leitmotifs that both signal revolt and emphasize the fact that it is the false Maria who is the real cause of the whole wretched business.

5

Enter the Sound Film

As far back as the earliest years of the silent film attempts were made to synchronize the projection of moving pictures with various kinds of recorded sound. Edison's employees, for example, had been working on this since the late 1880s. It was basically the phonograph that was the centre of their attention. The film strips were considered a supplement, an extra attraction that could underpin the commercial exploitation of the phonograph. This project resulted in the Kinetoscope (1894) and Kinetophone (1895) projection systems: viewers saw the film through peepholes in small cabinets and at the same time had rubber tubes in their ears through which they could hear the sound from a built-in phonograph. From the 1890s onwards inventors in the United States and Europe presented a number of similar systems, all of them based on showing film strips combined with the playing of gramophone records. In the first decade of the twentieth century, for example, hundreds of synchronized short films were produced for Gaumont's French Chronophone system and Cecil Hepworth's English Vivaphone.

None of these early systems really had a commercial breakthrough, mainly because they were based on an acoustic sound technique. They were weak in terms of volume and therefore could not be used in cinemas or other large halls, even though the German film pioneer Oscar Messter, for example, tried to use many gramophones at the same time and used vast funnel-shaped horns to amplify the sound.[1] A number of inventions in radio technology at the beginning of the twentieth century removed this obstacle.[2] And in the years after the First World War work was done both in Europe and the United States on developing film systems based on sound that was electronically amplified.

The American company Warner Brothers developed Vitaphone, a system that connected the film projector to a kind of gramophone, so that the film images could be shown synchronized with sound played on large records. The system was demonstrated in a number of short films in the course of 1926 and in the feature film *Don Juan*, which had its premiere in August of the same year. Many other companies were capable of synchronizing mechanically registered sound with film images at that time, but in the history of film *Don Juan* is usually considered to be the breakthrough of sound films aimed at larger audiences.

The paradox of the sound film

When the cinema manager Hugo Riesenfeld wrote the overview article 'Music and Moving Pictures' in 1926, he was dealing with music for the silent films. But he had already made the acquaintance of the Vitaphone system:

> The most recent development along the line of making the best music available to smaller communities is the Vitaphone. This invention is the best so far in reproducing synchronized music and films. It makes it possible for artists and orchestras of the first order to be heard in the smallest towns. The reproduction of the voice and music is very fine. It seems almost as though the performers were in the same room as the listener. It is not probable that the Vitaphone will ever entirely replace the orchestra, but it does make it possible for certain films requiring the finest musical accompaniment to be shown in places where there is no orchestra available.[3]

The quotation is interesting, not because Riesenfeld, like many others, underestimated the future and possible uses of sound films but because he formulates the paradox on which the breakthrough of sound films is based: the sound technology was developed with the aim of preserving that part of the cinema performance that was *not* film. The intention was for the system to be used to record music and live scene appearances so that audiences in the provinces would get the opportunity of experiencing popular artists who otherwise only appeared in cinemas in the big cities. It is clear from the demonstration films from 1926 that the Vitaphone system was conceived of as being used to preserve and reproduce music and singing and, on rarer occasions, to communicate important speeches to a large audience. This is also indicated by the fact that two types of loudspeakers were installed in the Vitaphone cinemas. The music loudspeaker was placed in the orchestra pit to simulate the sound of a cinema orchestra. Speeches addressing the audience were reproduced by a loudspeaker placed behind the screen.[4]

From sound-on-disc to sound-on-film

Don Juan was a film with continuous musical accompaniment. The following year, the Vitaphone system was demonstrated again, this time with the film *The Jazz Singer*, and now there was both music and speech on the sound discs. Posterity has considered *The Jazz Singer* to be the first real 'talkie', even though the amount of speech is restricted to a couple of sentences.

Warner Brothers was successful with its two sound films, especially with *The Jazz Singer*, which caused the other American film companies to speed up work on developing their own sound systems. Fox went for Movietone, a system that recorded sound directly on the strip of film. This and other similar systems based on *sound-on-film* soon proved to be considerably more practical than Warner Brothers' *sound-on-disc*. The fragile Vitaphone discs broke or got lost in the post. And the synchronization of sound and image was a recurring problem – as soon as the projectionist was obliged to remove a piece of ruined film, at the beginning or end of a reel for example, the sound no longer matched the images. Furthermore, the actual playback apparatus was sensitive and vulnerable. The needle jumped in the grooves, creating unintentional comic effects. The literature is full of anecdotes about actors talking while the soundtrack has the sound of a banjo or a dog barking. When the Vitaphone discs were played in the cinema the synchronisation between images and sound had to be checked constantly. In the Movietone films, on the other hand, the synchronization was done once and for all – the sound was printed on the strip of film.

For the sound film to be able to work the cinemas had to undergo a conversion process. This was no simple matter since each of the competing production companies assumed that the cinemas were equipped with their special sound system. As early as 1926, the year that *Don Juan* had its premiere, a number of the American companies set up a committee that was to establish a common system for the entire film industry. In 1928 agreement was reached on focusing on sound-on-film and on using the Western Electrics system as the industrial standard. In following years this sound system was installed in thousands of American cinemas, and during the period a number of technical problems concerning the recording and editing of sound were resolved. Cameras were soundproofed, unidirectional microphones began to be used, work began on multi-track recording, on after-synchronization and playback.

Many film companies attempted to maintain their silent-film production or at least to distribute films already produced in the hope of covering their investments, but by around 1930 it was clear that the sound film had become the norm. The era of the silent film was definitively over – in the United States as well as in Europe. In 1930 Western Electric and the German company Tobis-Klangfilm divided the world between them, reaching an agreement that made it possible to show American sound films using European systems and vice versa.

Goodbye to the silent film

By the turn of the 1930s the technical conversion had been carried out. Most of the major cinemas in the United States and Europe had installed the necessary sound systems. The national film industries were now geared to sound production, and film producers had long since understood that the public wanted to see and hear *films*, not filmed variety performances or educational lectures. The technological revolution led to changed forms of production and distribution, to the development of new aesthetic forms – and to social tragedies.

The silent film actors' high-flown, dramatic mode of expression was all at once completely superfluous and perceived as hopelessly out of date. Narrative information that formerly had to be made visible via expressive gestures and pantomime could now be effectively conveyed with the aid of a brief dialogue. Actors who did not manage to cope with the transition to the new, more sober style of acting fell out of the system. For cinema musicians the change had even more dramatic consequences. Throughout the 1920s the cinemas were by far the largest workplace within the music and entertainment industry. With the introduction of sound films the orchestras disbanded, with musicians and artists all over the world losing their most important source of income. A few large cinemas continued to use live music and appearances on a more modest scale, but the tendency was clear. Thousands of musicians became unemployed at a time when the entire Western world was in a deep economic crisis, with unemployment already at disastrous levels.

The switch to sound films had other, less dramatic consequences. The new technology led, for example, to a new perception of what films are. The entire history of film from this point onwards was understood from the perspective of sound films. What for thirty years had simply been thought of as *film* suddenly became *silent film*, i.e. deficient sound films. And at the same time the victorious sound film almost eradicated any recollection of the vanquished silent film. The film formats and forms of projection used during the first thirty years slipped from the collective memory, along with the memory of the versatility of early films in terms of musical solutions and materials.

The most characteristic feature of music for silent films was precisely its ungovernable, unstandardized diversity. In the thousands of cinemas that were established in the course of the first three decades of film, everything between heaven and earth was played: classical favourites, the very latest popular hits and newly composed pieces of music. Much was improvised; music from Tin Pan Alley was played, as were scores. Music was played by both amateurs and professional musicians, by pianists and organists, by small groups, by big bands, by symphony orchestras. But when a film theorist such as Siegfried Kracauer writes his reminiscences of the silent film era and its music in 1960, it is not the enormous musical range that he recalls but, quite symptomatically, the image of the solitary pianist in the old cinema, an image that has survived from the very breakthrough of the sound film as being the quintessential symbol of the silent film.

A transitional phase

The introduction of sound revolutionized the industry and changed the cinemas. But it was difficult to imagine when *Don Juan* had its premiere in 1926 that the new technology would also exert a crucial influence on the cinematic mode of expression and that it would come to radically change the role of music. Admittedly, the music had been recorded on discs and was more or less synchronized with the pictures on the screen, but apart from this, it was business as usual. *Don Juan* was a silent film accompanied by traditional compilation music plus a little newly written music. And *The Jazz Singer* was not much different. Here too the sound mainly consisted of instrumental music. Al Jolson in the role of the jazz singer only sang for a couple of minutes, and his famous line, the first words ever spoken in film history – 'Wait a minute, wait a minute, you ain't heard nothing yet!' – was an exception. During the rest of the film, the dialogue was presented via the traditional intertitles.

But the early sound systems did at least solve the practical problem that had plagued film companies throughout the era of the silent film. It was no longer necessary to entrust the choice of music and its perform-ance to random, unpredictable musicians in local cinemas. With the new systems it became possible to standardize the musical accompaniment. Music stopped being an 'external' site-specific part of one particular per-formance. From now on it was an integral part of one particular film.

On the face of it, it might seem as if sound film was only going to be this – silent film with a preserved musical accompaniment. That was at least the strategy of many American film companies. But the situa-tion was fluid. There were many other possibilities, and the first years of sound film were a period characterized by aesthetic and technical experiment, as well as by discussions as to how sound, and music in particular, was to be treated within the framework of the new system.

Film sound – parallelism or counterpoint?

'Sound-recording is a two-edged invention,' Sergei Eisenstein writes in the famous manifesto he and his colleagues Vsevolod Pudovkin and Grigory Alexandrov published in Leningrad in autumn 1928: sound will solve all the complex problems that it is impossible to overcome if one works exclusively with pictures,[5] but it can only do this if it is han-dled in the right way. The risk is that the new technical possibilities will mainly strengthen the position of mainstream films, that the new tech-nique will lead to increased cinematic realism, that sound will end up 'exactly corresponding with the movement on the screen, and provid-ing a certain "illusion" of talking people, of audible objects, etc.', and that that will lead to '"highly cultured dramas" and other photographed performances of a theatrical sort'.[6]

For Eisenstein and his colleagues, as well as for many other filmmakers of the time, it was a question of retaining the experimental

European montage culture that had functioned throughout the silent film period as an artistic alternative to mainstream films. For this reason they reject the synchronization of sound and image, calling instead for 'a contrapuntal use of sound in relation to the visual montage piece'. They imagine that in time this can lead to 'an orchestral counterpoint of visual and aural images'.[7]

The German film theorist and gestalt psychologist Rudolf Arnheim arrives at similar conclusions in his book *Film als Kunst* (1932), although he has a slightly different point of departure. His discussion of the aesthetics of sound film is based on a kind of information-economy argument: it is unnecessary to hear the sound of a bell if one sees a bell on the screen at the same time. 'The principle of sound film demands that picture and sound shall not do the same work simultaneously but that they shall share the work.' This is, as he writes, 'the principle of sound-film counterpoint'.[8]

Arnheim is well aware that it is impossible to avoid parallelism between sound and image, and he also emphasizes that the contrapuntal principle cannot apply absolutely, but he maintains that it is not sufficient for the sound to be simply justified on grounds of realism. If sound does not add something new, if it merely repeats the information provided by the image, it is superfluous. His point is that all the elements of the film must be 'essential' to be able to contribute to the overall *Gestaltung*. 'If essentials are mixed with superfluities, then the spectator cannot tell what is important and what is not.'[9]

Music and sound film

The contrast between parallelism and counterpoint was also the central topic of the early discussions concerning the role of music in sound films: should music run parallel with the images and, so to speak, repeat the action of the film using musical means? Or should it – can it – follow its own path and function as an independent, contrapuntal contribution to the whole?

'Usually music in sound films is treated merely as a pure accompaniment, advancing in inevitable and monotonous parallelism with the image,' Pudovkin writes.[10] And he explains how he himself chose a different path in the film *Deserter* (1933). At one point, a workers' demonstration is put down by the police. In the last pictures of their defeat, the workers raise their flag once more; it is passed from hand to hand, farther and farther away, 'establishing the moral if not the physical victory of the demonstration'.[11] The music does not follow the emotional curve of the revolt, via defeat to the hope of victory. It takes the form of a workers' march, 'with constantly running through it the note of stern and confident victory, firmly and uninterruptedly rising in strength from beginning to end'.[12] The sequence, according to Pudovkin, creates 'a great emotional upheaval' in a working-class audience, because it combines 'the objective representation of reality in the image and the revelation of the profound inner content of reality in the sound'.[13]

Kracauer discusses Pudovkin's example from *Deserter*, acidly remarking that it is difficult to imagine that even a sympathetic audience would have got this message. 'The uplifting music might as well express the feelings of the temporary victors.'[14] This does not mean, however, that Kracauer dismisses the idea of contrapuntal music. There is in fact a post-echo of the discussions of the 1930s in his own text about the intoxicated pianist who never took any interest in what was happening on the screen in the old silent-film cinema. Contrary to what one might expect, this text is not meant to be a criticism of the pianist's accompaniment. The very opposite is the case. Kracauer praises the unpredictable, surrealistic montage of film images and random music. The lack of coherence between the music and the action of the film caused him to see the story 'in a new and unexpected light'; it challenged him to lose himself 'in an uncharted wilderness opened up by allusive shots'.[15] His conclusion is, 'I never heard a more fitting accompaniment.'[16]

The realistic tendency

It was not only the film theorists and European representatives of the film and music avant-garde who busied themselves with these issues. The new technology had a massive impact on mainstream films in both Hollywood and Europe, raising a whole number of very general questions about the role of sound: How much sound should be recorded? What function should the sound have? What is 'realistic' sound? Similarly the transition from the live music of the silent-film cinema to the preserved music of the sound film meant changes both regarding the general conception of film music and the actual musical practice.

In some of the earliest sound films the music was organized as it was in silent films, as a continuous accompaniment, loosely coordinated with the sequence of images. *Don Juan* is an example of this. This practice, however, was soon abandoned. During the relatively long period from 1926 to the early 1930s there was no definitive answer as to what film music is, and how it ought to be used.

The introduction of sound, as Eisenstein and his colleagues foresaw, meant a consolidation of the realistic tendency in mainstream films. The musical consequence of this was that in many instances the choice was made to exclusively use 'realistic' music, i.e. only play music if music was actually played in the fictional world. The requirement for music to be diegetic led, among other things, to quite a number of films not having any music at all. Many of the films from the transitional period were *talkies*, adaptations of popular plays based on almost permanent dialogue, with music normally only being played during the opening and closing credits. The most popular genre of the time, the musical, was, on the other hand, completely based on music. The first of these, MGM's box-office hit *The Broadway Melody* (1929), was marketed as an 'all-talking, all-singing, all-dancing' film, but in this film too – and in most of the subsequent musicals – the music was actually diegetic. People who go to the theatre to see an operetta or a musical are used to the characters on stage suddenly bursting into song to express what they feel. During the first years of the sound film, such a movement back and forth between 'realistic' dialogue and 'unrealistic' song was out of the question. Songs and dance numbers had to be justified in terms of realism, which was why the early film musicals were practically always 'backstage musicals', films that go backstage at a theatre and tell a story of professional singers and dancers struggling to put on a music performance.[17]

In some cases, people went quite far to justify the presence of music. The composer Max Steiner states that a wandering fiddler could perhaps be introduced in order to legitimate the playing of music during a love scene in a forest.[18] And Kathryn Kalinak refers to Josef von Sternberg's film *Thunderbolt* (1929), where the music that accompanies the last hours of a condemned prisoner comes from an orchestra that, quite by chance, is rehearsing in one of the adjacent cells. Kalinak remarks that such absurd narrative tricks reveal that despite the many experiments belief in the power of music was never completely abandoned during this period.[19] And there are a number of examples of shorter or longer sequences of non-diegetic music being inserted into films that were otherwise based on diegetic music.

The studio system and Classical Hollywood

The history of the breakthrough of sound films is not just one of technological advances and aesthetic choices, but just as much one of economics.[20] For many decades the leading American film companies had been competing fiercely against each other for market share. Their most important strategy during the 1920s had been to go for 'vertical integration' of production, distribution and projection: the important thing was to control all stages in the movement of a film from script to cinema, which is why they established their own distribution companies and bought up cinemas all over the country. And also why relatively small companies such as Warner Brothers and Fox dabbled in sound films: to compete with the major companies within the cinema industry. By developing their own sound systems they hoped to gain control over the smaller cinemas.

The strategy proved successful. By the early 1930s Warner Brothers and Fox had become key players, and via a series of comprehensive mergers the American film industry was divided between eight large companies that together accounted for 95 per cent of the total film production. Apart from producing films, all the companies had their own distribution companies – and the five largest – Warner Brothers, Paramount, Twentieth Century Fox, MGM and RKO – also had their own chains of cinemas. It was the cinemas in particular that were important: even though the chains only accounted for 16 per cent of the market, they were the source of three quarters of the companies' income.

In other words film production was not the central economic link in the structure. Douglas Gomery calls the five main companies 'film corporations', remarking that the most correct way of characterizing them would be as 'diversified theater chains, producing features, shorts, cartoons, and newsreels to fill their houses'.[21] But the point is that the total system would not be able to generate a profit unless there was something 'to fill their houses' with. So films had to be produced, and it was important for this production to be as efficient and inexpensive as possible.

When film historians talk about the 'studio system' they are referring to the domination of the large film corporations from the early

1930s to the late 1940s, but also to the special production process that was developed within this structure. Film production was organized in a kind of assembly line system based on extreme division of labour in all phases, from the time the script was written until the film was edited. The individual production companies, or studios, were organized as strictly hierarchical industrial enterprises divided into departments led by department managers all of whom reported back to an omnipotent managing director.

Each studio tried to rationalize production, but also sought to differentiate itself from its competitors. This eventually resulted in a division of labour in terms of genre between the studios. At the same time as this differentiation took place, however, there was also a general standardization of the narrative technique. The basis of the standardization is what is referred to in film history as Classical Hollywood, a system of narrative conventions that indicate how one is to organize a narrative in a clear, effective way, and how one edits the film in such a way that the spectators forget the actual process of narrating and can concentrate on the action. These narrative conventions were developed relatively early during the second phase of the silent film and were consolidated in the course of the studio system period, since when they have been the predominant form of film narrative. David Bordwell, Kristin Thompson and Janet Staiger, who have written the standard work on the system, set a limit at 1960.[22] In reality, though, most of these classical narrative conventions are still in operation in mainstream films, not only in the United States but in most of the Western world.

A similar standardization takes place with regard to film music. Corresponding to the classical Hollywood narrative we have Classical Hollywood Music – a system of musical conventions that is laid down in the early 1930s. Like the narrative system the music system is a kind of common industrial standard and has been used in large parts of the world – as it still is. But while the narrative system has been relatively stable throughout the entire period, certain sections of the musical system disintegrated in the course of the 1950s. When dealing with film music, it is useful therefore to distinguish between the *classical system*, which covers the whole period from the 1930s until today, and *Golden Age* music, which refers to the special version of the system that was predominant until the late 1950s.

The establishment of the classical system

In the years following the breakthrough of the sound film a host of musicals were produced. In all other genres, however, music plays a very modest role. The musical wall-to-wall carpeting of the silent film disappears and is replaced by sporadic elements of diegetically motivated music. This continues until in the early 1930s a new model is established, based on non-diegetic music. In 1934 a special category of the Oscar was set up for this type of music, with the award the following year going to RKO for music for the John Ford film *The Informer.* The music was composed by Max Steiner.

Max Steiner (1888–1971) was an Austrian, born in Vienna. He had had a thorough grounding in music that included piano lessons under Johannes Brahms and musical studies under Gustav Mahler. He played several instruments, he had learned how to conduct, as a teenager he wrote operettas – and got them performed. When he was nineteen he emigrated to England, where he worked as a composer and conductor at various theatres. In 1914 he arrived in the United States. He orchestrated and conducted musicals in New York, but also did some cinema conducting on the side. In the late 1920s he came to Hollywood, where he orchestrated songs for RKO musicals on a one-year contract. Before the contract expired he was offered the job as head of the studio's music department, being employed on a monthly basis without a contract.[23]

It is often said that it was Steiner's music for such films as *King Kong* (1933) and *The Informer* (1935) that established the classical Hollywood system of film music. But Steiner was not solely responsible. He came to Hollywood at the same time as several other composers, all of whom had roughly the same background and career as he had.

• The Russian Dimitri Tiomkin (1894–1979) was a trained pianist and had worked as a cinema musician. After the Revolution in 1917 he travelled to Berlin and later to the United States. He arrived in Hollywood in 1929 in connection with the production of a musical.

• Alfred Newman (1901–1970) was the only one of the Hollywood composers of the time who was born in the United States. He started to work as a theatre pianist in New York at the age of twelve, became a conductor and later the musical manager of a Broadway theatre. He arrived in Hollywood in 1930, also in connection with the production of a musical.

• Franz Waxman (1906–1967), a German, had worked with film music both in Germany and in France. He arrived in Hollywood in 1935 and became known for his music for a number of horror films.

• Austrian Erich Korngold (1897–1957) was a musical child prodigy. He was an experienced pianist by the age of seven; he composed and performed his own works when he was ten, wrote music for a ballet when he was eleven; he had written two operas by the age of sixteen. In the 1920s he worked with the theatre director Max Reinhardt on several operetta projects. Reinhardt took him to Hollywood in 1929 in connection with a Shakespeare production. In 1935 Korngold returned, now as a refugee from the Nazis, and began to work as a film composer. He is particularly known for his lavish music for a number of adventure films starring Errol Flynn.

Though all of these composers – and more besides – contributed to establishing and consolidating the Hollywood system, Max Steiner is normally the man singled out in film-historical contexts. This is partly because he was so incredibly productive and because he perfected a number of the central features of the system, but also, as Kathryn Kalinak has pointed out, because it was his very first film score, the music for *Cimarron* (1931), that founded the system, so to speak.[24]

There is no more than ten minutes of music in *Cimarron*. In accordance with common practice around 1930 most of it is 'realistically' motivated, with a clear visual marking of the music source. And, also in line with the style of the age, some non-diegetic orchestral music accompanies the closing credits. But this concluding music begins during the last scene of the film, spilling over from there into the credits.

'The preview was a great success, and the next day both of the trade papers, *Variety* and *The Hollywood Reporter*, wanted to know who wrote the music and why there was no credit,' Steiner relates.[25] The music was also mentioned in the newspapers and, just as important, it was noticed by people in the film industry who considered it an interesting deviation from the implicit norm. Steiner was not the first composer to try adding non-diegetic musical elements in a sound film, but he was the first one to have his music noticed and talked about in public. The interest in *Cimarron* articulated both the norm and the breaking with the norm, which ultimately led to the norm being understood as one among many possibilities. As Kalinak puts it: with the music for *Cimarron*, Hollywood had acquired yet another musical alternative, 'selective use of nondiegetic music for dramatic emphasis'.[26] And in the course of the following years this alternative becomes the new norm.

Seen against the background of *Cimarron* Steiner's more famous music for *King Kong* (1933) is mainly a stabilizing of an already established system. Initially the intention was not for original music to be written for the film. The producers were well aware that there was a need of musical support if the story was to work convincingly; they thought 'that the gorilla looked unreal and that the animation was rather primitive', Steiner remarks. But RKO were in a state of perpetual financial crisis during this period, and the budget for the film had long since been exceeded. So they asked him for a cheap compilation score.[27] One of the film directors, Merian C. Cooper, intervened and promised to pay the expenses of an original score.

The music was recorded by an orchestra of 46 musicians, one of the largest orchestras in Hollywood at that time. In accordance with the plot the music is 'exotic', with predominant percussion and 'strange' chords. More interesting is that Steiner in this case had written an almost continuous accompaniment. It was as if, Kalinak remarks, the giant gorilla was in the process of going beyond the realistic framework and the music was to facilitate the leap into the world of fiction. The music assumed the responsibility for 'creating the credible from the incredible'.[28]

The continuous accompaniment in *King Kong* points back towards the musical practice of the silent film age but, as a whole, the music also points forwards towards what was going to be one of the characteristics of Steiner and the other composers of the Golden Age: the exact synchronization of music and images.

Synchronization

The early discussions about the music of sound films focused mainly on issues related to content. In the discussion about parallel and contrapuntal music the main question was whether the music was to underline and thereby highlight the action of the film by 'saying the same thing' as the pictures, or whether it was to offer a contrast to them, as, for example, when Pudovkin tries to mark opposition and optimism by adding a strict march to images of defeat. But the relationship between image and sound also has a more formal, technical side: to the contrast in terms of content between parallelism and counterpoint there is a corresponding contrast in terms of form between *synchronous* and *asynchronous* music.[29]

The most important technical task during the start-up phase of the sound film was to synchronize sound and image. If the film was to be convincing the dialogue on the soundtrack would have to be exactly synchronized with the movement of the actors' lips on the screen, and noises would have to correspond to the movement of objects. When it comes to music, however, things are more complicated. Diegetic music must of course be synchronized with the images. But the same does not necessarily apply to non-diegetic music. In both the era of the silent film and the transitional phase of the sound film there are many examples of non-diegetic music that is more or less coordinated with the images in terms of time without, for example, matching the movements of the actors in very detail. However, Steiner and his Hollywood contemporaries normally opted for a very close synchronization of music and image. This is called 'mickey-mousing', a derogatory term that refers to the cartoon films of the time in which each movement on the screen is accompanied by a striking musical effect. Steiner himself, though, used the term positively when he wanted to characterize his own compositional practice. In a note from 1940 he writes that mickey-mousing is the best musical technique that can be used in a filmic context: 'It fits the picture like a glove.'

> In other words, if I were to underline a love scene in a parlor and we were to cut away to a boat on the water, I would try and write my music so that the love theme would modulate into some kind of water music or what have you, as naturally the love theme would have nothing to do with the boat as the locale would be changed and probably would indicate time elapse.[30]

The opposite, according to Steiner, is composers from 'the over-all school', who 'totally' cover the film with music and who 'would keep right on playing regardless what happens'.

In Steiner's example the music is doubly coordinated with the action of the film. On the one hand, it corresponds in terms of content with the images: when the boat scene replaces the love scene, the 'love theme' is replaced by 'water music'. The musical transition, however, corresponds on the other hand to a formal transition: it is synchronized with the cut. Steiner must take most of the credit for this type of close formal synchronization becoming the usual practice in Hollywood. He tells of a scene in *The Informer*, for example, where water is dripping onto the main character in a prison cell. 'I wanted to catch each of these drops musically. The property man and I worked for days trying to regulate the water tank so it dripped in tempo and so I could accompany it.'[31]

During the years that followed Steiner worked on gaining complete technical mastery of synchronization. His predecessors used stopwatches to determine the duration of the individual sequences; Steiner developed the so-called *click track* technique, one that has been used in the industry up to the present day. A click track is a temporary soundtrack that the composer adds to the film when finally edited; the 'clicks' indicate the metronomic rhythm that must be kept if the music is to cover and follow the sequence with complete precision. The clicks are used both by the composer who writes the music and by the conductor and musicians when the music is recorded.[32]

Assembly line music

With the introduction of sound films, music becomes part of the film, and music production becomes part of the general production process. Practically all the Golden Age composers were contracted by one of the major studios. Like the actors, scriptwriters, photographers and technicians they were employed to carry out a limited, specialized assignment in a process based on heavy division of labour. They were subordinate employees in a subordinate section within a hierarchically constructed command system. Each of the major Hollywood studios had its own music department with contracted composers, conductors, musicians, music copyists and archivists. The department was run by a head of music who reported to the studio management. The relationship between employees and management was evidenced by the fact that when Oscars were introduced for film music, the first four awards did not go to the composers but to the music department. For example, it was not Max Steiner the composer, but Max Steiner the RKO Head of Music, who received an Oscar for the music for *The Informer* in 1935.

The film music was normally written last, after the film editing had been completed. This began with a so-called *spotting session*, where all those involved – producer, director, studio head of music, composer – watched the film and decided how music was to be used and where it ought to be placed. On the basis of this discussion, a 'music cutter' prepared a cue sheet that described the action in the individual sequences and indicated their precise duration. After this, the music was composed, orchestrated and recorded. Finally, it was mixed with the dialogue and other sounds.

On the face of it, it might seem that there was no great difference between this work process and the old accounts of how the conductors compiled music for the silent films.[33] But it is not that simple. Within the studio system the production of film music was a far more labour-divided process than in the era of the silent films. Normally the composers were only responsible for a very limited amount of the musical production process: they took part in the first meeting, and they wrote the pieces of music that had been agreed on, but the music was composed on the basis of cue sheets that other people had drawn up, and if a low-budget film was involved, even the composition work was farmed out to several people taking account of the individual composer's special skills.

The composer wrote the music in sketch form, as a kind of expanded piano score, using only a few staves. The rest of the process was passed on to others. The sketches went to an arranger, who indicated how the music was to be orchestrated. On the basis of the arranger's indications on the sketch, the copyists wrote out the orchestra parts. The music was then recorded by an orchestra led by one of the studio conductors, and finally it was mixed by sound technicians who had the right to change and edit it – or scrap it. Erich Korngold is said once to have remarked: 'A film composer's immortality lasts from the recording stage to the dubbing room', a statement that implies the dissatisfaction of the employee with this labour-divided process.[34] Bernard Herrmann, who came to Hollywood to write the music for Orson Welles's debut film *Citizen Kane* (1941), sums up in a newspaper article what the film composers normally complained about: first, the pressure of time, second, that they were seldom allowed or had time to orchestrate their own music and, third, that they did not have any influence on how the music was mixed and positioned in the total soundscape.[35]

The pressure of time was a recurring bone of contention. The composers, like other employees, worked to very tight deadlines – sometimes they had no more than two to three weeks at their disposal, Herrmann writes. Max Steiner says that he wrote the music for *The Lost Patrol* (1934) in eight days. The normal time-frame was four to six weeks, although in certain cases a composer was able to negotiate more time. Welles ensured that Herrmann was given twelve weeks to write the music for *Citizen Kane*. And Erich Korngold declares self-importantly that he has always worked under far more favourable conditions than his Hollywood colleagues. 'So far, I have successfully resisted the temptations of an all-year contract because in my opinion that would force me into factory-like mass production.' He refused to work on a tight schedule and only wrote music for two major films a year.[36]

That Korngold had a past as a relatively 'serious' composer perhaps gave him a certain advantage during negotiations with the companies. Other composers were worse off. Even Max Steiner, who was studio head of music and the most famous film composer of his age, had to accept 'factory-like mass production'. In his first years at RKO, he wrote music for 25–35 films a year. In the 1935–40 period while Korngold wrote the music for 11 films, Steiner wrote the music for 60.

The classical system

The industrial organization of the production process affected the style of the music. What in the literature is described as the classical Hollywood model is a system of rules that standardizes the composition work and makes it possible for several composers to work on the same score. In the next chapter, I will discuss the system in detail, but I here outline the most characteristic features and explain how the new system differs from the film music of the last phase of the silent films.

From compilation to composition

Typical silent-film music was a compilation of music that already existed, of well-known pieces of music or of mood music taken from the many manuals and anthologies – music that could fit a wide range of contexts, as an accompaniment to many different films. Classical Hollywood music, on the other hand, was an original composition, written with one film in mind and not intended to be re-used in other films.[37]

Non-diegetic and diegetic music

Hollywood music is reminiscent of that of the silent film since it mainly functions as a non-diegetic, 'external' commentary on the action of the film. The system, however, also contains diegetic music. If music is played in the story world, it is of course also heard on the soundtrack.

Discontinuous music

While the music of silent films was normally organized as a continuous sound-carpet, Hollywood music was used more selectively in order to achieve special dynamic or dramatic effects.

External and internal music

The 'external' commentary of silent-film music was also 'external' in relation to the film itself. While the audience of silent films experienced live music performed on the spot by local musicians to constantly changing films, the music of sound films is 'internal'. The audience hears music that it is impossible to separate from the film itself. The music of silent films was music played to a film. The music of sound films is a part of the film, in the same way as, for example, colours are an integral part of a colour film.

Late Romantic inspiration

All the above-mentioned elements are familiar from modern film music. In addition, however, there is the question of musical idiom and performance. Silent-film music was normally a collage of music from many different styles and, depending on the size and finances of the cinema, it was performed by every conceivable combination of musicians, from the solitary pianist to the big orchestra. In the Golden Age of the sound film – the period from the late 1930s to the late 1950s – Hollywood music was, on the other hand, written for a large orchestra, usually in continuation of the late Romantic symphonic tradition of the nineteenth century. The music that served as the immediate model for the Hollywood composers during this period can briefly be characterized as follows:

Experiments with tonal quality

The orchestral model that was established in the course of the eighteenth century broadened considerably during the nineteenth. New instruments were added, especially in the brass section, and composers began to emphasize the particular qualities and timbre of the individual instruments.

Experiments with the harmonic idiom

Tonal harmonics remained the foundation of nineteenth-century music, but its limits were constantly being challenged by the use of unprepared and unresolved dissonances and by chords that made use of the higher intervals of the scale, such as major and minor chords with added sevenths, ninths, etc.

Experiments with form

The simple, regular proportions of the classical period were replaced by freer, more dramatic forms, both in the large symphonic format and in chamber music.

Words and melody

Opera and *Lieder* became the central genres during the nineteenth century. This led to a strong emphasis being placed on melody and on melodic expressiveness.

Most of these features can be found in music from the Golden Age: it was written for relatively large symphony orchestras with a lavish, colourful orchestration, strongly influenced by the key composers of the nineteenth century. As far as harmonics are concerned, the chromaticized idiom of late Romanticism was predominant, and emphasis was placed on lyrical, expressive melodies, usually played by the strings.

On the other hand, the Hollywood composers were not writing music for the concert hall; they were employees working in an industry that produced entertainment for a diversified mass audience. Even if their music clearly points to late Romanticism, many of the more radical elements of the tradition are absent or considerably modified. Golden Age film music seldom goes to extremes. It is 'a strange anachronism, a relic of the late 19th century', Jan Swynnoe writes,[38] characterizing it as 'a generalized *Reader's Digest* idea of the romantic sound; something like a cross between Tchaikovsky and early Schoenberg'.[39] In addition it contains both elements from late nineteenth-century 'lighter' music and from contemporary popular music.

Why did composers like Max Steiner, Alfred Newman, Erich Korngold and Dimitri Tiomkin choose this particular musical idiom when they started to write music for sound films in the early 1930s? The secondary literature has, basically speaking, two answers: one of them historical-biographical, the other narrative-structural.

The historical-biographical explanation is the more widespread. Christopher Palmer writes in the 1980 edition of *New Grove* that the 'relatively conservative musical style' of Hollywood's Golden Age reflects the origins of the composers: 'the majority came from the Broadway theatres or the opera houses and theatres of middle and eastern Europe', and so their musical idiom derived from Tchaikovsky, Rachmaninov, Wagner and Strauss.[40] Fifteen years later Royal S. Brown writes in similar vein that since Max Steiner and Erich Korngold came from Vienna, and many of the other early Hollywood composers had a central European background, it is not surprising that the early Hollywood music had a late Romantic feel to it. 'Such diverse composers as Wagner, Puccini, Johann Strauss Jr., Richard Strauss, and Gustav Mahler all left their mark on melodic, harmonic, and instrumental profiles.'[41] Kathryn Kalinak points out that the music of the silent film era – at least the most ambitious part of it – was already relying on late Romantic models, and that the central Hollywood composers of the 1930s, who themselves had been trained in this late Romantic idiom, were really only strengthening an already existing practice.[42]

In other words, the Hollywood composers wrote the music they had learnt to write. But why did the heads of the large film studios employ such composers? Why did they want to have precisely this type of music for their films? Perhaps because it accorded with their own musical taste and that of their environment? Graham Bruce, for example, believes that it was Hollywood's general predilection for the grandiose and extravagant that made the large symphony orchestras attractive.[43] Nor can we ignore the possibility that social snobbery played a role. In most people's ears the sound of late Romantic orchestral music was, and is, synonymous with 'serious music' and 'high culture'. And when an adapted imitation of such music was used in Hollywood, this was, among other things, in order to evoke these connotations, in order to signal that the films were quality products. It is presumably considerations of this nature that are hovering in the background when Brown writes that the studio managers made a financial gain by exploiting their own 'philistine sensitivities'.[44]

But the background of the composers and the social aspirations of the studio managers can hardly be the whole explanation. The late Romantic idiom would of course never have been used if it were not profitable, if it did not 'work'. One must assume that the Golden Age music had certain qualities that fitted and enhanced the film narrative.

Roy M. Prendergast, who is a spokesman for the structural explanation, points at the similarity between opera and film music, and writes that Steiner and the other Golden Age composers simply solved their narrative problems by taking over models from Wagner, Puccini, Verdi and Strauss.[45] Narrative functionality is also Kathryn Kalinak's main explanation, although she gives the argument a twist by adding that the strong emphasis in late Romanticism on melodics in some form or other corresponds to the emphasis of the classical Hollywood film on the narrative. The Romantic musical idiom is based on 'the subordination of all elements in the musical texture to melody giving auditors a clear point of focus in the dense sound'. On the basis of how strongly the classical narrative film attempts to draw the spectator into the film, the Romantic idiom seems to be a logical choice.[46]

This analogy between narrative and melody seems a trifle forced – and it is actually unnecessary in order to underpin the structural explanation. The main function of the Golden Age music was to enhance the spectators' understanding of the action by directing their attention towards the crucial narrative information that was conveyed by image and dialogue. Furthermore the music was to create formal and narrative continuity between shots and scenes, to fill in 'holes', etc. Among the musical possibilities available, the late Romantic musical idiom was especially well suited to this, not only because of its melodic expressiveness but also, and most important, because of its use of irregular, dramatic forms. These forms could be shaped and adapted in many directions, as well as shortened and expanded whenever necessary during the editing process.

Film music inspired by late Romanticism and performed by a large orchestra went more or less out of use during the 1950s. But in the mid-1940s the Golden Age model was still very much intact. In the following chapter, we will take a closer look at how it works in one of the major crime films of the period.

6
Film Music from the Golden Age: *The Big Sleep*, 1946

The Big Sleep is a crime film, a *film noir* version of Raymond Chandler's debut novel from 1939.[1] When the director Howard Hawks planned the film for Warner Brothers Chandler himself was working as a scriptwriter in Hollywood, but he was employed by Paramount. For that reason the task of adapting the novel had to be entrusted to others. Hawks chose the novelist William Faulkner, providing him with a young crime writer, Leigh Brackett, as his assistant. At a late stage in the process the writer Jules Furthman was hired to add a finishing touch to the manuscript.[2]

Many changes were necessary for Chandler's novel to become a film. It has a formidable array of characters and a complex, intricate plot. As always in such cases the scriptwriters removed a great number of characters and altered the plot considerably. Furthermore, Hawks wished from the outset to emphasize the relationship between the two main characters of the film, Philip Marlowe and Vivian Sternwood, who were played by Hollywood's new star couple, Humphrey Bogart and Lauren Bacall. This led to the roles being drastically altered in comparison with the book. All these changes make the story quite difficult to follow.[3] The film became even more incomprehensible after a final rewrite in January 1946, because a number of the explanatory dialogues were excised to make room for some new scenes between Bogart and Bacall.

A beginning

The story is complicated. To begin with, however, everything is simple and easy to grasp. Once the opening credits have left the screen, we see a close-up of a door, a large brass plate with the name Sternwood and a finger pressing a bell. There then follows a small sequence of interconnected events. The door is opened by a butler. The man at the door presents himself: his name is Marlowe. 'The general is expecting you,' the butler says. He goes off, leaving Marlowe alone in the large hall. While he is waiting, he meets a young woman who, rather clumsily, attempts to interrogate and seduce him. The butler returns, interrupting them in a somewhat embarrassing, uncomfortable situation. He explains that the young woman is Carmen Sternwood, after which he leads Marlowe into a large conservatory, where the old general is waiting for him.

This 'opens' the narrative. In the course of this first scene two important characters have been introduced, and at the same time a field of possibilities and tensions has been established. Who is Marlowe? Who is the general? Why has Marlowe been summoned? What is the problem with this strange Carmen? Some of the many uncertainties and tensions are resolved then and there; others are resolved in the following, quite long, scene where the general introduces Marlowe, and us, to the case that the rest of the narrative is going to deal with. But the uncertainties linked to the character of Carmen remain throughout most of the film. They are not resolved until the very last minutes of the film and the narrative.

The introductory events are accompanied by a cohesive piece of music that itself is organized in 'events'. The transitions between the major sections of the music are synchronized with the movements of the characters, their glances and their dialogues. The music 'matches' and underlines the parts of the narrative, indicating how as a spectator one ought to read or articulate what one sees and hears. Let me outline this series of musical events.[4]

A musical opening

The film starts with the Warner Brothers logo and accompanying fanfare. Then come the opening credits accompanied by a dramatic, 'heavy' overture, marked *Grandioso* in the score.[5] At the end of the overture, the music moves towards a resolution, but the expected final chord does not come. Instead, a new, 'different' musical section begins, just as we see a close-up of Marlowe's finger pressing the Sternwood bell button. The rhythm slows down; the new, musical event is indeterminate as regards harmony and theme; it has all the characteristic features of an 'introduction'.

We expect the music to move on, but cannot predict which direction it will take. The field is relatively open.

The musical uncertainty and our undefined expectation of a continuation is further emphasised by three clearly separated notes (C–E–E^b) in the low strings. They indicate a possible direction, but do not coagulate to form a melody. We hear them while Marlowe hesitantly moves a little further into the large hall. The uncertainty of the music corresponds to the general narrative uncertainty of the first shots. The music then changes character: we hear a descending motif played by the woodwind at a brisk pace.

6.1: *The Big Sleep*: Descending motif

Musically speaking, these bars function as a resolution of the introductory tension and uncertainty. In relation to the visual sequence, they therefore function as a kind of unspecified anticipation. They simply signal that something else is now about to happen, that events are going to move in an as yet unspecified direction. And this imminent change is further emphasized by Marlowe gazing at something taking place off-screen (illus 6.2).

Only now do we see Carmen, as some kind of 'answer' to the preceding shot: here is the person Marlowe was looking at. The uncertainty

Marlowe looks up   Carmen on the staircase

6.2: *The Big Sleep*: Marlowe meets Carmen

is removed for the time being, the narrative has acquired its specifying direction. And the shot of Carmen on the staircase is also a specifying 'answer' to the musical statement: we understand that this was the event signalled by the first two bars. The music itself underlines the specification: while Carmen descends the staircase, the two last chords are repeated twice, as a kind of echo.

6.3: *The Big Sleep*: Carmen on the staircase

While Carmen crosses the floor of the hall, pausing at a small table, we hear the whole section yet again, now sequenced, transposed a semitone up and played at a slower tempo by the strings.

The short section (illus. 6.3) where the music accompanies Carmen's movement down the staircase, is a kind of *mickey-mousing*, but can better be described as a mutual *mapping* between image and music. Because the visual and musical events are coordinated, our attention is directed at the quick, rhythmic movement that the events share, while other possible aspects – in the music and the image – fade into the background.

There is a corresponding example a moment later, when Carmen asks Marlowe what his name is and is given the ironic reply 'Doghouse Reilly'. 'That's a funny kind of name,' she exclaims, while we hear a striking theme in F minor (illus. 6.4). The theme sounds 'funny'. It is played by cor anglais and clarinets, which give it a cackling, Donald Duck-like sound. So the music underlines an element in the dialogue, but itself is also interpreted by the dialogue. It is Carmen's reply that causes us to focus on the 'funniness' of the theme, while, for example,

6.4: *The Big Sleep*: Doghouse Reilly

the 'ascending' line of the melody or the 'skewed', 'knotted' rhythm fade into the background.

Any piece of music can be described in many different ways. Which aspects are emphasized in a given description depend on the context. In the staircase example it is the image of Carmen and her movement that dictate the choice; in the Doghouse Reilly example it is the dialogue. And because such a mutual selection takes place, both image and music are affected. In the staircase example the music emphasizes the contrast between Carmen's swift downward movement and Marlowe's slow horizontal movement. At the same time, and similarly, the images specify the musical transition from uncertainty to certainty by underlining the high register and accented rhythm of the descending theme, thereby bringing out the contrast with the deep register of the introduction and its slow, hesitant rhythm.

Immediately afterwards, Carmen lets herself fall into Marlowe's arms, and this time there is a *mickey-mousing* that is quite unmistakable. The fall is accompanied by a descending arpeggio on the harp. Then she flatteringly remarks: 'You're cute!' to the tones of a short, 'bluesy' motif. And when the butler returns, she gets up and leaves the hall accompanied by a longer version of the same motif (illus. 6.5).

6.5: *The Big Sleep*: Blues

The music then returns to the register of the introduction; the deep notes from the strings are repeated. Marlowe resumes his forward horizontal movement, leaving the hall in the opposite direction from Carmen. This concludes the first section of the narrative and begins a new one, at the same time as the music, in corresponding fashion, is taken to its conclusion, only to disappoint our expectations once more: the final chord does not come. A new, open field is established, and the music dies away while Marlowe enters the conservatory and meets the general.

Marlowe's first encounter with Carmen is thus placed in a sense in double brackets. The first bracket is a visual one, marked by the opposing directions in the fictional space: Carmen represents a narrative deviation from the correct course; she literally crosses Marlowe's path and halts his progress from the door through the hall, until he breaks free and resumes his forward movement through the door into the general's conservatory, into the story. Second, there is a musical bracket: the melodic phrases that are heard during the incident in the hall are distinctly different as regards rhythm, instrumentation, etc. from the music that precedes and follows.

Precisely because the interaction between image and music triggers off this double emphasis, it becomes clear – both 'visually' and 'aurally' – that the incident in the hall is not a chance 'insignificant' deviation from the right course. With the aid of this extremely effective visual and musical underlining, the incident is singled out as being something special. It is actually related here, using quite subtle means, that Carmen is the real obstacle in the narrative we are about to experience. But it takes an hour and a half before Marlowe – and we – understand this.

A first outline

The hall scene can be used as a point of departure for some remarks about the positioning and function of the music, both in this particular film and in films from the Golden Age in general.

Musical idiom

The music during the credit titles is an 'overture', an 'opening' which signals that this is going to be a 'strong', 'dramatic' film. From a musical point of view, too, we are dealing with an opening. Here, before the actual narrative has got underway, the musical idiom of the film is defined and a musical framework is established. The large orchestra, the symphonic music, the instrumentation, indicate that the music of the film is based on a late Romantic ideal. This does not necessarily mean that all *the music in the film* is going to be late Romantic, but precisely that *the music of the film* is this, and that other types of music are to be heard and measured in relation to this musical idiom.

Non-diegetic and diegetic music

The music that can be heard during the hall scene is obviously non-diegetic. This is true of most of the music in the film. There are, though, a couple of characteristic exceptions. At one point Marlowe meets the general's eldest daughter, Vivian, at a nightclub where a pianist is playing in the background. Immediately afterwards, Marlowe leaves for the gangster Eddie Mars's casino, where the guests are being entertained by a swing orchestra.

In both cases, 'live music' is played in the fictional space, i.e. diegetic music. The examples also demonstrate that 'music in the film' can be quite different from 'the music of the film', and that the stylistic difference conveys meaning. While the late Romantic musical idiom functions as a neutral background, the music of the bar pianist and the swing orchestra is used to characterize the environment of the night club and the casino.

Music as attraction

On his way round the casino Marlowe sees some people together in a small room. He looks inside and catches sight of Vivian, who is standing there singing for the guests, accompanied by a small group of musicians. The scene has no narrative function; it is quite clearly a 'time-out', a show-like performance determined by circumstances outside the narrative. The name of the song is 'And Her Tears Flowed Like Wine'. It was written by Stan Kenton and was his first big hit. When the shooting of *The Big Sleep* started in October 1944 the record version by Kenton's big band was at no. 4 on the music magazine *Billboard*'s hit list. That is the real reason why Vivian suddenly starts singing in this scene: the action is broken off, the film becomes a *spectacle*, the main female character of the narrative steps outside her role and presents one of the most popular melodies of the time. We hear the original big band version rearranged for piano and rhythm section, with Lauren Bacall as a surprisingly good replacement for Kenton's singer Anita O'Day, 'The First Lady of Swing'.[6]

The close connection between Hollywood and the music industry of the time did not only find expression in musicals and show films. The boundary between narrative and attraction was always fluid. Twenty years after the entry of the sound film, it was still common practice to pep up films, even a gloomy crime film, with show numbers and popular melodies of the time. The little scene with Vivian in the casino demonstrates that it was perfectly possible to deviate from the late Romantic musical idiom and insert elements of contemporary popular music as spectacular effects in the course of the film.[7]

Discontinuity

The opening scene is 'covered' with music, and on several occasions Steiner makes use of *fermatas*, prolongations of notes, to stretch the music so that it can fill the allotted time. On the other hand, the music fades out when Marlowe enters the conservatory to meet the general. And there is no music, either, in the following scene where he meets Vivian for the first time. In these two scenes Marlowe gains a lot of the necessary information about the mysteries of the past, characters, actions, special interests, that are crucial for what is to come later. Only when he leaves the house do we hear music again.

This pattern recurs during the rest of the film: the music comes in at regular intervals, but after a while it is discontinued. At times the music is introduced during the transition to a new scene and broken off at the next change of scene; at others it is quietened down and fades out a little later on, and sometimes it pops up in the middle of a scene, for example to emphasize an emotional point. This pattern is typical of the classical Hollywood system. Unlike the music of the silent film era, which covered the entire film, the music of sound films is discontinuous.

Continuity

Measured in terms of the narrative as a whole, the music is discontinuous, but when music actually occurs during a scene, it is continuous. Classical Hollywood music does not consist of isolated effects; it is always constructed as cohesive pieces, designed to cover a given section of the narrative and to create narrative coherence. Even though, for example, the music of the opening scene of *The Big Sleep* consists of a series of musical events that have clearly been designed to fit the dialogue and images, we are nevertheless dealing with a cohesive composition. The individual sections of the music are linked together with the aid of transitions, modulations, etc., and the coherence of the sound makes the actual scene in the hall 'hang together', marking it off as an independent unity.

This linking function is particularly important in transitions between *scenes* that are separate in terms of time or space, as well as in *montage sequences*, i.e. narrative 'overviews', where a lengthy piece of action is summarized, or where it is simply indicated that time passes. An example occurs at the beginning of *The Big Sleep*: when Marlowe leaves the Sternwood house after his conversations with the general and Vivian, the music starts up again while he is still in the hall on his way out. It continues during the following: a cut and zoom in on the entrance to a library; then a cut and zoom out from a book about famous first editions and a hand taking notes; finally, a shot of Marlowe placing the note in his pocket, getting up from a table in a reading room, going over to a counter and handing over the book he has been reading from. During the entire sequence, the music has a linking function: it softens up the spatial leap from the Sternwood house to the library. By means of its presence it assures us that even if the two next shots are taken somewhere else and show neither Marlowe nor any of the other characters, they are nevertheless part of the same narrative. At the same time the music 'expands' the time of the narrative. The first shots from the library follow immediately after each other and are kept on the screen for only a short time, but the music gives us the feeling of a longer time having passed since Marlowe left the Sternwood house.

Music, dialogue and noise

The fact that there is no music during the introductory conversations of *The Big Sleep* is just one of several expressions of the central importance of dialogue in this film, as in the films of the period in general. The rule of thumb is that the volume of the music is reduced during dialogue and that it stops if the characters exchange information that is crucial to an understanding of the story. The diegetic music is subject to the same rule: the piano music we hear when Marlowe meets Vivian at the nightclub is part of the 'realistic' sound of the environment; even so, it is turned down considerably as soon as they begin to talk. And even though Bacall's song in the scene at the casino is clearly part of the film's attraction, the narrative has nevertheless top priority. After a while the camera turns back to Marlowe as he listens; one of the hostesses at the casino comes to tell him that Eddie Mars is waiting for him; the song quietens down and fades away while Marlowe returns to the narrative. That the music is turned down is a signal that the events are being conveyed to us via a 'narrator'. There is an authority outside the diegesis that selects what is important and how the information is going to be presented to us.[8]

The dialogue is more important than the music, and the music is generally speaking more important than all other sounds. During the opening scene, one only hears sounds, for example, during the transitions between the decisive events – the bell at the beginning of the scene, the door being opened, the steps of characters from time to time. Like most of the other films of the time, *The Big Sleep* is not a sound film, but a 'talkie', accompanied by music and with very discreet sound effects. Only if non-musical sounds have vital narrative functions do they come into the foreground – as, for example, the sound of shots being exchanged.

Themes and leitmotifs

When the opening scene is over and Marlowe disappears into the conservatory, we have heard musical 'fabric' or 'material', an articulated composition that is easy to understand and easy to follow with the ear. In the rest of the film parts of this 'fabric' reappear from time to time. What initially were only musical 'events' now change into recognizable themes or motifs, which are repeated, varied, transformed.

Marlowe

As soon as Marlowe has left the Sternwood house, we hear the Doghouse Reilly theme again (illus. 6.6); for the first time while he is sitting reading in the library, for the second time when he stops in front of a second-hand bookshop. And as the narrative progresses we hear it again and again: a long, two-part phrase in the woodwind (a + b) which is answered by a short motif with muted brass (c). Sometimes, the entire question/answer construction (a+b | c) is played, at other times, only the question (a + b) or the answer (c), and in some cases, only one of the two halves of the question (a or b).

6.6: *The Big Sleep*: Marlowe

This is clearly the main theme of the film. And it always occurs in connection with Marlowe being on screen, i.e. it is a leitmotif: 'the Marlowe theme'. But it is a somewhat strange leitmotif. It is of course possible that the angular ascending minor theme is conceived as a kind of musical 'portrayal' of the main character, but that is a reference that never comes to play any role. And since Marlowe is on screen for practically all the film, the theme has little of the traditional signal function of a leitmotif.[9] In virtually all cases it is used as a simple, formal marker, anticipating or underlining Marlowe's actions. Only on one occasion does it deepen the narrative – at the very end, when the gangster Mars is dead, and Marlowe tells Vivian how he intends to explain the complex case to the police. Vivian says that he must have forgotten her. 'What is wrong with you?' he asks. 'Nothing you can't fix,' is her reply. The screen goes black and is replaced by *The End*. And here we hear the Marlowe theme for the last time, now in the major, 'triumphantly' announcing that *The End* is a happy ending.

The staircase

The staircase theme (see illus. 6.1) is heard once again as Marlowe is strolling to the second-hand bookshop, and later when he crosses the street to another bookshop. Later in the film it reoccurs on several occasions, but it never really develops into a leitmotif. It is partly used as a marker in transitions or dissolves between scenes, and partly as an accompaniment for brisk movements. It is usually linked to Marlowe, but is also used on one occasion when Vivian walks through the hall of the Sternwood house.

Carmen

Early in the film Marlowe is sitting in his car, keeping an eye on the house of the book dealer Geiger. A car stops in front of the house; a woman enters. We cannot see who it is, but Marlowe goes over to her car and checks it out for us. He finds Carmen's name on the car papers, while the music plays the 'bluesy' theme we heard in the first scene (see illus. 6.5). During the rest of the film, the theme reoccurs a couple of times, always in contexts where Carmen herself appears or is mentioned in the dialogue. The theme is a traditional leitmotif. It is linked to Carmen when it is introduced in the hall, and this connection is marked again, demonstratively, when Marlowe finds her name in the car. The motif represents her and is also a character motif: first, the jazzy style of the theme refers to the bars and casinos she normally frequents; second, the 'deviating' musical idiom and the deviating 'spooky' instrumentation imply that she too is a deviant in some way or other.

Analytical units

In summarizing the characteristics of music in the Golden Age, K. J. Donnelly refers to Max Steiner, writing that he 'steadfastly' used leitmotifs as building blocks to give the film 'structural unity' and to underpin 'the relationship between the music and the action on the screen and its narrative development'. Apart from the principle of leitmotifs, the Hollywood model also comprised 'the use of a full orchestra, the provision of a "wall-to-wall" fabric of music throughout the film, and the general matching of the dynamics on screen'.[10]

My account of the introductory scene from *The Big Sleep* gives rise to a couple of clarifying remarks about such summaries, both regarding Steiner's musical practice and, more generally, the Golden Age system. Many of the characteristics mentioned by Donnelly can naturally be found in *The Big Sleep*: the large orchestra, the leitmotifs, the music that is synchronized with the pictures and matches the action. But, generally speaking, this characterization is far too coarse-meshed: There is, for example, no wall-to-wall music in either this or most of the other films of the period. The late Romantic symphonic form and the large orchestra are not completely universal. And the leitmotifs are used along with many other musical techniques.

However, the literature about Steiner and the music of the Golden Age has been particularly preoccupied with the leitmotif technique. This is perhaps not so remarkable: synchronization and the use of leitmotifs were precisely Steiner's trademark when he established himself as a film composer in the early 1930s. He is often cited in the literature for the opinion that 'every character should have a theme'. This remark was made in connection with the Oscar-awarded music for John Ford's *The Informer* (1935), where he used a theme to, as he put it, 'identify' the main character Gypo: 'A blind man could have sat in a theatre and known when Gypo was on the screen.'[11]

The identifying theme is the simplest form of the leitmotif: a melodic phrase that constantly refers to a particular character every single time that character is on the screen. 'Music aids audiences in keeping characters straight in their minds,' Steiner said in 1935.[12] And in *The Informer* he used the reference technique almost automatically. But over the following years, the system was varied and developed considerably and, as the examples from *The Big Sleep* indicate, the recurring motifs often have many other tasks than to mark the presence of the characters.

Nevertheless, the music of the Golden Age is normally described as a series of simple, semantic functions based on the 'persistent' use of leitmotifs as building blocks. Even though it cannot be contested that the music can have semantic functions, such descriptions tend to simplify the case by repressing the complex networks of formal matchings that are established in the interaction between music, images and dialogue while the narrative unfolds. If one is to try to capture such relations, the analysis will have to be far more sensitive to context than the traditional descriptions of the semantic functions of music. An important aspect of this issue is the question of *analytic units*. What units are relevant when we are attempting to analyse, not the music 'in itself', not the 'inherent' meaning of the music, but the role of music as a functional element in a narrative that unfolds in a forward-oriented progression? Here we cannot make do with referring to the fact that the music in question carries out simple, semantic or referential functions, nor can we rely on the fine-meshed analyses of musical structures carried out in traditional musicology. We must attempt to develop analytic units which in some way or other 'match' the matchings we ourselves construct when, as spectators and listeners, we follow a film narrative. Let me illustrate this by means of another example from *The Big Sleep*.[13]

An example

Hawks's film is often used in film literature as an example, of the crime film genre, or *film noir*, or Classical Hollywood etc. 'Take as the example twelve shots from The Big Sleep', wrote Raymond Bellour in 1973, in an influential essay 'L'Évidence et le code', a text which in itself is an example of a particular semiotic-structuralist conception of the classical Hollywood narrative.[14] Below, I begin by following Bellour's example.

The twelve shots that Bellour is so interested in come right at the end of the film. They 'open and close on lap dissolves', he writes.[15] And, it can be added, the demarcation does not only take place at the formal level. In terms of narrative action the sequence is marked off by two dramatic shoot-outs. The first takes place in Realito, a small town outside Los Angeles; Vivian has freed Marlowe from Mars's gangsters; a shoot-out ensues; Vivian and Marlowe manage to flee in a car. The other shoot-out is the final scene, where Eddie Mars is killed by his own people. The twelve shots mark, in other words, a narrative transition: the series deals with what happens 'between' two narrative climaxes; it tells of Marlowe and Vivian's flight, and of how they get from Realito to Los Angeles.

Bellour calls this a *segment* – defined as a closed narrative element in which 'dramatic or fictional unity' coincides with 'identity of setting and characters of the narrative'.[16] So it is the narrative, the narrative functions, that are the central thing here. But what really happens at this point in the narrative? Not very much, according to Bellour: Marlowe and Vivian get into a car; they drive off from Realito towards LA; during their trip they admit for the first time that they love each other. In other words: two declarations of love. Where does the narrative take place? Again, according to Bellour, mainly in the dialogue, but also in the images, for example, when Vivian, towards the end of the segment, after Marlowe's declaration of love, touches his arm in a tiny, almost imperceptible gesture.

'Take as the example twelve shots from *The Big Sleep*,' Bellour writes. And his analysis is precisely this, a discussion of these twelve shots, of how the segment is formally structured. He presents his observations in a small table indicating the framing of the shots, their relative length, camera movements, camera angles, etc. The relation from shot to shot is based on similarity/difference: each shot is different from the preceding one, but most of them are repetitions of shots one has seen before in the segment. This creates a number of transverse symmetries and, according to Bellour, it is this 'regulated opposition between the closing off of symmetries and the opening up of dissymmetries' that produces the narrative.[17] In his analysis Bellour deals exclusively with images and dialogue, and most of all he is preoccupied with the repetitive elements in the segment – the two shoot-outs in the frame, the two declarations of love inside the frame, the regular alternation between series of identical shots throughout the segment, etc. And it is of course precisely the repetitions, the formal 'mirrorings', that are most salient if one is studying and analysing the film at a cutting table or using a video player. But when one sees it *in flux*, it actually has considerably more narrative impetus than is apparent from Bellour's description.

6.7: *The Big Sleep*: Twelve shots

The segment (illus 6.7) is ultra-short. It only takes one minute and 45 seconds, yet it is even so an example of how a classical narrative *scene* is constructed – just as David Bordwell describes it in *Narration in the Fiction Film*.[18] There is an *opening* that defines the situation in relation to the scene immediately preceding it: the two main characters are on the run. There is a *middle section* with conflicts and actions – in this instance we have the classic 'double' conflict of the Hollywood film: if Marlowe is to sort out the crime mystery, he must at the same time resolve his relationship with Vivian. The actions in the middle section – the mutual declarations of love – establish precisely this resolution. In the middle section there is also the well-known marking of a *deadline*: time is running out. Very soon Marlowe and Vivian will have to confront the gangsters in Los Angeles.

Compared to the classical paradigm, however, it would seem at first glance as if something was lacking – end, closure, narrative transition to the following scene. It is, among other things, here where music 'comes into the picture'. For even if Bellour does not mention music with a single word in his analysis, there is actually music being played throughout this scene – a composition for a large orchestra.

72 bars of music

'Take as the example 72 bars of Max Steiner's music for *The Big Sleep* . . .' If we were to follow in the footsteps of Bellour, we would have to add various new aspects to his overview of the segment. We would have to identify the musical 'events' and describe their positioning in the sequence as well as their relationship to the individual shots. We would have to describe the changes in the instrumentation, in the thematic material, in the harmonic structure, etc.

If we were to attempt to expand Bellour's table with these new parameters, it would soon become completely confusing. Formal descriptions of this type have a tendency to become so when used to give an account of complex textual constructions. And the question naturally is whether such a description would be at all relevant. Bellour's own analysis is to an extent a cautionary example. His point of departure was that via the analysis of the twelve shots he would be able to determine the characteristic features of the classical narrative segment. The result was a list of repetitions and mirroring effects that are unable to capture the narrative dynamics of the segment, yet which he even so claims are 'fundamentally characteristic of American films'.[19]

There is an indirect criticism of this kind of analysis in Edward Branigan's *Narrative Comprehension and Film*, where he writes that 'separation of material and structure' is a 'fundamental principle of the analysis of narrative'. Two basic processes are at work when we try to interpret our sense impressions. On the one hand, we construct meaning with the aid of so-called *top-down* processes, i.e. the sense impressions are interpreted on the basis of expectations, prior knowledge, etc.; on the other, we draw direct conclusions from the actual sense impression with the aid of so-called *bottom-up* processes. Branigan's point is that our understanding of narrative and narration is 'critically dependent' upon top-down cognitive processes. It is not determined by 'the formal boundaries of the material on screen, the "techniques" for displaying material, phenomenal categories that describe material, nor bottom-up cognitive processes'.[20]

But if material and structure are not identical, if we are unable to use Bellour's method and capture the narrative structure simply by describing the formal boundaries in the available material, what procedures and what analytical units ought we then to use instead? How should we advance to determine how the cinematic material is 'partitioned and reformed' by the spectator?[21] A discussion of how Steiner's music works in the car scene from *The Big Sleep* can give us an idea of how these questions can be answered in practice. Let us consider the quite different descriptions we get when we 'read' Max Steiner's score, 'listen' to the music from the soundtrack, and 'see' the music in its almost visual articulation as part of a narrative that unfolds in time.

Reading and listening to music

In a score music is represented as a stable, graphic configuration. By reading the score we gain a visual impression of the overall musical structure. In descriptions based on such readings it seems reasonable to use the bar as the basic unit, but even in this case Branigan's 'fundamental principle' applies concerning 'the separation of material and structure': When we focus on important features like tempo, thematic organization, part writing, instrumentation, we have to work with units of very different dimensions, often within one and the same description. Nevertheless, descriptions based on score-reading are often of a somewhat 'formalistic' nature; they are preoccupied with forms and structures, with balances, mirrorings, etc. When we read Steiner's score, for example, we see that the 72 bars of music have been constructed as a series of short, regular sections – four bars, eight bars, sixteen bars, etc., and that both the composition as a whole and the individual sections are based on regular, symmetrical forms.

A description based on the experience of listening to music played in a concert hall or on a disc will naturally focus on many of the same features as a description of the score, but the basic analytical unit in this case is the listener's spontaneous partitioning of the actual piece, one that is usually based on motifs, themes, melodies and corresponding larger structures. The short piece of music from *The Big Sleep*, for example, forms a closed whole that seems to be almost of a 'classical' nature: first we hear an introductory section; then thematic material is presented; the material is transformed and varied and the piece concludes somewhat abruptly. It is the organizing of the thematic and melodic material that forms the basis of this partitioning, but it is underpinned by, among other things, changes in the instrumentation of the music.

Let me attempt to provide a more detailed description of the music as an acoustic phenomenon. Such a description naturally requires references to the music itself, to the realization in sound, which is difficult to practise when one is obliged to undertake both the description and the references in a text. In the following, I will attempt to compensate for this by 'illustrating' the description, using brief references to the score.

Introduction

The music begins with an introductory, 'preparatory' section that is clearly divided into four almost identical parts. The first part lasts four bars: strings and woodwind play a motif-like cell four times (illus. 6.8).

6.8: *The Big Sleep*: Cell

The second part is a repeat of the first four bars, apart from the fact that the music has been transposed up a semitone; the same takes place in the third part. In the fourth part this sequencing is broken. The music returns to the point of departure and the first part is repeated.

Here, we already have an example of the difference between reading and listening to music. If we rely on the score, we will presumably consider the individual parts of the sequence as a series of four identical bars. When we listen to these bars being played, the bar line loses its subdividing function, however, and we hear an insistent, rising chromatic motif that cuts across the division into bars. It begins on the third beat of the bar and ends on the second beat of the following bar.

As can be seen the entire introduction is based on repetitions: the first cell is repeated four times after which the first four bars are sequenced upwards, etc. Via these constant repetitions of the ascending theme, an intensity is created that increases with each new sequence. In principle the sequencing could continue ad infinitum, with constantly new transpositions, but it is broken off by the variation in the fourth part, which returns the music to its point of departure, and a new arch of intensity begins.

Repetition, then, but also variation: in the third part of the introduction one hears muted trumpets and horns play two short, rhythmic motifs:

6.9: *The Big Sleep*: Muted brass

In the fourth part, the low brass twice play a falling phrase:

6.10: *The Big Sleep*: Low brass

Heard on the soundtrack, the movement of the music through these sixteen bars is intense, with forward impetus, but without any particular direction. The repeating figure in the strings and the falling phrase in the low brass are harmonically speaking undefined, and the figure of the muted brass (see illus. 6.9) is based on an ambiguous, dissonant chord that points in many different directions – the score indicates that it is a B minor chord with a diminished fifth and an added ninth.

Theme

The thematic cell changes slightly in the next section, but the basic pattern is the same. A new theme, played by violins and cellos, is now added (illus. 6.11). It is based on large triplets, creating a tension between the basis four beats to the bar and an implied waltz beat.

6.11: *The Big Sleep*: 'Waltz'

The waltz theme is repeated and we hear a kind of 'answer' in quadruple time:

6.12: *The Big Sleep*: Answer

When the 'waltz theme' is introduced, the music acquires a certain melodic direction and, when it is repeated, we have a reasonable idea where the music is heading. Harmonically speaking, too, this part has a defined direction. The waltz theme is in the major, and we expect it to 'come to rest' on the tonic chord after the two run-throughs. But these expectations are dashed by the 'answer' chords. Once again, a look at the score can make this more precise: we expect an E^b major chord, instead, there is a chord that consists of G-C#-F#. This opens up the music: the chord is undefined and can be interpreted in many different ways – as a 'blue' E^{b7}, as an A^7 with an added sixth, as a $F^{\#7}$ with a diminished ninth, as a Gm with a major seventh and diminished fifth, etc. None of these 'fits' the major key signature of the waltz. And the harmonic ambiguity is not resolved: in the following two bars, the chord is simply moved chromatically up and down.

Variation

A number of melodic, rhythmic and harmonic tensions have now been established, and in the next bars we hear the cell pattern with the quadruple rhythm underneath, the two motifs of the brass on top, and a repetition of the waltz theme. Once again, repetition, and variation: when the waltz theme is repeated, it is not played through twice, but broken off by a dissonant chord. A new musical motif is also introduced – a blues-like figure in E^b major that is first played by piano and vibraphone and later repeated by the horns:

6.13: *The Big Sleep*: Blues

The conclusion

The piece concludes with two run-throughs of the waltz theme played as a 'straight' repetition of the first occurrence, which means that the last bar ends once again with the ambiguous 'answer' chord (E-B-D$^{\#}$). The whole piece then comes demonstratively to rest: the harmonic tension is resolved by two bars of abrupt, strong marking of the key of B^{b} major.

Visible music

What happens when we 'see' the music, not in a score but at the cinema? A first observation is that the music has many different functions in this short scene. It is used, for example, to add continuity and unity to the narrative. The cohesive 72-bar composition immediately indicates that the scene is a *formal* unit, and that it is to be understood as a coherent *narrative* unit.

As I implied above, the scene, narratively speaking, has an unfinished feel to it. After Marlowe and Vivian have declared their love for each other, the rest of the scene is basically an in-between time, the time until deadline, until the new scene where they are to meet the gangsters. The music helps here to shape the scene and to round it off: during the introduction, a forward-oriented but undefined intensity is created, after which the sequence acquires a more precise direction with the introduction of the waltz theme; with the 'disappointing' harmonic turn, a musical tension is established, an expectation that is not resolved until a point much further on; the clearly marked final chord rounds off the sequence, functioning as a kind of punctuation mark in relation to the course of the events in the film narrative.

And let me remark, in passing, that when we listen to the music we can hear that Bellour was mistaken when he used the two dissolves as outer boundaries of his segment: the music continues after the final dissolve, thereby stating that the following image – where one sees the car come to a halt – is actually part of the same formal unit, that the segment, in other words, does not consist of twelve but of thirteen shots (illus. 6.14).[22]

Within this formal framework various other types of interaction are established between music, images and dialogue. The musical point of departure is the 'cell' sections (see illus. 6.8). During the introduction

6.14: *The Big Sleep*: Shot 13

of the first four-bar section, we see images of a misty night-time landscape swiftly gliding past the car windows. The images have to do with speed and flight, and the tempo of the music, combined with its constant chromatic movement, matches them. This combination of images and music is kept constant throughout the scene, but very soon other elements are added to the basic mood of tempo and hectic forward movement. There is dialogue; new musical elements are introduced; new connections are established between music and narrative.

This begins in the second four-bar section: Marlowe asks Vivian how far it is to the nearest telephone from Realito. 'Why?' she asks. The question and Marlowe's answer are synchronized with the first entry of the brass at the beginning of the third section (see illus. 6.9). The brass figures are *stingers*, short musical signals that draw the attention of the spectators to the fact that something important is happening. In this case, it is Marlowe's answer that is emphasized: as soon as the gangsters in Realito get to a telephone, they will ring and warn Mars. And Vivian will herself become involved, Marlowe adds during the fourth section, with the undefined, descending theme in the low brass matching the open-ended, uncertain nature of the situation (see illus. 6.10).

At this point the waltz theme is introduced (see illus. 6.11). In relation to the musical context built up during the first sixteen bars, this theme stands out conspicuously – it is in a different, slower rhythm and is not played by the brass but by the strings. We have heard it twice before, in both instances as an accompaniment to Marlowe kissing Vivian. But we do not have to have seen the whole film to understand that the theme is about 'love', for its appearance is exactly synchronized with Vivian's declaration of love to Marlowe: 'I guess I am in love with you.' The waltz marks a change at the musical level that 'corresponds' to the new, different element that this declaration brings into a dialogue which, until then, has dealt with their uncertain flight and the hazardous aspects of the crime story.

The waltz breaks off without the expected harmonic progression being completed. Instead, the 'answer' (see illus. 6.12) comes, which is harmonically ambiguous and marks a return to the original quadruple basic rhythm of the music. In the following action, this pattern of equivalents I have outlined is maintained. On the one hand, Marlowe continues to talk about the criminal case, about the dangers he and Vivian are facing, and this is accompanied by music that mainly comprises variations on the first sixteen bars; on the other, the waltz theme is occasionally played, each time where there is an emotional turn in the dialogue.

The first repetition of the waltz comes in bar 35, at the point where Marlowe adopts a gentler tone and tells Vivian that he will not report her to the police. Immediately afterwards, however, in bar 37, we are once again 'disappointed', musically speaking, the expected repetition does not come; the theme is abruptly broken off by a dissonant chord, while Marlowe picks up once more the story of his problems, with the music returning to the basic pattern. Twice in the following section we hear the 'blues theme' (see illus. 6.13) instead. We have also heard this theme before, but in our little scene it functions in a slightly different way to the waltz theme. When the waltz theme is played during Vivian's declaration of love, its function does not depend on its earlier appearances; it can immediately be matched in terms of structure with the clear, obvious shift in the dialogue. This is not the case with the blues theme. It functions in this context as a leitmotif that provides both a 'referential' and 'connotative' underlining of individual, local points in Marlowe's lines. We recognize the blues theme as 'Carmen's theme', and when Marlowe, in the car scene, talks about Vivian's family problems, we understand that it is Carmen he is referring to.

Towards the end of the scene, the waltz reappears, this time played in full. The first run through is synchronized with Marlowe's declaration of love. Vivian asks him why he wants to help her. 'I guess I am in love with *you*,' he replies. The rest is silence. She places a hand on his arm, while the music steps into the foreground and one hears the second half of the waltz theme, followed by the strong ending.

A musical narrative

Steiner's way of composing has often been criticized. His music is schematic, people say; it is a series of signal effects, simple musical comments on the action of the film, etc. The example from *The Big Sleep*, however, demonstrates that things are not quite so simple.

Admittedly, there are examples of music that consists of short phrases, music that is used to make a section 'hang together', music that is to set up a state of tension and that then, at some suitable point, when the images and dialogue call for it, releases it, only to begin to build up a new tension. But, as the example shows, there is also music that in a fairly complex and effective way interacts with the narrative sequence as conveyed in images and dialogue.

The cell pattern is the point of departure, a musical basis that is immediately established and is then used as a kind of contrasting background for a series of markings by means of short motifs and themes. The most ear-catching in this progression is the tension between frame and waltz theme – a tension that is made greater because of the 'disappointing' harmonic resolutions and the delayed ending, and that is emphatically released in the final bars. These simple, formal contrasts in the musical material are, as we have seen, exactly coordinated to correspond to the narrative conflict which emerges during the dialogue, the conflict between the criminal intrigue and the love story. The dialogue begins with Marlowe talking about the flight and impending dangers; Vivian interrupts him with a declaration of love that brings a new element into the scene; he becomes uncertain, picks up the thread of the criminal case once more and after a couple of delays, finally makes his own declaration of love.

The formal arch of tension in the music matches the narrative arch of tension in the dialogue and helps articulate it. But once this matching has been established, once the linking of music, images and dialogue has been set up, a movement takes place in the opposite direction. I said above that 'the music comes into the picture'. But the picture and, in this case in particular, the dialogue also come 'into the music'. The narrative of the film, as conveyed by images and dialogue, has a counter-effect, supporting the music and releasing its narrative potential. First, the inner articulations of the music are made clear: The narrative causes the 'classical' formal structure of the composition to stand out: opening, thematic conflict, development, closure. And, second, this formal structure is 'semanticized'. When the course of the narrative matches that of the music, the music acquires a local, external reference. It is as if we can *hear* the narrative in the music, as if the thematic conflict of the music 'is about' something. About flight, fear, love.

7

Other Ways: *North by Northwest*, 1959

When *The Big Sleep* had its premiere in 1946 Max Steiner was 58 years old. He was head of music at one of Hollywood's major film studios; he had been a central figure in the development of the musical aesthetics of the sound film; he had written music for hundreds of films. He had been Oscar-nominated for Best Music every year since 1935 and had won the award three times, and his productivity was still as astounding as it had been when he started in Hollywood. Every year throughout the 1940s he wrote music for ten new films. In the 1950s the tempo slowed. He wrote music for fewer films, gained no Oscars and Oscar nominations were further apart. Time was running out, not only for Steiner but for his entire generation of Hollywood composers and the music they stood for. There are several reasons for this.

The last days of the empire

Classical Hollywood music developed at the same time as the consolidation of the studio system. It was a practical, effective answer to the requirements of the system, and it corresponded to the expectations and musical preferences of the large cinema audience. But the days of the studio system were numbered. Ever since the end of the 1930s government authorities, independent cinema owners and small film producers had attempted to break the large studios' vertical integration of production, distribution and projection. They finally succeeded in 1949 when a Supreme Court decision forced the five major studios to give up their cinemas, depriving them of their most important source of income. At the same time the entire film industry began to feel the competition from television.

The collapse of the studio system meant the closing of the large music departments with their many employees, high division of labour and streamlined, industrial production. But if film music altered its nature in the course of the 1950s it was also a result of changes in the public's attitude towards films and film music. General modernization processes such as increased urbanization and industrialization, the development of new family patterns in connection with the entry of women into the labour market, etc. are part of the underlying cause. The economic depression of the 1930s and American participation in the Second World War were also contributory factors when the cinema public in the 1940s began to make new demands as regards the content and style of films. Admittedly, the industry continued to produce films in the old, well-known formats – crime films and westerns, extravagant musicals and melodramas, escapist adventure films, romantic comedies. But the emergence of a phenomenon such as *film noir* was one of several signs that something new was taking place, in both the industry and the film-going public.

At the turn of the 1950s the mood changes. The public feels that the grandiose Hollywood productions are old-fashioned. The task of the film producers is now to make films that are on a par with the new preferences of the audience. How does one produce modern films for a modern audience? And what is the role of music in modern films?

Experiments

The 1950s is a decade of new departures, where alternative types of film music are tried out, often in connection with the development of new types of film. A number of producers go in for low-budget films about everyday life and recognizable social problems. Inspired by Italian neo-realism, film-makers move out of the studios and shoot semi-documentary stories on location. In such productions traditional opulent Hollywood music would seem out of place. So in some cases the practice from the first experimental phase of sound films is reverted to, with music only being used if it actually occurs in the story world. The demand for the music to be diegetically motivated sometimes results in there being no music at all on the soundtrack.[1]

In other films non-diegetic music is still used, but experiments are carried out with alternatives to the late Romantic musical idiom of the Golden Age. Early in this period Alex North writes jazz-inspired music for *A Streetcar Named Desire* (Elia Kazan, 1951), and over the next few years he and other young Hollywood composers such as Elmer Bernstein, Johnny Mandel and Henry Mancini sometimes include jazz elements as a stylistic effect or a signal of modernity in films about big cities and crime. In a couple of instances well-known jazz musicians are also encountered in the role of film composers, for example, Duke Ellington (Otto Preminger's *Anatomy of a Murder*, 1959) and John Lewis (Robert Wise's *Odds Against Tomorrow*, 1959).

In the 1950s film composers also experiment with various types of modernistic idioms. Leonard Bernstein's music for *On the Waterfront* (Kazan, 1954) and Leonard Rosenman's music for *East of Eden* (Kazan, 1955) and *Rebel Without a Cause* (Nicholas Ray, 1955) are inspired by earlier atonal experiments as well as the twelve-tone music of the Schönberg circle. And Louis Barron and his wife Bebe, two pioneers within American electro-acoustic music, construct with the aid of tone generators 'electronic tonalities' for MGM's large-scale science fiction film *Forbidden Planet* (Fred M. Wilcox, 1956). Other examples of untraditional film music solutions could be mentioned. But, if one considers the 1950s as a whole, it is nevertheless difficult to claim that the classical system has disintegrated. The late Romantic influenced scores and the sumptuous melodies on the strings that characterized the Golden Age admittedly disappear in connection with the modernization of the music. But it is still 'symphonic' music that is the preferred solution for Hollywood's mainstream films. And the more basic conceptions of what film music is, where it ought to be placed in relation to the narrative, and what its functions are do not change to any appreciable extent.

Herrmann, Hitchcock and *North by Northwest*

Bernard Herrmann is one of the few composers of the period who shake the foundations of the classical Hollywood system in a more radical way. He came to Hollywood after the first generation of composers had already established themselves. Many of the heads of music told him there was no room for a person like him. 'They had a tight little corporation going,' he remarked later.[2] Throughout his career he was opposed to this tight corporation. His film music can be considered a series of attempts to develop sustainable alternatives to common practice.

Herrmann was an American, born in 1911 in New York.[3] He gained his basic musical education at New York University, where the Australian composer Percy Grainger was among his teachers. He subsequently qualified as a composer and conductor at the Juilliard School of Music. At the age of twenty, he established the New Chamber Orchestra, an ensemble that specialized in the performance of contemporary music. While the older film composers had a background in musical theatres and silent film cinemas, Herrmann came to Hollywood via the radio. He became attached to the CBS network in 1934, where he began to make music programmes. In 1937 he started to write music for radio dramas. Most important was his cooperation with Orson Welles, who in 1938 began producing *Mercury Theatre on the Air* for CBS, a series of radio dramas based on famous novels and short stories. 'I learned to become a film composer by doing two or three thousand radio dramas,' Herrmann said later. 'Each week was different. Radio was the greatest place to train one's dramatic sense.'[4]

When Welles set out for Hollywood in 1940 to shoot *Citizen Kane* for RKO, Herrmann accompanied him as composer. During this period he also worked on other films, and received an Oscar for his music for William Dieterle's *The Devil and Daniel Webster* (1941). In the succeeding years he worked as a film composer for Twentieth Century Fox and at the same time was the head conductor of the CBS Symphony Orchestra. In 1955 he was asked to write the music for Hitchcock's *The Trouble with Harry* for Paramount. This marked the beginning of a cooperation that was to last for ten years. During this time Herrmann wrote music for many other directors, while keeping up a career as a composer and conductor outside the Hollywood system, but it is his collaboration with Hitchcock that is normally regarded as his most important musical contribution. When this collaboration ended in 1965 Herrmann left Hollywood. He spent some time in England in the following years, writing music for a couple of European films including François Truffaut's *Fahrenheit 451* (1966) and *La mariée était en noir* (1968). In 1973 he returned to Hollywood, where he wrote the music for Brian de Palma's *Sisters* (1973) and *Obsession* (1976) as well as for Martin Scorsese's *Taxi Driver* (1975). He died in 1975.

I intend to use the music for Hitchcock's *North by Northwest* (1959) as a point of departure for a discussion of Herrmann's alternatives to the Golden Age model. *North by Northwest* is the second of three films thought to mark the culmination of Hitchcock's American production, and of Herrmann's career as a film composer. The first, *Vertigo* (1958), is a complex mystery film with a tragic ending; the third, *Psycho* (1960), is a dark thriller, remembered for one of the most famous horror scenes of film history. *North by Northwest* is a kind of entertaining interlude – a light, elegant thriller comedy. It was produced by MGM. Shooting began at the end of August 1958 and was completed on 16 December the same year. According to Herrmann's score, he started to write the music on 10 January 1959 and finished it on 2 March.[5] The film had its premiere in summer 1959.

Like most of Hitchcock's thrillers *North by Northwest* is built around what he himself called a *McGuffin* – a narrative element that is virtually unspecified, yet nevertheless plays a key role for the characters in the story, and therefore pushes the plot forwards. In *North by Northwest* the McGuffin is 'government secrets'. What secrets these are we are never told, but the prospect of a group of spies handing over the secrets to some unspecified 'foreign powers' is – in the story world – the 'realistic' explanation for all the incredible events that the main character, advertising executive Roger Thornhill (Cary Grant), experiences in the course of the film.

Spanish opening

North by Northwest begins with credit titles projected onto a green surface. As the titles appear there is a dissolve to a picture of the CIT building in New York, filmed obliquely from above. In the glass facade one sees the reflection of traffic on Madison Avenue. There then follows a series of shots at street level. One sees crowds hurrying past, people on their way to the subway, pedestrians crossing the street, women bickering over a taxi. And, last, the obligatory picture of Hitchcock himself, this time arriving too late for a bus.

The entire opening presents the hectic life of a modern metropolis. However, Herrmann has chosen to accompany it with a *fandango*, an old Spanish dance form. A traditional fandango is a quick, rhythmically accented piece of guitar music in 3/4 time, accompanied by castanets and hand-clapping. Herrmann's fandango is written for a full symphony orchestra, but he retains the time and tempo, and gives the percussion section the central role: the music track is dominated by drums, cymbals, castanets and tambourines. The result is a violently rowdy composition with piccolos shrieking above strident brass and noisy percussion.

This is not typical 'big city music' in the style of the 1950s, and yet the intense, aggressive overture, played *allegro vivace e con bravura*, manages to match the nervous big city atmosphere of the images.

The fandango starts with the kettledrums playing a short rhythmical motif twice, followed by a contrasting 'answer' from the low strings (illus. 7.1).

7.1: *North by Northwest*: Overture: basic structure

This theme is played six times in all, with changing instrumentation of the 'answer' section. Then the opening credits begin and the real overture gets underway. The rest of the piece is based on two rhythmical-melodic themes both of which are derived from the basic theme. The total composition emerges, so to speak, from the very first four bars. A few ultra-short, rhythmical motifs or 'cells' are linked together to form almost identical themes, and the themes are linked together into larger, regular units. The music has a 'Spanish' feel to it, with ambiguous chords being used freely for percussive effects. Nevertheless, one gets the feeling that the overture is moving forwards in a particular direction towards a particular goal – a result of the tremendous rhythmic drive of the music, not least the violent, dynamic curve that is built up from the almost inaudible kettledrums of the introduction to the thundering crescendo of the finale.

An overture is normally used to indicate the mood of the ensuing narrative and to lead the spectator into the musical universe of the film. In it the musical idiom and style is determined, and it is often here that one introduces the main musical themes of the film. Herrmann's overture to *North by Northwest* does neither of these. There is no narrative connection between the Spanish mood of the overture and the plot, and in terms of music, the symphonic fandango is quite atypical – the rest of the music is written in a different style and orchestrated for various chamber ensembles. And even though sections of the fandango reappear during the film, we cannot say that the overture is used to present the main themes of the film, for it does not actually contain a single traditional theme. The overture, to quote Royal S. Brown's words, is 'totally unhummable'.[6] It is made up of simple, rhythmic structures that are repeated and after a while recognized, but there is no melodic material to get hold of.

Exposition

Even though the unorthodox overture is somewhat isolated from the following music, it serves nevertheless in its own way as an excellent introduction – not to Hitchcock's film but to Herrmann's musical universe. It takes quite a while, however, before we have the chance of getting to know this universe more intimately. The narrative opens with a long, unaccompanied sequence where Roger Thornhill is presented.[7] We are in New York, on Madison Avenue. Thornhill is dictating a letter to his secretary while hurrying off to a meeting in the bar of the Plaza Hotel. Meanwhile, we are given various pieces of information that are necessary for us to understand the events about to take place.

When he arrives at the Plaza and enters via the lobby, we can hear the hotel orchestra playing the song 'It's a Most Unusual Day' in the background, a small piece of diegetic music that at the same time is an ironic, non-diegetic omen of something unusual about to happen.[8] Thornhill meets some business connections in The Oak Room Bar, where the fatal misunderstanding takes place: when he leaves the lobby for a moment in order to send a telegram, he is stopped by spy chief Vandamm's men, who believe he is a certain George Kaplan. He is confused and wishes to continue on his way, and it is at this point in the film that the real, non-diegetic film music starts.

Most of Herrmann's film scores consist of short compositions with titles that indicate where they are to be placed in relation to the plot. The first composition in *North by Northwest* is called 'Kidnapped' and functions as a kind of musical transition while the two gangsters abduct Thornhill and the action shifts from the Plaza Hotel in New York to a country house on Long Island. 'Kidnapped' starts with a *fortissimo* note on the horns and a small *forte* figure on the strings – a *stinger* that indicates that the action has taken a surprising turn: Thornhill has a pistol pointed at him. The stinger also opens the music: the note on the horns is part of a motif that consists of

7.2: *North by Northwest*: Kidnapped (1)

a descending series of notes played by clarinets and bass clarinets (illus. 7.2).

These two bars form the point of departure for a sequencing: the slow motif (*molto moderato*) is played four times, each time from a lower position, while we follow Thornhill and the men out of the hotel into a waiting car (illus. 7.3). The stinger is heard twice here, in the fifth bar, while the bad guys are leading Thornhill out of the hotel, and in the seventh bar, while they are getting into the car.

7.3: *North by Northwest*: Kidnapped (1a)

There is now a shift to 3/4 time. While Thornhill tries to get the two men to explain what is going on, the strings play an open fifth (A-E) followed by an E^b major chord (illus. 7.4). The same pattern is then repeated in 4/4 time.

7.4: *North by Northwest*: Kidnapped (2)

A dissolve signals that time has passed. The car drives in through the entrance to a large park and the music changes tempo and nature: A long, angular line in 12/8 is played by strings in unison, alternating with clarinets and bass clarinets in unison:

7.5: *North by Northwest*: Kidnapped (3)

The line is then repeated twice, accompanied the first time by a descending unison line on bassoons and horns, then played by the strings on their own. When the car stops in front of the country house, the piece ends with a repeat of the slow, descending motif from the introduction (see illus. 7.1).

Thornhill is now led into a large library and is told to wait. When the door is closed behind him, the next piece, 'The Door', begins. Its starting point is slow chords on the strings (A minor, G minor, A minor) and an ascending motif played in parallel thirds on the horns (illus. 7.6). On the last note of the horn motif, the chords on the strings return. The horn motif is repeated three times.

7.6: *North by Northwest*: The Door

The music ends when the door of the library opens. Vandamm enters and questions Thornhill in the belief that he has got hold of Kaplan. Since Thornhill, for very good reasons, is unable to divulge anything at all, Vandamm orders his men to get rid of him. The music starts once more when Vandamm's secretary pours out a large glass of whisky and says 'Cheers!' First, the strings play the ascending horn motif from 'The Door', then the horns repeat it. While there is a cut to a shot of two cars on a deserted mountain road, the music changes to double tempo and the strings play a variation of the horn motif (illus. 7.7).

7.7: *North by Northwest*: Cheers

The same motifs are heard while the two gangsters get out of the second car, dragging the highly intoxicated Thornhill. They place him behind the wheel of the front car and start the engine. The aim is clearly for Thornhill to drive over the edge of the ravine, but he manages to straighten up the car at the last moment. During the following scene, with the car rushing down the mountain road and constantly almost colliding with oncoming traffic, one hears the fandango from the overture. The scene ends with Thornhill being pursued by the police. He manages to stop the car, but causes a concertina collision that is marked in the music by some dissonant chords.

There then follows a whole series of scenes without music. Thornhill is taken to a police station; an alcohol test is taken; he phones his mother. The following day he is in court; his mother and a lawyer are present; Thornhill tries to explain what took place the previous day. The judge sends them off to investigate escorted by a couple of policemen. There is a dissolve to a shot of their car arriving at the country house, accompanied by the piece 'Return', a variation of the unison melody in the strings from 'Kidnapped'. The music stops when they enter the house. A woman receives Thornhill as if he is a close friend of the family. She tells the police that he was at a party at the house the day before, that he got drunk but insisted on driving home in his own car. Thornhill cannot find anything to support his own version of the story. As they leave the house, a variant of a theme from the overture is heard, which concludes with some menacing chords, while the camera pans, revealing one of Vandamm's men disguised as a gardener.

Hermann's musical universe

This marks the end of the narrative exposition: Thornhill has been exposed to some harrowing experiences. He has narrowly avoided being killed. But no one believes his story. Now the detective work begins. He has to find Kaplan and extract an explanation from him.

At this point, the musical exposition is also over. In the course of these first scenes we have been presented with most of the material Herrmann uses in the rest of the film. We can begin to form an idea of his musical universe.

Melodies and modules

Herrmann's small pieces break with the classical Hollywood system in a number of ways. First, there are no fine singable melodies, neither in the overture nor in the first part of *North by Northwest*. The unison theme in 'Kidnapped' is the only thing that is reminiscent of a melody in the traditional sense – and it is not particularly tuneful, it is angular, 'unhummable'. In the other pieces the melodics is restricted to very simple stepwise movements. Herrmann's music is clearly not melodic in its orientation. All the pieces in the exposition, and most of those in the rest of the film, are made up of ultra-short motif-like cells that are repeated or sequenced and linked together to form larger units.

In an interview Herrmann gives a functional explanation for why throughout his career he refused to write melodies:

> You know, the reason I don't like this tune business is that a tune has to have eight or sixteen bars, which limits you as a composer. Once you start, you've got to finish – eight or sixteen bars. Otherwise, the audience doesn't know what the hell it's all about. It's putting handcuffs on yourself.[9]

Melodies take time. They arouse expectations of continuations, developments and conclusions, and can therefore quickly clash with the movement of the film narrative. The obvious advantage of Herrmann's compositional strategy is that music made up of short modules can be broken off or change direction to keep pace with the narrative progression without the spectator experiencing the changes as a breach of musical expectations regarding a continuation. This type of music can also be changed more quickly if a film sequence is edited or shortened later on in the production process. Herrmann's score for *North by Northwest* is an excellent example of that. There are pencil deletions everywhere that reveal he has shortened the pieces after having written them. 'The Door', for example, originally comprised twelve bars; in the film version the last three bars are missing. During the process two modules have been cut, without the music sounding amputated for that reason.

Harmonics

Herrmann breaks with the harmonics of Golden Age music. His music gives the impression of tonality, but it is often difficult to determine the basic key or whether the piece is in the major or minor. The pieces in the exposition, for example, are all open and indeterminate, with none of them ending in a traditional, tonal cadence.

Many of the pieces consist of short, simple unison lines. In certain cases a descending or ascending line may be added. Both the one-part and two-part passages are harmonically ambiguous and invite many different interpretations. For example, the first motif in

'Kidnapped' (see illus. 7.3) suggests an underlying B major seventh chord; in a traditional context one would perhaps expect a transition to E minor with the descending line of the melody to end on an E. Such expectations, however, are dashed by the three subsequent sequencings, which suggest an underlying series of seventh chords that are transposed stepwise downwards: $G^{b7} \mid E^7 \mid E^{b7}$. The same pattern is also found in those instances where proper three- or four-note chords occur in the music. The chords are not placed in traditional functional series but are usually set up against each other without any mediating transitions (as, for example, the series A minor, G minor, A minor in 'The Door'). In some cases they may be linked with the aid of minimal stepwise movements (as, for example, when the A-E fifth in 'Kidnapped' is transformed into an E^b major chord).

The brisk two-part motif on the strings in 'Cheers' is another example of harmonic ambiguity (see illus. 7.7). Each time violins and violas play the first two notes in unison (C-D) and then collide on the third note. In the first bar the violins play $D^\#$ against the violas' E; in the second bar, the violins play E against the violas' E^b, etc. The melodics suggest C major with a dissonantal tinge, but the lower part in the second violins (A^b-B-C) points in other directions.

Instrumentation

That this constructivist, minimalist music does not feel thin or dry is partly due to its original instrumentation. Herrmann's older colleagues in Hollywood composed symphonic music for a large orchestra and were seldom able to influence the final sound of the music. The instrumentation was done by assistants trained to give the music a uniform, streamlined feel in the preferred style of the time. Herrmann, on the other hand, insisted on doing his own instrumentation, preferring to write for many different, and often untraditional, combinations of instruments. In a newspaper article from 1941 about the music for *Citizen Kane*, he writes that he tried to avoid 'the realistic sound of a large symphony orchestra': 'The motion picture sound-track is an exquisitely sensitive medium, and with skillful engineering a simple bass flute solo, the pulsing of a bass drum, or the sound of muted horns can often be far more effective than half a hundred musicians playing away.'[10] In an interview, many years later, he clarifies his view of traditional Hollywood orchestration. The large symphony orchestra is designed to perform a comprehensive musical repertoire ranging from the mid-eighteenth century to the present day. 'But since a film score is only written for one performance, I could never see the logic in making a rule of the standard symphony orchestra.'[11]

The music for *North by Northwest* is an excellent illustration of this point of view. With 'Kidnapped', Herrmann establishes a distinctive sound universe that he is to use for the rest of the film, and that is constructed for precisely this one 'performance', this one film. The simple descending lines in the first part are played by clarinets and bass clarinets against a background of strings and horns in unison. The theme in the second part, which is heard when the car arrives at the country house on Long Island, is played first time round as a conversation between strings, clarinets and bass clarinets, second time round by strings and clarinets accompanied by a descending line in the bass clarinets, bassoons, double-bassoons and horns, and the third time round by the strings on their own. Although Herrmann on several occasions later on in the film uses the large symphony orchestra, it is these combinations of instruments that dominate and that create the film's sound universe: strings, low woodwind and horns.

Musical 'numbers'

Herrmann's older colleagues used leitmotifs in order to create cohesion in the music and to link it to the changes in the narrative. Here too, Herrmann deviated from the norm. 'I am not a great believer in the "leitmotiv" as a device for motion picture music,' he wrote in 1941.[12] In articles and interviews over the years he stresses this opposition time and again. He suggests that one could instead use Verdi's opera technique and write film music as a series of independent, musically unrelated 'numbers'.[13]

His own film scores do to a certain extent remind one of the traditional 'number operas' of pre-Wagnerian times. But even if each of Herrmann's numbers is given its own title, they can seldom be considered as separate compositions. If, for example, one gets the feeling of moving along in an interconnected musical and narrative universe in *North by Northwest*, this is not only due to the common sound quality of the pieces but also – and just as importantly – to the fact that the short modules are repeated and varied from piece to piece. The rising horn motif in 'The Door' is repeated and varied in 'Cheers'; a variation of the unison 12/8 theme from 'Kidnapped' is used in 'Return', and the same theme appears in a number of different variants towards the end of the film. In all such

instances musical links are created with the aid of repetitions and variations between the single pieces – at the same time as narrative links are
suggested between the corresponding elements of the action.

Leitmotifs

Herrmann's resistance to leitmotifs did not prevent him using the technique himself occasionally when he felt the narrative called for it. There
is an example of this in the second part of *North by Northwest*.

Thornhill is suspected of a murder he has not committed. He flees
to Chicago to find the mysterious Kaplan. On board the train, he
meets a woman, Eve Kendall, who helps him avoid being taken in a
police check. Later, they are seated at the same table in the dining car.
During the first part of this scene, we hear the sound of the train, the
conversation of the guests, the noise of cutlery – and underneath this
something that sound like typical restaurant muzak.[14] Eve tells Thornhill
she knows that he is wanted for murder. She then gives him a clear,
erotic invitation and asks him: 'You know what I mean?' The diegetic
muzak suddenly stops: 'Now, let me think,' he replies ironically. While
he is thinking, 'Interlude', a piece of non-diegetic music, starts up. It
begins with a rhythmical motif in the strings (illus. 7.8), played so softly
that it can hardly be distinguished from the sound of the train against
the rails.

7.8: *North by Northwest*: 'Interlude' (1)

'Yes, I know exactly what you mean', he says. Something is heard
that could be a train whistle. Then the volume of the music increases
and the musical imitation of a 'train journey' changes into a slow,
descending melody that is played *dolce e amoroso* by an oboe against a
background of chords on the strings (illus. 7.9).

'Interlude' is the first – and only – proper melody in *North by
Northwest* – a simple ABBA structure with traditional harmonics. But
even here, where Herrmann writes a fairly long piece of melody, his
sense of module-based music does not desert him. All four sections of
the melody are constructed as repetitions and variations of the first

7.9: *North by Northwest*: 'Interlude' (2)

four bars – and these four bars themselves are based on a repetition: the falling whole-tone step in the first bar is repeated a fourth lower in the third bar.

After the oboe has presented the melody, the clarinet plays the basic theme twice. The music then stops: Roger has to leave the dining car because two detectives have boarded the train. He hides in Eve's sleeper, first from the detectives, later from the sleeper conductor. From time to time they take up their flirting from the dining car, and each time one hears the 'Interlude' melody or variants on the falling whole-tone step. The mood in the sleeper becomes increasingly erotic and intense. Finally the melody comes to rest, and the scene concludes with a virtuous cutaway. At this point the 'Interlude' theme is clearly connected to the relationship between Roger and Eve, but it is not a traditional 'love' motif, for their relationship is fairly complex, characterized by deception and misunderstanding: he is in love with her; she is possibly gradually falling in love with him, but she is Vandamm's mistress and has begun seducing Thornhill as part of Vandamm's plans. When the theme reappears later in the film, it is used to indicate the psychological game going on between them.

Asceticism

Module-based music, restricted melodics, ambiguous harmonics, colourful instrumentation – these cue words point to certain characteristic aspects of Herrmann's musical universe. But how does his music function as film music?

If one has just seen one of the older Hollywood films, *The Big Sleep*, for example, *North by Northwest* inevitably seems very ascetic. It is as if there is hardly any music in it. The Golden Age composers wrote long, cohesive compositions that were precisely adjusted to the action and that were often designed to cover an entire scene. Herrmann, on the other hand, writes very little music. The exposition in *North by Northwest*, from the beginning of the narrative until the point where Thornhill leaves the country house for the second time, lasts 24 minutes, but there is only music for a quarter of that time. Roughly the same ratio is found in the whole of *North by Northwest*: only 40 minutes out of the film's 136 minutes are accompanied by music. Most of this comprises ultra-short pieces that normally last less than a minute. 'The Door' lasts 52 seconds, 'Cheers' 37 seconds, etc.

'Kidnapped', which lasts two minutes, is quite a long composition in such a context. It is probably also the most traditional of Herrmann's small pieces. The introductory stinger marks a dramatic change in the action and is followed by other stingers that scan the abduction of Thornhill – the slow, indeterminate music of the first part seems menacing and functions as an intensification of an intense moment in the action. As a whole, the music covers the transition between two scenes, marking with the unison 12/8 theme the arrival at the country house on Long Island. Everything takes place in perfect accordance with the classical system.

In the rest of the film Herrmann occasionally uses music in a similar way, to cover geographical or temporal transitions between parts of the narrative. But normally such traditions are marked without music, just with the aid of a clear change in the diegetic sound as, for example, when there is a cut from a quiet government office to the noisy, echoing Central Station in New York, where Thornhill tries to buy a ticket for the train to Chicago. A little later in the same sequence, he is pursued by the police and runs down onto the platform, where he is seen running alongside the train. Herrmann could have intensified this scene with some suitable 'flight music', e.g. 'The Street', which he uses later in corresponding situations, but here all one hears is the sound of Thornhill's feet.

There is a similar example at the beginning of the film, when the confused Thornhill arrives at the country house and meets Vandamm for the first time. The scene, which lasts about four minutes, is used to deepen and underline the fact that Vandamm confuses Thornhill with Kaplan as well as to illustrate that Thornhill's life is in danger. It is full of surprising information and dramatic turns, with a tension that gradually intensifies as the initially diffuse threat becomes more specific. According to the classical system the entire scene ought to have been covered with music. There ought, at least, to have been music from the crucial moment when Thornhill suddenly understands that Vandamm is planning to kill him. Herrmann, however, chooses neither of these solutions. The scene has no music at all, and perhaps for that reason has a particularly menacing feel to it. At the same time, the shock effect is even greater when Vandamm's secretary says 'Cheers!' and the music starts again after the long pause.

Tempo and tension

Herrmann differs from the older Hollywood composers in seldom using music to underscore a narrative section when the events are obvious or exciting enough in themselves. He prefers to use music as an independent narrative effect, to indicate the tempo of a scene, for example, or to create tensions or to intensify a mood.

The main character in *North by Northwest* finds himself in an incomprehensible situation. He is forced to be constantly on the move, fleeing both from the police, who want to arrest him for a murder he has not committed, and from unknown persons who, for unknown reasons, want to take his life. Many of Herrmann's pieces are used to underline and intensify the experience of movement and drive. Thornhill's arrival in Chicago is typical of this. A group of policemen is running round the station searching for him. The tempo of the action is not all that high. The arrival hall is full of travellers walking calmly around; the confused policemen seem almost clumsy and a trifle comical. But when Herrmann accompanies the episode with close chords played fast and staccato, first on the horns, then the clarinets and bass clarinets, the whole scene gets a feeling of hectic, headlong activity (illus. 7.10).

7.10: *North by Northwest*: The Station

'The Station' is a typical piece of 'hurry' music.[15] It reoccurs in many other contexts later on in the film and is used every time in the same way – to create an impression of high tempo or nervousness.

Another of Herrmann's preferred effects is an ultra-short, extremely simple motif that is used to evoke a mood or to increase the intensity of a scene: Thornhill's flight from the dining car in the Chicago train is accompanied by nineteen seconds of 'tension' music that consists of a single stepwise movement in the lower strings accompanied by a rhythmical figure on the violins and violas. An ambiguous question to Eve after he has discovered her connection with Vandamm is accompanied by a short series of chords.

Herrmann had learnt this technique from writing for radio. In a radio drama all the scenes have to be linked by means of sound, 'so that even five seconds of music becomes a vital instrument in telling the ear that the scene is shifting', he writes in the article about the music for *Citizen Kane*. This is not necessary in films where the spectator can see the transitions between the scenes. Even so, he recommends using *radio scoring*: in films with sharp and sudden contrasts 'a brief cue – even two or three chords might heighten the effect immeasurably'.[16]

Musical focalization

Herrmann's view of music as a tempo- and tension-creating element was established quite early on. In a newspaper article of 1945 he writes about the functions of film music, emphasizing that it can 'invest a scene with terror, grandeur, gaiety, or misery. It can propel narrative swiftly forward, or slow it down'.[17] But the very first thing he mentions in this connection is that music can 'seek out and intensify the inner thoughts of the characters'.[18] This is a view he often later reiterates. In an interview towards the end of his career, he says, for example, that 'film music expresses what the actor can't show or tell'.[19] Thornhill's arrival at the country house at the beginning of *North by Northwest* illustrates how Herrmann uses music to 'intensify the inner thoughts of the characters'.

When the car enters the park the unison theme in the strings in 12/8 starts. Initially it functions as a traditional musical underlining of the dissolve. We realize that the action has shifted in time and space. When the theme is repeated it accompanies a sequence that begins with three shots. The first two shots establish an *eyeline match*: we see Thornhill lift his head and look at something off screen; then we see what he is looking at, the park seen through the car window. The third shot is a *reaction shot*: it shows his reaction to what he has seen (illus. 7.11). There are numerous sequences like that in the classical Hollywood film. They are used to suggest subjective experiences and to get the spectators to identify themselves with the fictive characters.

7.11: *North by Northwest*: Eyeline match and reaction shot

This is the first time Hitchcock uses the eyeline match/reaction shot construction in *North by Northwest*. Until this point in the film we have seen events and Thornhill 'from the outside'. Everything we know about him as a character we have arrived at by hearing him talk and observing his behaviour. Now, for the first time, we move in closer and get some sort of an insight into how he experiences the situation. In the reaction shot we get a close-up of him. He turns his head and first looks to the left, towards one of the bad guys who is outside the frame; then he looks straight forward; finally, he looks to the right towards the other bad guy, who is also outside the frame. There then follows another eye-line match and reaction shot: we cut to a shot of the country house in the distance and then back to a close-up of Thornhill, who frowns.

In these two sequences Thornhill is established as a *focalizer* of the narrative.[20] The camera has zoomed in on him; he is 'in focus'. He is not only a character who lives and acts in the story world, we also experience this world from his position. The sequences are examples of *external focalization*: we gain access to Thornhill's consciousness, but only to a limited extent, only 'from the outside', so to speak. The shots of the grounds and the country house show what he sees, but are not seen 'through his eyes'. A *point of view shot*, a shot that was taken precisely from his angle of vision, and that showed precisely what he saw, would be an example of *internal focalization*.[21]

When the car enters the park, the music functions as a 'neutral' narrator. It helps us gain an overview of what is happening. In the course of the eyeline match/reaction shot sequences it changes character. Because Thornhill is made the focalizer, the music is linked to him, to his experience. Admittedly, the focalization only gives us access to his *visual* impression of the experience. The music itself is not 'his' experience, not something he, or the other persons in the car, hear. It continues to be an external, non-diegetic comment on the events. But because of the coordination with the eyeline match/reaction shot sequences, it nevertheless becomes 'linked' to him and his experience. The music is no longer a general comment on the narrative as a whole, it comments on one of the characters in the narrative. It places a subjective experience 'in focus'.

The next piece of music functions in the same way. After arriving at the country house, Thornhill is shown into the library and asked to wait; the door behind him is closed. And the music – 'The Door' (see illus. 7.6) – begins. At the beginning of the scene we see Thornhill at a distance while he takes a leisurely look at the library. He then becomes a focalizer by means of three eyeline matches:

> He picks up a parcel from the writing desk; in a point-of-view shot we see the name and address on the parcel from his point of view while the volume of the music increases.

> He looks out of the window; through it we see one of the gangsters call a man dressed in black.

He hears the door open behind him; he looks up; we see Vandamm enter.

The first and the last of the eyeline matches are followed by reaction shots of Thornhill. The whole sequence shows us the situation seen from Thornhill's point of view, underlining his increasing sense of disorientation. Meanwhile, the music is 'linked' to his subjective experience.

It is difficult to decide what the music actually 'says' in cases like that. While the car drives through the park and approaches the country house, Thornhill's facial expressions signal 'surprise', 'amazement' and increasing 'thoughtfulness'. But the pictures do not reveal any more than that. And 'Kidnapped' does not specify what he is actually thinking about. The angular 12/8 theme, the slow tempo, the descending figure in the woodwind give the arrival at the country house a majestic, stately feel that contrasts strangely with the speed of the car on its path through the park. Perhaps Thornhill is sitting there speculating on what the connection can possibly be between the bad guys in the car and the apparently genteel, prosperous people that live in this imposing, elegant building? The music does not provide an answer. It does not have a simple, clear sign function. It does not *represent* Thornhill's thoughts. It emphasizes the fact that he *is thinking*. It *refers to* his subjective experience and vaguely suggests his mood.

'The Door' functions in a similar way. The sudden crescendo when Thornhill sees the address on the parcel in a point-of-view shot emphasizes that he is thinking, but does not tell us *what* he is thinking. The piece as a whole does, however, convey an impression of his emotional reaction to the incomprehensible events. The slow, restrained chords on the strings and the rising theme in the horns function as a kind of unanswered musical question that intensifies the impression of his bewilderment and disorientation.

Later on in the film the music is used on several occasions in the same way. It refers to subjective but unspecified experiences. There are, however, also occasions when the music expresses 'what the actor cannot show or tell', especially in scenes that involve the mysterious Eve Kendall. Eva Marie Saint plays her with a cool, expressionless face that hardly ever reveals what she is thinking or feeling. The fact that as a spectator one nevertheless gains an impression early on that Eve is both in love with Thornhill and having problems with her relationship with Vandamm, is not least due to Herrmann's music. A single example from the arrival in Chicago illustrates this.

We see Eve and Thornhill walking together along the platform to the arrival hall, filmed with a camera that tracks backwards. While the tracking continues there is a cut to her alone in a medium-close shot while the music starts. There is then a shot of Vandamm and his secretary following them along the platform; then once more a picture of Eve looking to the right, and finally a picture of Thornhill walking beside her. The sequence of shots shows first something we already know, that Eve is in league with Vandamm. Second, it establishes Eve as focalizer, the music underlining the fact that something important is happening here. She does not betray what she is thinking via her gestures or facial expressions. But since the 'Interlude' theme starts up here on the music track, we are given a hint that her relationship to Thornhill is more complex than we had assumed so far.

A transitional figure

The music for *North by Northwest* has a number of characteristic features that are to be found in most of Herrmann's production. However, it is difficult to speak of a particular Herrmann *style*. As David Cooper remarks, Herrmann was not interested in codifying a particular compositional technique; he was 'an empiricist who relied on his experience and instinct'.[22] Every new film was a new challenge that called for new solutions. Throughout his career he experimented with all musical parameters.

For that reason, he never became a model for other composers as, for example, Max Steiner did. But he paved the way for the younger generation of film composers that established itself during the 1950s,[23] and he anticipated central features of much of the film music of the subsequent decades. His greatest importance in this forward-looking perspective is that he functioned as an example to be imitated. All his scores demonstrated that it was possible to develop alternatives to music from the Golden Age.

As far as *musical* parameters are concerned, he broke with the old system on practically all points:

He demonstrated that symphonic-style music written for a large orchestra is only one possibility among many, and that chamber-music solutions and experiments with untraditional combinations of instruments and timbres can often be more effective.

On certain occasions he chose to write in a Romantic/late Romantic style, but normally he preferred a more modern idiom based on 'free' tonality.

He seldom used traditional melodies; his music was made up of short, flexible modules.

Taken as a whole his music was not based on leitmotifs; he created musical and narrative cohesion via a repetition of musical cells and thematic material.

The traditional Golden Age style of film music went more or less out of fashion during the 1950s. As discussed, the disintegration of the studio system as well as general changes in the aesthetic sensibility and musical tastes of the public played important roles in this development. There is, however, also a third factor to be included: the increasing film 'literacy' of the audience. Herrmann's most significant contribution is perhaps precisely that he relied on this literacy. He assumed that modern spectators would be able to understand the gist of a plot via basic information conveyed by images and dialogue. So he seldom used music to scan and clarify the narrative. He broke with the demand that there should be long, coherent compositions that cover entire narrative sequences, writing instead short pieces or 'numbers'. Because his music was not mainly designed to guide the spectator through the maze of the plot, he could use it for other purposes – to colour a scene, to suggest a general mood, to intensify a narrative or emotional tension.

It is especially this last feature that points forwards. While the music of the Golden Age was a kind of pedagogical commentary that ran parallel to the film and pointed out the most important moments in the narrative, Herrmann demonstrated that music can be integrated into the plot itself and be just as flexible a medium as lighting, camera movement or editing.

8

Striking a New Note: Film Music after the Golden Age

Bernard Herrmann's collaboration with Alfred Hitchcock ended in 1965 with a row over the music for *Torn Curtain*.[1] The managers at Universal were dissatisfied with Herrmann's experimental style. They wanted popular music that could appeal to a wide audience. And they wanted an ear-catching title song that could be used in marketing and earn extra income via record sales. Hitchcock, who agreed to a great extent with these views, made it clear to Herrmann what was expected of him. Herrmann replied by writing dissonant music for flutes, brass, deep strings and percussion, plus two anvils, tuned to different pitches.

Hitchcock turned up at the studio to listen to the recording of the music. He only got to hear the first bars of the music for the title sequence before he exploded. He was entitled to 'a great pop tune', he shouted, enraged. To which Herrmann replied: 'Look, Hitch, you can't outjump your own shadow. And you don't make pop pictures. What do you want with me? I don't write pop music.' Hitchcock stopped the recording and hired the English composer John Addison to write new music. Addison's music was not particularly popular in tone, but he did at least supply *Torn Curtain* with a theme song – which no one recalls today. It was 'Love Theme from Torn Curtain', sung by the popular Johnny Mann Singers.

The story of Hitchcock, Herrmann and *Torn Curtain* says a great deal about the situation of film music in the 1960s. Hitchcock was not the only director of the time who dreamed of marketing his films with 'a great pop tune'. And the managers at Universal were not the only ones who wanted popular music instead of artistically ambitious experiments. The 1960s in general was a period where the links between films and popular music were strengthened.

Films and popular music

Throughout the history of film-making there have been close connections between the film industry, radio, theatre and the recording
industry. The first cue sheets were based on popular songs from the
music publishers in Tin Pan Alley and from Broadway musicals.
Throughout the silent film period the performance of contemporary popular songs was an important element of the cinema programme. The era of the sound film was ushered in by Al Jolson with
The Jazz Singer (1927), and the first great box-office successes were
film versions of Broadway musicals. Popular music was also used in
many other kinds of films. The major hits of the time were borrowed and used in order to give the films an extra attraction. And
there are also many examples of traffic in the opposite direction, of
melodies that were originally written for a film gaining their own
popularity. Many evergreens and standards come from Hollywood
films that have long since been consigned to oblivion. For example,
hardly anyone nowadays recalls that Harry Warren and Mack
Gordon's indestructible song 'There'll Never Be Another You' originally came from the film *Iceland* (H. Bruce Humberstone, 1942), one
of Sonja Henie's skating films.

The film studios were quick off the mark in using both title
melodies and theme songs in their marketing. In some cases such songs
could gain a commercial afterlife independently of the films themselves. An example is the music by the composer David Raksin for
Laura (Otto Preminger, 1944), which is based on a single, ear-catching
theme. After the premiere of the film Raksin and the film company
were approached by people who wanted to buy the theme music. This
led to the company asking the lyricist Johnny Mercer to collaborate with
Raksin, which eventually resulted in the song 'Laura'. It was released as
a record in 1945, was in the charts for fourteen weeks, and has since
been recorded in hundreds of versions.[2] Another example is the record
of Anton Karas's zither melody for *The Third Man* (Carol Reed, 1949).
When the film had its US premiere in 1950 the record was on the Top
40 for over three months.

At the time such success stories were isolated cases, and title
melodies and theme songs were not something that every film simply
had to have. Hitchcock's films from the 1950s did not have them, for
example. When he insists on having a pop song from Bernard

Herrmann in 1965 for *Torn Curtain*, it is an indication of a change in the economic conditions of the film industry.[3]

Title melodies, theme songs and theme scores

In the age of the studio system film production was a large-scale operation. One and the same company produced several films at the same time, using the same model and broadly speaking under the same conditions. After the breakdown of the studio system each film became an individual project. The 1950s is the decade when independent producers make their entry into Hollywood and when the surviving film studios begin to produce films as independent single projects. Under the new conditions the producer has the overall responsibility for all the details of the process, from financing and shooting to the sale of the end product. The director, the actors and the rest of the production crew are no longer members of a permanent staff, but specialists who are engaged to solve one single, defined task.

In the age of the studio system the deficit incurred by a single film could be offset by the profit from the studio's other films. With the new mode of production every single film had to be self-supporting and cover its own expenses. This leads to increasing demands for the films to generate extra income, and it is at this time that the hunt for title melodies and theme songs gets seriously underway. The film that demonstrated the independent commercial potential of film music more than any other was Fred Zinnemann's meta-western *High Noon* (1952), which was produced by Stanley Kramer, one of the independent producers of the period. Kramer requested the film's composer, Dimitri Tiomkin, to weave a western ballad into the music. This resulted in 'Do Not Forsake Me, Oh My Darlin'', performed by the singing cowboy star Tex Ritter. Dimitri Tiomkin won Oscars both for the music as a whole, 'Scoring of a Dramatic or Comedy Picture', and for 'Original Song'. But the most important thing, from a financial point of view, was that the song became a huge hit on its own.

Tiomkin's success led to a veritable mania for title melodies and theme songs, and for *theme scores*, film music constructed round a single theme.[4] Roy M. Prendergast even believes that Tiomkin's song 'rang the death knell for intelligent use of music in films'.[5] This is probably an exaggeration, but it is clear that many producers were inspired by Tiomkin's example, insisting the music for their films had to contain a song or an instrumental number that could make the charts. While music had previously been adapted to fit the film, it was now also to be adapted to circumstances outside the film itself. It had to be able to live its own life, independent of the film. One result was that a number of films were provided with popular-music elements that had almost nothing to do with the action or general mood of the film.

One of the composers who lived up to the producers' expectations was Henry Mancini, who had an indisputable talent for writing ear-catching tunes. When an LP with his jazz-inspired music for the TV series *Peter Gunn* (1958–61) was issued in 1958, it broke all existing records. It was no. 1 on *Billboard*'s hit list for ten weeks and stayed on the list for almost two years. Blake Edwards, who directed *Peter Gunn*, then hired Mancini for a number of film projects. Mancini's music for *Breakfast at Tiffany's* (1961) included the theme song 'Moon River', which was no. 1 on *Billboard*'s hit list for twelve weeks in 1961, ending up as one of the most sold and most recorded tunes in the 1960s. Instrumental music could also make the charts. Mancini proved this with his melody 'Baby Elephant Walk' from *Hatari* (Howard Hawks, 1962) and with the title melody for *The Pink Panther* (Blake Edwards, 1963).

Interest in the economic potential of film music led to changes in the institutional framework. Under the studio system film music was rarely considered to be an independent commercial asset. When a film had been completed the companies normally sold the music rights to a third party. Under the new production structure, however, the companies began to set up or invest in record companies and music publishing firms in order to be able to fully exploit the economic potential of the combination of film and music. It turned out that not only title melodies or theme songs could be sold or could make the charts. After the introduction of the LP format in the early 1950s it became common to release edited versions of film music on 'sound track albums'. A well-known example is the LP with Maurice Jarre's music for *Doctor Zhivago* (David Lean, 1965), which sold 2 million copies and was on the hit lists for 70 weeks.

Teenage music

Hitchcock felt he was entitled to a great pop tune and so did many other film producers of the 1960s. They were interested in popular music for their films, but in particular they wanted pop and rock music, the music of teenagers and the new youth culture. The targeting of film music to the tastes of young audiences is yet another expression of the changed conditions film production was facing.

With the breakthrough of television in the early 1950s films gained a serious competitor. Large sections of the traditional film audiences preferred to stay at home and get their entertainment from the little box in the living room. The film companies tried to tempt people back to the cinemas by going in for lavish productions and technical innovations. But neither the large-scale historical dramas, 3D films, stereophonic sound nor such widescreen formats as Cinerama, CinemaScope or Vistavision were able to change the course of developments. Cinema audiences were changing character. Films were in the process of becoming a medium for the young, and producers became interested in using music to capture the young audience.

The first films for young people with pop and rock music on the soundtrack appeared in the mid-1950s. Bill Haley's version of 'Rock Around the Clock' caught people's attention when it was played during the opening credits of *Blackboard Jungle* (Richard Brooks, 1955). The following year it became the title melody of *Rock Around the Clock* (Fred F. Sears, 1956), a film that caused teenage riots in both the United States and Europe, and that put the combination of rock music and teenagers on the mass media agenda for good. 1956 also saw the premiere of *Love Me Tender* (Robert D. Webb, 1956), the first of a long series of films with Elvis Presley in the leading role, and from the late 1950s onwards there was a flood of youth films with pop and rock music on the soundtrack.

The great success story in this respect is not a Hollywood film but *A Hard Day's Night* (1964), Richard Lester's untraditional music film starring The Beatles. It was produced with a highly restricted budget and became the greatest box-office success in the history of British films at that time. And the LP with the songs from the film went to the top of the charts all over the Western world. By 1966 the American distributor had earned $2 million on the record – almost four times as much as it had cost to produce the film. Profits of this magnitude were not of course an everyday occurrence, but examples such as this demonstrated at least that there were large profits to be made in the borderland between the film and music industries.

Many of the youth films of the 1960s were modernized backstage musicals, where the story of some pop group's way to its major breakthrough forms a flimsy framework to various music numbers. But pop and rock music also appeared in many other types of films, creating shifts in the traditional relationship between diegetic and non-diegetic music.

In the Golden Age of film music, non-diegetic music was composed for a particular film, while diegetic music was often based on already existing material; think, for example, of Lauren Bacall's cover version of Anita O'Day's hit in *The Big Sleep*. Furthermore there was a kind of division of labour as regards style and taste. The non-diegetic music was written in a broad, symphonic style, while the diegetic music was taken from – or in some cases written with reference to – the lighter repertoire of the time. The increasing use of jazz as non-diegetic music in the 1950s is a sign that this distinction was breaking down. In the course of the 1960s an ever-decreasing number of symphonic scores were written, but after a while jazz also disappeared, with pop and rock music becoming the new musical idiom of films.

In certain cases the pop music was written directly for one particular film as, for example, John Lennon and Paul McCartney's songs for *A Hard Day's Night* and *Help!* (Richard Lester, 1965), Burt Bacharach's songs for *Butch Cassidy and the Sundance Kid* (1969) or Isaac Hayes's songs for *Shaft* (Gordon Parks, 1971). Often, though, the non-diegetic music was constructed with the aid of already recorded material. Films such as *Easy Rider* (Dennis Hopper, 1969) and *Zabriskie Point* (Michelangelo Antonioni, 1969) are some of the first examples of modern film-makers returning to the practice of the silent film era of using compilations of already existing music as an accompaniment.

Mike Nichols's *The Graduate* (1967), one of the first box office hits with compilation music on the soundtrack, illustrates some of the narrative problems that arise when films are accompanied by songs, and song texts, not originally written for that purpose.

Difficult songs: *The Graduate*, 1967

During the planning of *The Graduate*, Mike Nichols contacted Paul Simon of Simon & Garfunkel and asked him to write some songs for the film.[6] Simon agreed to do so, and Simon & Garfunkel's record company bought the rights to the film music. An LP with the music would be able to generate its own income in the slipstream from the film, while also functioning as part of the marketing of Simon & Garfunkel's next album, *Bookends*.

It turned out, however, that Simon had difficulty working on commission. He wrote two songs that Nichols rejected. After that, he got stuck. When the shooting of the film was complete and the editing process was to begin, Nichols therefore began to use some of Simon's old songs as *temp tracks*. A temp track is a 'temporary soundtrack', used in the cutting room to indicate the length and mood of a sequence before the real music is written. During the editing Nichols gradually became convinced that the temporary soundtrack could be used in the final film. The result was that Simon's contribution to the film consisted of two songs from the album *Sounds of Silence* (1966), two from *Parsley, Sage, Rosemary and Thyme* (1966) plus a bit of a new, unfinished song, the later so famous 'Mrs Robinson'.

The film had its premiere in December 1967. The soundtrack album which was released in February 1968 only contained fifteen minutes of material by Simon; the rest was filled up with diverse diegetic muzak composed for the film by Dave Grusin, a cha-cha-cha piece played on a radio, a foxtrot that is played by a dance orchestra, etc. Despite the paucity of content, the record topped the LP charts for nine weeks in 1968. It was finally ousted by *Bookends*, which contained the final version of 'Mrs Robinson' and topped the charts for seven weeks. The single 'Mrs Robinson' was no. 1 on the singles list for three weeks. Another single with music from the film made it to the eleventh spot. Simon's music for *The Graduate* was, then, a massive success on the record market. The film marketed the record; conversely, the songs helped market the film. *The Graduate* was the film that earned the most money in the United States in 1968, and the music was clearly part of the film's attraction.

The reason why Nichols wanted Simon & Garfunkel on the project in the first place was that he had heard the album *Parsley, Sage, Rosemary and Thyme* and felt that this was a type of music which the main character, young Benjamin Braddock (Dustin Hoffman), would be interested in. In the final film, however, there is only one scene where Ben actually listens to one of Simon's songs, and it is clear he does not really like it: he asks some teenagers to turn down the noisy car radio playing 'Big Bright Green Pleasure Machine' (from *Parsley, Sage, Rosemary and Thyme*). In this instance Simon's song appears in the story world, it functions as diegetic music. But what about the other songs? We know that Paul Simon has written them and that Simon & Garfunkel are singing them. But what is the meaning of their appearing in the film? Where 'do they come from' in a narrative context?

The film starts with an unaccompanied close-up of Ben's face. He is sitting alone, staring expressionlessly in front of him. The camera zooms out; he is on board a plane, surrounded by a lot of people. Then the camera isolates him again: he is standing alone in the picture, motionless on a speedwalk at an airport. This is where the opening credits start, as does the song 'The Sound of Silence'.

The lyrics present a religiously tinged criticism of mass society. The narrator observes his robot-like fellow human beings: 'People talking without speaking, people hearing without listening. / People writing songs that voices never shared, no one dared disturb the sound of silence.' He tries to rouse them to an authentic life, but in vain: 'But my words like silent raindrops fell and echoed in the wells of silence. / And the people bowed and prayed to the neon god they made.' Simon's text about the contrast between the lonely narrator and the unconscious people around him seems at first sight to be a comment on the picture of Ben, standing there alone on the speedwalk, and to point forwards to the following scenes which reveal that Ben has come home to Los Angeles after having been at college out east. He feels alienated from his well-off parents and their superficial friends. He is unsure of himself and what to do with his life.

Perhaps, though, the song is more than an external comment telling us that Ben is an outsider, someone who does not fit. He is established as a focalizer in these first images, and the focalizer function is underlined in the many following scenes via a profusion of eyeline match/reaction shot sequences and spectacular use of point-of-view shots.[7] The images invite us to experience the world via his consciousness, and since the song 'The Sound of Silence' is linked to him in the introductory sequence, it becomes in a way part of the focalization.

There are many kinds of focalization. In an article on the function of songs in modern Hollywood films, Todd Berliner and Philip Furia write, for example, that even though it is not Dustin Hoffman who sings 'The Sound of Silence', the song nevertheless expresses Ben's loneliness and fear.[8] This is an example of what Edward Branigan calls 'external' focalization.[9] We experience Ben 'from the outside', yet even so gain an impression of what is going on in his mind. According to Berliner and

Furia, something similar happens towards the end of the film: Ben loves Elaine, but she is going to marry someone else. Ben, who wants to prevent this, does not reach the church until after the marriage ceremony is over. He calls out to her and they run off together. The film ends with them sitting on the back seat of a coach, surrounded by strangers, driving off. There is a general mood of 'happy ending' about this scene, until the closing credits start and 'The Sound of Silence' is heard once more on the soundtrack. The two main characters do not say anything, but the mood changes. 'The melancholy song, already linked to Ben's sadness, loneliness, and indecision, works in tandem with the image to help undermine the otherwise happy ending.'[10]

When Berliner and Furia sum up these observations, however, they go a step further. The song 'The Sound of Silence' does not only *refer to* Ben's thoughts, it *is* his thoughts, and, they believe, that is how Paul Simon's songs work in the film in general – as 'internal songs', as a kind of modern, film-parallel to the 'external songs' familiar from operettas and musicals, where it is quite common for the characters to 'spontaneously' burst into song to express their feelings.[11] According to this point of view, we are dealing with a kind of focalization here: internal songs give us 'indirect access to the characters' thoughts', they write.[12] We experience Ben's consciousness from the inside. Here Berliner and Furia share the view of Mike Nichols, who had originally imagined that Simon's songs would not only characterize Ben as a person but also function as his mouthpiece or his inner monologue. It is, however, not possible to maintain this point of view regarding the music as a whole.

For example, 'The Sound of Silence' accompanies a montage sequence early on in the film that summarizes Ben's summer. He has begun a relationship with Mrs Robinson (Anne Bancroft), who is married to his father's business partner. The sequence begins where he is together with Mrs Robinson in a hotel room. He turns out the light, the screen goes black, and one hears Simon & Garfunkel sing 'Hello darkness, my old friend, I've come to talk with you again.' The word 'darkness' creates a superficial link between song and narrative. But it is not possible to link Simon's poetic lyric about modern mass society and the lonely crowd in the subway more directly to the subsequent images of Ben lying in his parents' swimming pool or in bed with Mrs Robinson. The song as a whole does not grant us access to Ben's actual thoughts about the situation; it only suggests, as in the introductory sequence, a certain feeling of alienation.

This is also true of the other songs. 'April Come She Will' (from the *Sounds of Silence* album), which replaces 'The Sound of Silence' and accompanies the last part of the montage sequence, is based on an English nursery rhyme about the cuckoo who comes in April and dies in September. In Paul Simon's version it is the point of departure for a lyrical text about a love relationship. The fact that the text ends with 'August, die she must, / The autumn winds blow chilly and cold; / September I'll remember / A love once new has now grown old' can perhaps be seen as a kind of parallel to the concluding images of the sequence, where we realize that Ben has begun to tire of his relationship with Mrs Robinson. But we are not dealing with more than a superficial parallel here. It has been clear from the start of the film – the main point, even – that their relationship was not based on love.

The last of Simon's songs used in the film is his fantasy based on the folk song 'Scarborough Fair' (from *Parsley, Sage, Rosemary and Thyme*). It accompanies a montage sequence where Ben sees, from a distance, Elaine leave to study at Berkeley, and it is used a couple of times in the following scenes, where Ben follows her and settles in Berkeley. Here too it is possible to see a certain parallel between the song and Ben's story: the lyrics deal with a man who dreams about winning back his lost love. On the other hand, the song has a clear anti-war theme that cannot be linked to either Ben as a person or the film in general.[13]

Many later films have demonstrated that songs on the soundtrack can convey what goes on in the mind of a fictive character, even though they are sung by someone else. The reason why it is difficult to consider Simon's songs as Ben's inner monologue or 'internal songs' is not that they are sung by Simon & Garfunkel, but simply that they were not written with *The Graduate* in mind. The lyrics are actually not *about* Ben – which means that connections between the lyrics and his thoughts have to be established at a more general level. The only piece of text that Simon wrote directly for the film, the four lines of 'Mrs Robinson', have, strangely enough, no connection to the Mrs Robinson of the film: 'And here's to you, Mrs Robinson / Jesus loves you more than you will know, wo wo wo / Stand up tall, Mrs Robinson / God in Heaven smiles on those who pray, hey hey hey. Hey hey hey.' It is 'as though Simon and Garfunkel knew little about *The Graduate* except that one of the characters was named "Mrs Robinson",' Berliner and Furia remark.[14]

Instead of considering the songs as examples of focalization, as the diegetic expression of Ben's thoughts, one could perhaps imagine that they came from a non-diegetic narrator, from a kind of troubadour who is standing outside the story world and commenting on it. But here one runs into the same problem as before. Because there is no immediate, concrete connection between the lyrics and the narrative of the film, it is difficult to comprehend what the troubadour actually feels or wants to express. In one of the scenes from Berkeley it is clear that it is the recycling of Simon's lyrics that is the real problem. After Ben has found a place to live, we cut to a scene at the university where Elaine is seen walking among the students. Synchronized with this cut, 'Scarborough Fair' starts up, now played on an acoustic guitar, flute and glockenspiel. The instrumental version functions as a completely traditional piece of non-diegetic music: the rhythm matches Elaine's movements; the folksong-like melody gives the scene a lyrical touch, with both the melody and instrumentation matching the environment. Such music could be heard at Berkeley and similar student environments during this period.

Most of the songs in the film function in the same way, as non-diegetic accompaniment. They support a few scenes and montage sequences; they are used to shape the course of events and to suggest a mood or emotion. But, because they are provided with lyrics, we inevitably regard them as something more than traditional, non-diegetic mood music. The lyrics indicate that 'someone is speaking' here and, because they are coordinated with the narrative of the film, we inevitably try both to link them to the action and to place the speaking subject in relation to the story world – and have considerable problems on both counts.

Presumably it is – paradoxically enough – precisely these problems of interpretation that are the reason why the songs actually work excellently within the context of the film. The lyrics clearly deal with something other than the film itself. But because the songs run parallel with the narrative, and because as a spectator one always listens to them in anticipation of their giving narrative meaning, the lyrics acquire a kind of metaphorical function. One feels that they are dealing with something 'corresponding', that they are saying something 'similar', even though one never completely gets the point and can only contrive to get text and narrative to cohere at a completely general level. Because of the lack of coordination in terms of content the songs create an impression of 'meaning' and 'depth' around the relatively simple story; they imply a larger common universe of which both they and the narrative about Ben are a part.

It is difficult, generally speaking, to get the songs in *The Graduate* to tally with habitual conceptions of how film music works. Take a song like 'The Sound of Silence'. Is its function diegetic or non-diegetic? Does it express Ben's subjective experience, or is it an external comment on the action of the film? Or should it perhaps more be considered as a kind of theme song that is relatively independent of the film? Does it always have the same function? Or does it function in three different ways the three times it is heard during the film? It is not only Mike Nichols's use of Paul Simon's music that raises such questions. The breakthrough of compilation music in the 1970s challenges at a general level the traditional categories of film music, creating fluid transitions and diffuse intermediate forms. One of the most interesting examples from this period is *American Graffiti*, George Lucas's trendsetter from 1973.

Chameleon music: *American Graffiti*, 1973

It starts with a black screen and strange, incoherent sounds – someone is surfing frequencies on a radio, finally arriving at the right station. One hears a jingle. Then 'Rock Around the Clock' blares out – at the same time as the opening credits of *American Graffiti* start up. We are in front of Mel's Drive-In in a small town in California's Central Valley, in late summer 1962. It is Saturday, sunset, time for the classic American teenager ritual of cruising. As soon as it gets dark, the town's teenagers begin to drive along the street in their big cars. They meet their friends, flirt, fall in love, argue, race each other.

For Curt (Richard Dreyfuss) and Steve (Ron Howard), this will be their last evening in town. The following day they are to travel east to go to college. Steve is determined to leave, while Curt has begun to have doubts. He drifts around the town, spending most of the evening looking for a mysterious blonde who is cruising in a white Ford Thunderbird. Steve is with his girlfriend Laurie (Cindy Williams), who is trying to convince him to stay in the town. In the course of the evening, they fall out and go their separate ways, although they patch things up the following morning. Terry (Charles Martin Smith) is the nerd of the group; he normally does not have any success with the girls, but this evening he borrows Steve's car and experiences some eventful hours with Debbie (Candy Clark). John (Paul Le Mat) is the eldest of the group. He works as a car mechanic and is the best racing driver in The Valley. During the evening, he is challenged by the new arrival, Bob Falfa (Harrison Ford). The duel takes place outside the town at sunrise. John wins because Falfa's car leaves the road and explodes. Several hours later, the friends are all at the airport to say goodbye to Curt. Steve will not go after all; he has decided to stay with Laurie.

Music and sound

The musical universe of the film is established by the sound of the radio and 'Rock Around the Clock' during the opening credits. This is a film with classic American pop and rock music on the soundtrack. At the beginning of the film there are a couple of scenes from a school dance where live music is played. The rest of the music comes from the teenagers' car radios, all of which are tuned in to a programme with the legendary disc jockey Wolfman Jack. In the course of the film a total of 41 songs from the 1955–62 period is heard, in an almost constant stream that is only interrupted by radio commercials and jingles and people phoning in to send greetings to their sweethearts.

The music from the car radios has to compete with all sorts of other sounds in the story world. Throughout, we hear teenagers shouting and screaming to each other, sometimes in the background, 'behind' the music, at other times in the foreground. And we hear the sound of cars – cars revving up or starting or braking. At one point the music is completely drowned out by a train driving past close by but, when it has passed, the radio is still playing the same song. The music is there all the time. When a song is to end, it fades out, and Wolfman Jack announces the next number. If the action moves to some other part of the town, there is no cut in the music. The sound quality changes, but the music continues, telling us that teenagers everywhere in this town are listening to the same station and the same song, and that the visual cut only marks a leap in space, not in time.

In other words, we are dealing here with diegetic music. But that is not the end of the story. The 41 songs admittedly belong to the story world, but they do not function merely as some 'realistic' background. They have many different narrative functions. They are used, for example, to blur the temporal relations in the narrative.

Syuzhet and fabula

As one watches the film it seems as if there is a coincidence in time between the *syuzhet* of the film (the 'plot', the events that are actually depicted in the progression of images and sound) and its *fabula* (the 'story', the course of events one can reconstruct having seen the film).[15] This, though, is of course an illusion: the film lasts less than two hours, while the time of the fabula stretches from sunset on the one day until well after sunrise on the following day. In other words the syuzhet is a summary of a much longer course of events. Because of the music, however, these shortenings are seldom noticed. Two examples demonstrate the technique.

Steve and Laurie are at a dance at their old school. They are standing in the middle of the gym and beginning to move forwards between the dancers. There is a cut, and in the next shot we see them walking away to Laurie's car at the school parking lot. Apparently, nothing of importance took place as they left the gym, walked through the school and out to the parking lot. An 'unimportant' piece of the action has been edited out, but there is no cut in the music. The song 'Louie, Louie', which the band was playing inside the gym, can still be heard, without any break, after the cut; the sound has merely changed its character: we notice that the gym lies a long way from the parking lot.

In this instance we can 'see' the time-shortening, because Steve and Laurie appear in shots on both sides of the cut. Larger leaps forward in time, however, are 'invisible'. These take place in the transitions between the main sections of the narrative, where there are not only cuts between various locations but also from one group of people to another. There is an example of this just after the school dance: Steve and Laurie are standing by the car. Wolfman Jack's voice comes from a car radio not far away. When they get into the car, the radio starts to play 'Little Darlin'' by The Diamonds. The song continues into the next scene, where we see Terry and Debbie sitting in front of Mel's Drive-In. Presumably there has been a leap forward in time, but because the song plays through the cut, it seems as if the two scenes are consecutive. The continuity of the music hides the discontinuity of the syuzhet.

Who is it that is manipulating the transitions between the scenes via the music? George Lucas and his staff would be an obvious answer. On the other hand they are 'outside' the film or 'prior to' the film. As soon as we begin to watch a film, this or any other, we normally forget the historical persons who have actually constructed it. Instead we begin forming hypotheses about how the various types of information are to be placed 'within' the space of the text, hypotheses about who is telling what and why. These hypotheses colour our experience of the information and its function, and also influence how we would describe and interpret the various elements of the film in an analysis.

The narrative information in a film, including its music, typically comes from three positions within the text. A couple of examples from *American Graffiti* demonstrate how.

Diegetic information

At Late at night Steve is sitting alone at Mel's Drive-In. Two girls come in and ask him where Laurie is. He replies that he doesn't know. 'We know where she is,' one of the girls says, 'She was with a really cute guy in a really boss car.' The information that he, and we too, obtain here comes from a character in the story world and has to be judged accordingly. The malicious girl is part of the diegesis – she is a *diegetic narrator*.

Any of the characters in a film can function as a diegetic narrator. In *American Graffiti*, for example, we gain some of the most important information simply by listening to people talking, telling each other what has happened since they last met. Diegetic narrators are 'first person narrators' – they tell of their own experiences in the first person, referring to themselves as 'I'. In some films there is a single diegetic narrator who is superior to all the others, so that the entire story has ultimately to be understood as this particular person's account. Voice-over in the first person and past tense are the typical techniques used in such films.[16] If the scene with Steve and the two girls had been presented in this way, it could have started with us hearing Steve's voice on the soundtrack: 'As Laurie had thrown me out of the car, I went across to Mel's Drive-In and drank a cup of coffee. Karen and Judy came in . . .'

In many instances, we do not need diegetic narrators to explain to us what is going on. Most films include long sections where we just 'witness' the events as if we were 'invisibly' present in the story world. When, for example, we see Steve come running out of Mel's Drive-In and demanding his car back from Terry, the information does not come from an actual diegetic narrator, but such a narrator is 'implied'.[17] We experience the scene as a chance passer-by *could* have experienced it and, at some later point, talked about it in retrospect: 'I saw Steve come running out of Mel's Drive-In . . .'

Practically all the music in *American Graffiti* is diegetic music in this sense. It is part of the story world, and we hear it as it sounds in that world, not necessarily the same way that the characters on the screen hear it, but like a person placed where the camera was positioned would have heard it. Sometimes it seems as if the music is coming from a car radio in the distance; at other times it is as if we were sitting in the car. The nature of the sound adds a spatial 'perspective' to the music, marking an 'implied' narrator's position in relation to the sound source.

Non-diegetic information

At the end of the film Curt flies out of town. The final shot shows the plane as a small speck against a blue sky. Over the image appear old school photographs of the four main male characters, plus some brief information: 'John Milner was killed by a drunk driver in December 1964. Terry Fields was reported missing in action near An Loc in December 1965. Steve Bolander is an insurance agent in Modesto, California. Curt Henderson is a writer living in Canada.'

Who is telling us this? Perhaps a diegetic narrator, one of the characters we have seen during the film, for example. Now, in 1973, this person is thinking back, telling us what happened in 1962, and what happened to John and the others since then. On the other hand, nothing at all in the entire preceding film has suggested that the narrative was to be understood as the recollections of one particular person. So it is not possible to link an actual 'I' to this concluding information. The style of the four sentences is more reminiscent of the way certain novels are narrated, by a narrator who does not live and act in the story world, but who has insight into it and is capable of mediating it to us. The person who writes the four concluding sentences in *American Graffiti* is presumably such an 'impersonal', *non-diegetic* narrator who sees the story world from the outside and writes about the characters in the third person. As is clear from the texts, this narrator 'believes' in the fiction: the characters in the film are real persons; they were alive in 1962; now two of them are dead. A non-diegetic narrator is located outside the diegesis, but inside the *fiction*.

The entire story of *American Graffiti* can be understood as being told by a non-diegetic narrator. Admittedly, we experience most of the scenes 'from the inside', from an implied diegetic narrator's perspective, but 'someone' or 'something' ensures that we are moved from place to place within the story world so that we gain the relevant information in the relevant order. In a novel the non-diegetic narrator would write: 'While Steve was talking to the two girls, Terry and Debby drove into the parking lot outside.' In the film, the information is presented in two scenes, separated by a cut. The function is the same.

The non-diegetic narrator organizes the information for us, including the music. Every time characters converse and have something important to say, and every time important events take place, the music is turned down so we can hear what people are saying and concentrate on what is shown on the screen. In spite of the fact that the music is diegetic and that we experience it from an implied diegetic narrator's position, there is another authority in the fiction – a non-diegetic narrator – who controls the course of events and intervenes so as to ensure that the diegetic music does not get in the way of the conveying and understanding of the story. It is the same narrative authority that turns up the music again and that sometimes changes the volume and sound to indicate that a new part of the account of the evening's events is about to start.

The non-diegetic narrator also ensures that the music continues to play even though there is a cut in the events and 'unessential' parts of the action are omitted. Think, for example, of Steve and Laurie leaving the school dance and arriving at the parking lot. In a novel the non-diegetic narrator would write: 'While the music continued, Steve and Laurie went out to the parking lot.' In the film, something similar happens: before the cut 'Louie, Louie' is a piece of diegetic music; after the cut it is a non-diegetic comment that says: 'The music continues.' Before the cut we hear an actual bit of an actual song being performed; after the cut, we hear a generalizing summary, some music that means 'dance music played in the distance'.

Extra-fictional information

At the end of the film, after the non-diegetic narrator has finished his information about what subsequently happened, the closing credits begin to scroll up over the screen with information about the actors and the crew: Curt was played by Richard Dreyfuss, Steve by Ron Howard, etc. Another kind of narrator has taken over here, one who knows that the characters are not real, and that the entire narrative is a fiction that many people have helped construct. This is an *extra-fictional narrator* who is present in the *text* but stands outside the fiction.

163

While the closing credits are scrolling, 'All Summer Long' by the Beach Boys is played on the soundtrack. Unlike most of the music in the film this song does not have any spatial perspective. The sound is pure and clear. The song is clearly not coming from inside the story world. It exists at the same level as the closing credits. This is extra-fictional music, music that is in the text, but neither in the diegesis nor the fiction.

'Rock Around the Clock', which is played during the opening credits, has the same clear sound and accompanies the same type of extra-fictional texts as 'All Summer Long'. It can be described as an extra-fictional overture. It marks the fact that the film has begun, and it finishes when the opening credits are over and the fiction begins. On the other hand, the film-as-text really starts with the sound of a car radio being tuned, after which there comes a jingle, and only then 'Rock Around the Clock'. Perhaps this whole sequence is the start of the fiction, the narrative? Perhaps 'Rock Around the Clock' is just the first record played after an anonymous person has managed to tune in to his or her favourite station, i.e. a piece of diegetic music? Or perhaps it functions as a non-diegetic representation of 'music that is typically played on car radios' in the story world? The point is that all these possibilities can be argued for. The music is the same, but the description of it changes character according to what frames of reference it is measured against.

When it comes to the opening credits themselves there can be no doubt. They have been written from a position outside the fiction. The opening credits of a film, like its closing credits, are the typical, explicit presentation of extra-fictional information. But there can also be moments in a film where one more implicitly marks the presence of an extra-fictional narrator. For example, the radio starts to play 'Why Do Fools Fall in Love?' by Frankie Lymon and the Teenagers the first time Curt sees the mysterious blonde. The song continues into the next scene, where John invites a girl over into his car. She rejects him because she is going steady with another guy. John calls out that he is available if she felt like accepting his offer some day. At the same time the radio starts to play 'That'll Be The Day' by Buddy Holly.

Are these songs – with precisely these refrains – chosen at random? Is it purely by chance that the radio plays 'I Only Have Eyes For You' while Terry kisses Debbie, and 'Only You' when Curt finally makes contact with the blonde? If we see the music as diegetic, the answer is of course 'yes'. For in the story world it is Wolfman Jack who has chosen these songs, and naturally he has not tried to get the refrains of the songs to fit the experiences of some random teenagers. But one and the same narrative element can perfectly well be described from several different perspectives. It is possible to consider the songs as numbers in a radio programme in the story world and at the same time understand them as extra-fictional comments on the action and the characters. In this way *American Graffiti* can be considered the last link in a long tradition that started in the early phase of the silent film, where the cinema pianists often functioned as extra-fictional narrators. It was usual to accompany the films with popular songs, the titles of which could be understood as comments on the events taking place on the screen.[18]

Chameleon music

Edward Branigan writes at one point about the chameleon effect of the narrative text: textual elements change 'colour' – meaning, function – according to where they are positioned.[19] The use of music in *American Graffiti* is a good example of this phenomenon. In many cases one and the same piece of music is played during a fairly long sequence of events, but functions differently at different points in time, because the nature of the context changes. In other cases one and the same piece of music can be experienced in several different ways at the same time and be described in relation to a number of different interpretative contexts. A couple of remarks about the music in the final scenes of the film will sum this up and give an impression of the virtuosity with which music is used to shape our experiencing of the narrative.

It is early in the morning. The duel with Falfa is over. John goes over to his car with Terry. As they get into the car to drive home, 'Only You' by The Platters starts up on the soundtrack. The song continues while there is a cut to a shot of Curt's car seen from above. The music is clear and distinct, but as the camera zooms in and there is a cut to a shot of the car taken at street level, the volume is turned down and the music now has an unmistakable spatial character. The abstract, pure sound in the beginning of this sequence is a non-diegetic marking of the fact that a new, important section of the narrative is now beginning, information that is underlined visually by our seeing this new scene in an overview, from an 'Olympian' perspective. As the sound changes we are taken into the story world. A diegetic narrator who stood where the camera is positioned in relation to Curt's car would have heard 'Only You' in this way, played on a car radio a little way off.

A telephone rings several times. We see Curt asleep in the car; he suddenly wakes up; he rushes over to a telephone box and picks up the phone. It is the mysterious blonde who is calling. As he starts talking to her, the volume of the music is turned down. After their conversation he stays for a while inside the telephone box. 'Only You' finishes, and we hear Wolfman Jack's voice, clearly and distinctly. What do these changes in the sound mean? One possibility is that this is yet another example of a non-diegetic narrator organizing the narrative information for us. In this case the music is turned down so we can hear everything the woman says to Curt. Another possibility, which does not exclude the first one, is that we are hearing the diegetic music from Curt's perspective. He is so absorbed in his telephone conversation that he hardly hears the music at all; not until the conversation is over does he once more hear Wolfman Jack's programme. Described in this second way, the music is part of a focalization: the change in the sound reflects Curt's subjective experience.[20] The woman's voice can be described in the same way. We do not hear it as a distant, indistinct sound in a telephone receiver but clearly and distinctly, either because the non-diegetic narrator has decided that we are to hear what she says or because we are hearing it with Curt's ears.

The woman says goodbye and hangs up, without having given her name. We hear a kissing sound from the radio. Then Wolfman Jack says 'A little kiss on your ear. Goodnight sweetheart. I'll see you later.' It is as if he is commenting on the conversation or expressing what Curt is thinking. But then he adds: 'Oh, the Spaniels'. He was actually introducing the next song. And when The Spaniels begin to sing 'Goodnight Sweetheart' there is a cut to the airport. The song is heard in the background during the departure scene that now follows – a scene that clearly takes place many hours later. In other words, the music changes character in this cut: it is not coming from some car radio in the background. It is only we, the spectators, who hear it. It is no longer diegetic, but 'accompanies' the departure scene in the same way as traditional non-diegetic film music. And even though the slow pop tune does not perhaps resemble traditional 'departure music', the lyrics do at least give the scene an extra-fictional comment that underlines what it is all about: 'Goodnight sweetheart, well it's time to go.'

The Empire strikes back: *Star Wars*, 1977

Measured in relation to the original investment, *American Graffiti* was the greatest economic success in the history of Hollywood to that date. The enormous profit only underscored what a number of earlier films had shown – that there are financial gains to be had in compilations of pop and rock music. From 1970 to the present day this type of film music has played a predominant role, not only in Hollywood but in Western film production in general. And not only in films for younger audiences such as *Clueless* (Amy Heckerling, 1995) or *Legally Blonde* (Robert Luketic, 2001), but in many other genres, from the dance films of the 1970s, *Saturday Night Fever* (John Badham, 1977) and *Grease* (Randal Kleiser, 1978), via the popular fighter pilot films of the 1980s, *Top Gun* (Tony Scott, 1986) and *Iron Eagle* (Sidney J. Furie, 1986) up to Quentin Tarantino's gangster and martial arts films (*Pulp Fiction*, 1994; *Kill Bill 1–11*, 2003–4).

American Graffiti was Lucas's second film. When he began shooting it he was almost unknown. After the premiere he was one of the biggest names in Hollywood. And he had earned a fortune. He invested his share of the profits in developing and realizing his grandiose science fiction project *Star Wars*. From a film music perspective there is a certain historical irony in the fact that the man who had earned a fortune by using pop and rock music in *American Graffiti* was to be the one who, via *Star Wars*, gave traditional film music an unexpected renaissance.

It has been claimed that the composer John Williams's score for *Star Wars* revived the classical Hollywood system. This is not completely correct. The actual system – understood as a collection of rules of the trade as to *where* film music is to be positioned and what narrative *functions* it should have – had never really been ousted from the cinemas. Most compilations of pop and rock music, for example, were quite clearly used in accordance with the old rules. What John Williams revived was the music of the Golden Age, the special version of the classical system that is based on late Romantic music for a large orchestra. That type of music had more or less gone out of fashion during the 1960s and 1970s. It now returned to the cinemas and mass audiences.

John Williams (1932–) is a jazz pianist, but also had a classical education at the Juilliard School of Music. In the 1950s he began to work in Hollywood, first as a pianist, then as an assistant for the leading film composers of the day. He orchestrated for, among others, Franz Waxman, Alfred Newman, Dmitri Tiomkin and Bernard Herrmann. In the late 1950s he began to write his own music, first for TV series and later for films. He gradually became known for being able to write effective, hard-hitting music for 'big' films, and was Oscar-nominated for, among other things, his music for two of the 1970s' great disaster films: *The Poseidon Adventure* (Ronald Neame, 1972) and *The Towering Inferno* (Irwin Allen and John Guillermin, 1974). He consolidated his position with the music for two of Steven Spielberg's major productions: *Jaws* (1975) and *Close Encounters of the Third Kind* (1977). And then came the music for *A New Hope* – the first film of the *Star Wars* series.[21]

Science fiction has traditionally been a film genre where composers were allowed to let themselves go and experiment with unusual sounds and modernistic forms. Bernard Herrmann's music for Robert Wise's *The Day the Earth Stood Still* (1951), for example, was written for electronic organ, amplified strings and an old-fashioned tone-generator, a Theremin, which produces a strange, spooky sound. When Stanley Kubrick completed *2001: A Space Odyssey* (1968), the most advanced science fiction film, technically speaking, prior to *Star Wars*, he used works by the Hungarian avant-garde composer György Ligeti as an accompaniment to the central scenes.

One would perhaps have expected Lucas to have used similar experimental, advanced music for *Star Wars*, but instead he chose to turn back the musical clock. Which in a way makes sense, when one sees the film. For *Star Wars* is quite clearly not any run-of-the-mill science fiction film. It is both future and past at one and the same time: a fantasy about a futuristic hi-tech world carried out using the most advanced film technology, and at the same time a tribute to the primitive SF films of the 1930s about Buck Rogers and Flash Gordon. The action takes place 'a long time ago in a galaxy far, far away' and is an amazing blend of genres where the princesses and wizards of the adventure and fantasy universes meet fighter pilots, Western heroes and robots.

When Lucas started editing the film, he used a temp track with music by Gustav Holst, Antonin Dvorák and William Walton. He also used part of Miklós Rózsa's grandiose music for William Wyler's *Ben-Hur* (1959). Initially he imagined that the final music would be something similar, a compilation of popular, classical orchestral works. He mentioned his plans to Steven Spielberg, who suggested that he should instead let John Williams write original music for the film. Spielberg had collaborated with Williams and knew that he was capable of working in many different musical genres. The result was that Williams was included in the project and wrote a score according to Lucas's specifications.

The opening

The film starts with the Twentieth Century Fox logo and its fanfare.[22] Then the Star Wars logo appears, followed by another fanfare, after which – without the usual opening credits – we are directly introduced into the fiction with the aid of a text that outlines the pre-history and context of the action that is to come. The text is accompanied by an overture that is reminiscent of the opening to a Golden Age film. Like many of the overtures to old Hollywood melodramas, the Star Wars overture is divided into two sections, based on a musical contrast between a 'hard' masculine and a 'soft' feminine theme. It begins with a 'heroic' fanfare-like march theme played by the brass section, with blaring trumpets at the top and thunderous percussion at the bottom:

8.1: *Star Wars:* Main theme (1)

After being played twice, the march is replaced by a more flexible, romantic theme played by the strings:

8.2: *Star Wars:* Main theme (2)

The first theme returns and, while the last of the text is scrolling over the screen, the overture concludes with a violent crescendo,

dominated by drums and percussion. The music dissolves into indeterminable sounds played by flutes and harps. On the screen we see a
dark starry sky with a planet in the distance. A spaceship bursts into
the picture. The story begins.

In terms of melodics and harmonics this opening is fairly simple,
but the sound of the large symphony orchestra sends a clear musical
message. And the references to an earlier era in film history are rein-
forced when we enter the story world. Williams makes use of a traditional musical idiom, but just as importantly uses the music in the same
way as the Golden Age composers. If one comes to *Star Wars* with the
flexible film music of the 1960s in one's ears, it is like being thrown
back to one of Max Steiner's or Erich Korngold's films: the sound is
massive, and it feels as if the music is playing continuously. This is not
completely correct, but there is a great deal of music on the soundtrack: a total of 86 minutes, i.e. about three quarters of the 120 minutes that the film lasts.

The music plays uninterruptedly, for example, for the first seven
minutes, where we see the forces of the galactic Rebel Alliance defeated
by the Imperial stormtroopers. The formidable Imperial Commander-
in-Chief Darth Vader enters the rebels' spaceship; he demands to have
their plans handed over, but their leader, Princess Leia, manages to get
them sent away, together with the robots R2-D2 and C-3PO, who escape
in a space capsule. The capsule lands on the deserted planet Tatooine.
Only here does the music stop for a brief moment while the robots discuss what they are to do.

Reading aid

Here and in the following the music functions first and foremost as a
reading aid. When the action changes from place to place, or when
there are decisive shifts in the narrative, the transitions are emphasised
by music. The firing of the space capsule is underscored by a crescendo.
In other instances the transition is marked by a new, different type of
music, usually adapted to the mood of the narrative at that particular
point. The imperial starship hurtles through space accompanied by a
full orchestra; when there is a cut to the robots in the desert, the music
dissolves into indeterminable sounds played by flutes. In some cases
the music follows the action so closely that one could almost speak of
mickey-mousing. From time to time Williams intensifies the scenes
with the aid of familiar formulas that in some cases go right back to

the period of the silent films. There is 'hurry' music when things happen fast; there is 'spooky' music when the action takes a nasty turn, etc.

Leitmotifs

As the narrative proceeds we gradually start to recognize certain themes and to understand that the music does not only function as a formal subdividing of the course of the action. It is also being used for more content-defined markings. At one point we find ourselves on a remote farm. A young man comes out to meet some travelling scrapdealers. A woman's voice calls out: 'Luke, Luke!' While he runs back to the farm, we hear the march theme from the overture being played on a distant horn. In short: a character is emphasized in the picture, we hear that person's name and at the same time we hear a striking musical theme. It is hardly possible to establish a leitmotif more pedagogically. In other cases this is done less demonstrably. The first time Princess Leia appears in action, we hear a brief melody, but it is much further on in the film that it becomes obvious that this melody is linked specifically to her:

8.3: *Star Wars*: Princess Leia

As time passes most of the important characters have a leitmotif linked to them. And, as was the case in the old films, these themes are often ambiguous, or are used as a reference to something more than the characters themselves. The theme that is linked to the Jedi Master Obi-Wan Kenobi at the beginning of the film is later used as a broader reference both to the Jedi Knights and the old republic that the rebels are defending, and to the Force, the magic 'power' that the Knights as well as Luke possess (illus. 8.4).

8.4: *Star Wars*: Obi-Wan Kenobi

The themes are not just signals. In most cases they characterize the referent using musical effects. This characterization is particularly evident in the mutual contrasts between the themes: Luke's theme is normally played as a 'majestic' march, while Leia's theme is played 'like a mild and gentle flow', according to the tempo designation in the piano version.[23] Luke's theme is in the major and has a simple, straightforward harmonization. The march that signals Darth Vader and the evil Imperial stormtroopers, on the other hand, is based on a series of disconnected minor chords – Gm | E^{b}m | C$^#$m:

8.5: *Star Wars*: The March of the Empire

Musical loans

In the literature on *Star Wars* a number of Williams's themes are characterized as quotations or loans. A whole range of classical composers, from Tchaikovsky to Bartók, has been quoted as sources. On closer inspection it normally transpires that we are dealing with fairly superficial similarities, but the martial music in *Star Wars* is, at least, clearly inspired by 'Mars, the Bringer of War' from Gustav Holst's *The Planets* suite.

Hollywood composers such as Max Steiner and Erich Korngold have also been mentioned as sources. For example, Luke's theme is usually thought to be a direct loan from Korngold's music for the film *Kings Row* (Sam Wood, 1942; illus. 8.6). There are certainly similarities between the themes. Both start with a triplet upbeat, a 'heroic' upward leap of a fifth in the first bar, a stepwise descending movement in the second bar. But if one listens to the themes in the actual musical context it is obvious that the similarity is only superficial. The rhythm in the descending figure is different in the two themes, and the figures have completely different functions. In the *Kings Row* theme the figure

8.6: Erich Korngold: Theme from *Kings Row*

is part of a movement that brings the music to rest; in the *Star Wars* theme the figure is a triplet that forms the upbeat to yet another upward 'heroic' leap.

When so many spectators nevertheless feel that they can recognize *Star Wars* music from works by classical composers or from other films, this is because Williams exploits his comprehensive knowledge of Romantic and late Romantic music as well as of the composers of the Golden Age in order to evoke moods and associations that match the action of the film. We are seldom dealing with direct quotations or loans of themes, rather with a virtuoso exploitation of established formulas and techniques, of melodic turns of phrase, harmonizations, instrumentations.

Spectacle

When interviewers ask Williams to characterize the *Star Wars* music, he often refers to its 'heroic' and 'idealistic' qualities. His task was to underpin Lucas's mythological narrative of the struggle between the forces of good and evil, but also to give the narrative a musical lift by intensifying the visual experience. At one point he talks, for example, about the fact that the introduction to the film was 'visually so stunning' that strong music was called for which could 'smack you right in the eye'.[24] Claudia Gorbman is considering something similar when she writes about the spaceships hurtling through the galaxy accompanied by the 'orchestral grandeur' of the main theme. In such situations, the music helps to make the events on the screen 'larger than life'. It enables us not only to see the narrative but also to see the images and be stunned by them *as* images – as a *spectacle*. In this way, the music adds an 'epic dimension' to the events on the screen: it makes us 'view' the narrative rather than get involved in it.[25]

A success story

Star Wars had its premiere in May 1977. The rest is history – both film history and film music history. The film broke all previous sales records, as did the film music. It was released in July of the same year on a double album that contained 78 of the total 86 minutes of music Williams had written for the film. The album was on *Billboard*'s Top 20 list for 18 weeks, and at no. 2 for five weeks. The great success of the film with the mass audience is of course an important part of the explanation, but the fact that it was possible to sell a double album of film music, and that this album is to date one of the best selling releases of symphonic instrumental music in the history of the music industry, would seem to indicate that Williams had struck a chord not only in the film but in the public as well.

The *Star Wars* music established Williams as Hollywood's leading composer. His filmography includes both blockbusters and films with 'big', 'serious' themes. There is *Superman* (Richard Donner, 1978), the 'Indiana Jones' film *Raiders of the Lost Ark* (Steven Spielberg, 1981) and *Jurassic Park* (Steven Spielberg, 1993), and there is *Schindler's List* (Steven Spielberg, 1993) and *Saving Private Ryan* (Steven Spielberg, 1998). Many of the fantasy and adventure films have developed into longer series. Williams has, for example, written music for all the subsequent episodes of *Star Wars*, for the *Superman* films, the *Indiana Jones* films, etc. He wrote the music for *Harry Potter and the Sorcerer's Stone* (Chris Columbus, 2001) as well as for the subsequent *Harry Potter* films.

For film producers the *Star Wars* success was an example to be followed. Since 1977 it has been the rule that 'big' productions must of necessity be accompanied by 'big' music in the old style. This has resulted in a veritable renaissance for symphonic film music and several younger composers have made a career by following in Williams's footsteps: Bruce Broughton, James Newton Howard, Danny Elfman, James Horner, Hans Zimmer, to name but a few.

The sound of the future: *Blade Runner*, 1982

There was not only grandiose orchestral music in *Star Wars*. There were also remarkable sound effects: Luke's humming lightsabre, the laser guns of the imperial stormtroopers, the rebels' starfighter planes – all objects of the futuristic universe were accompanied by strange, suggestive sounds created by the sound designer Ben Burtt. He used fairly unorthodox methods to get the right effects: the sound of Luke's flying landspeeder was constructed by recording the noise from a Los Angeles freeway through the pipe of a vacuum cleaner; the humming of the lightsabre is a blend of the sounds of a TV set and a film projector; the droid R2-D2's 'voice' is generated electronically and mixed with the sound of water pipes and flutes.

At the Oscar awards in 1978 Burtt won a Special Achievement Award for the sound effects, and *Star Wars* also won in the category Best Sound, for the *Star Wars* sound was much more than Burtt's special effects. The total sound universe of the film was revolutionary. Lucas had reintroduced stereophonic sound to the cinema. Stereo was used in the 1950s when the film companies tried to entice the TV public back to the cinemas with technical innovations. The first CinemaScope film, *The Robe* (Henry Koster, 1953) has stereophonic sound, and other major productions of the time continued along the same path, but after that the technique went more or less out of use until Lucas came along with *Star Wars*. There was stereophonic sound and tremendous spatial acoustics with a vengeance. And at the same time the overall film sound had been dramatically improved with the aid of the Dolby system.

New sounds

The Dolby system, developed in the mid-1960s by an American sound engineer, reduced background noise on tape recordings. It also increased the frequency range it is possible to record and play back. The system was first used in the record industry and was a necessary condition for the breakthrough of cassette tapes in the early 1970s. In 1975 Dolby presented a version that could be used in film production. In the years that followed the system was used in a few films, but the breakthrough with regard to the film industry and the cinemas came in 1977 with *Star Wars* and with Spielberg's *Close Encounters of the Third Kind*. Since then, there have been a number of new versions of the system, the most important being Dolby SR from 1986 and Dolby Digital from 1992.

The introduction of the Dolby system meant a dramatic improvement in the sound of film music. The noise reduction makes the music clear and sharp, while the expanded frequency range offers the film composers completely new possibilities. One can, for example, work with effects in the deeper register that would have been inaudible with the old sound technology, and the system can reproduce large fluctuation in volume without the sound becoming distorted. It is also possible to mix music completely differently to how it was done before, for it is not only the music but the sound of the film as a whole that has become clearer. This means that the individual sounds are clearly demarcated from each other and can be manipulated in new ways. With the breakthrough of the Dolby system, 'sound design' became an important function in the international film industry.

The 1970s was also the period when synthesizers had their breakthrough both as an instrument on the ordinary music market and as an aid in film music. A synth generates sounds and notes electronically. One can play on a synth as if it were a piano, and manipulate the sounds according to a whole range of parameters such as duration, intensity, sound. One can use the synth to imitate traditional instruments or to create sounds that lie outside the register of these instruments. The first synths were based on traditional sound technology; later versions generated sound with the aid of computer programmes and various digital techniques.

Giorgio Moroder was the first composer to get an Oscar for synth-based film music. The film was *Midnight Express* (Alan Parker, 1978), where Moroder occasionally imitates the sound of a large film orchestra, but first and foremost creates a musical universe with clear references to the synth-based popular music of the age. At the beginning of the 1980s the film companies began to use increasingly advanced electronic equipment. In certain cases the new technology was mainly used to create musical special effects, but during the 1980s more and more films were produced where all the music had been electronically generated. Older film composers started to experiment with electronic music, e.g. Jerry Goldsmith (the music for Michael Crichton's *Runaway*, 1985) and Maurice Jarre (the music for Adrian Lyne's *Fatal Attraction*, 1987). New names also emerged, composers with a background in pop and rock music, such as Vangelis, who was awarded an Oscar for his music for Hugh Hudson's *Chariots of Fire* (1981). The following year Vangelis collaborated with Ridley Scott on the science fiction film *Blade Runner*. The music for this film is an interesting example of experimental use of popular electronic music and in addition the film demonstrates some of the possibilities offered film creators by the new sound technology.

Future noir

Blade Runner is an unusual science fiction film. The action takes place in an urban universe that is not reminiscent of anything else in the history of film. The old SF films always took place in spotless, functionalistic surroundings. In Ridley Scott's version Los Angeles 2019 is just as dark and rainy a city as Los Angeles 1946 in *The Big Sleep*. But, unlike Howard Hawks's *film noir*, the cityscape of Scott's *future noir* is characterized by overpopulation and chaotic decline. The city centre is a meltdown of every known architectural style, and the tangled, overgrown urban space teems with people of all nationalities. Above the city the headquarters of the mighty Tyrell Corporation soars into the sky like some modern Mayan temple. In impressive overview shots one looks out over a dark urban sprawl that is occasionally lit up by violent flashes of lightning and explosion-like blow-outs from colossal derricks. Everywhere in the city one comes across strange electronic apparatus – talking traffic signals, picture phones and cash points. The sky is criss-crossed by advertising airships and flying cars, the so-called *spinners*, while down at street level there are people cycling, riding in rickshaws or taking the subway.[26]

In this confusing, hard-to-grasp universe we meet *replicants* and *blade runners:* the replicants are high-functional androids; blade runners are state-hired assassins who eliminate replicants if they become too troublesome. The shabby private detective Deckard was once a blade runner; he has now been ordered to resume his former job. He is to find and kill a group of escaped replicants.

An opening

The film has rightly been praised for its visual complexity. But its sound effects are just as intriguing and overwhelming. The mysteries start already while the opening credits are being shown against a black screen. Two thunderous, powerful explosions are heard – or maybe they are drumbeats? There is a long, resounding echo, suggesting an enormous space. While the noise dies away, a high whining note starts up, an E^b, which is gradually followed by the notes F, C and finally B^b (illus. 8.7). But what sort of an instrument is this? A violin, an electric guitar, an electronically amplified sawblade? Or something else entirely?

8.7: *Blade Runner.* Introduction: The first four notes

When we hear the final note, we realize that this could become a melody, or at least a melodic motif, one that will descend from B^b and come to rest on the tonic A^b. But this expectation is dashed: the B^b is held for an extremely long time, ending in a distorting, descending glissando that is followed by new explosive drumbeats. Because the four notes are played very slowly and no audible basic rhythm is indicated, it is difficult to identify the precise contours of the motif (illus. 8.8 gives a suggestion).

8.8: *Blade Runner.* Introduction: First motif

After the drumbeats, the notes Eᵇ and F are heard again. A new, hovering motif is suggested; this time the melodic line ends on a high G that keels over into a glissando, followed by new drumbeats. The rhythm is still unclear.

8.9: *Blade Runner.* Introduction: Second motif

Both motifs are repeated, followed by drumbeats. The sound then changes character. The *fiction* begins. While an explanatory text about replicants and blade runners scrolls upwards across the dark screen, we are led into a complex acoustic space. It is difficult to decide if it is the music that has shifted to a different register, or if we are listening to diegetic sounds. 'Underneath' there is a rhythmical pattern of something reminiscent of church bells. Above that lies the sound of a traffic signal. There are also some deep sirens in the distance. At one point towards the end of the scrolling text it seems as if a large vehicle is drawing nearer and nearer while the sound becomes deep and resonating. Then there are new drumbeats and the sound of a large gong. On the screen it says *Los Angeles 2019*.

The sound now changes character once again. While we are shown an impressive panorama view of the city, an ascending arpeggio is heard, played by a harp-like instrument; to which the sound of a gong is added, the sound of explosions from distant derricks and a deep synth-sound as pedal point. A spinner flies noisily straight at the camera and disappears out of picture. The two motifs from the introduction reappear, played this time with a trumpet-like sound, accompanied by some kind of strings. The motifs now form a coherent melodic line that is prolonged and ends with a leap up to a high Eᵇ. But the melody is not taken down to the expected conclusion on A^b; it ends on the high E^b, which keels over into a descending glissando. In this musically speaking undefined situation, there is a cut to a new narrative space. The sound changes character. The introduction is over.

Point of view and 'point of hearing'

An obvious comparison can be made between this introductory sequence and the opening of *Star Wars*. In *Star Wars* the musical universe is crystal-clear from the very first fanfare, and in the following scenes the sound space is easy to grasp and thoroughly structured. It is clear that the music exists in a universe separated from that of the other sounds. In *Blade Runner* the individual sounds are even more sharply defined, but they are used to create a space where everything is just as complex and hard to grasp as the cityscape shown on the screen. In general it is difficult to determine the musical idiom used. And it is difficult to decide which instruments are being used – something that has to do with the fact that most of the music is electronically generated. It imitates the sound of traditional instruments, but at the same time the sound is manipulated and distorted in many different ways so that one is constantly unsure of what one is actually hearing. Added to which it is difficult to decide where the boundary lies between Vangelis's music and other forms of sound.

This complex sound universe is maintained throughout the rest of the film. The recurring pattern is that sound is used to characterize and separate the individual scenes from each other. Each time there is a visual cut to a new location the sound quality changes character, often with quite dramatic effect. The expanded sound register of the Dolby system is exploited to the limit here. Every narrative space has its own sound, its own background noise, its own buzz, its own echo. Even with cuts within single scenes the sound changes character. The voices of the characters change according to what position the camera sees them from, and the diegetic sound sometimes gives us access to their 'inner' experiences. In two of the most dramatic scenes of the film, for example, we hear the thudding heartbeat of the replicants.

The action is seen from the camera's point of view. The stereophonic sound indicates a 'point of hearing'. It divides the narrative space into many different sound spaces. In certain cases these sound spaces have enormous breadth and depth. The first time we meet Deckard, he is sitting outdoors in the rain, waiting to get a seat in a sushi bar. We hear music played on an Asian string instrument, pop music sung in a foreign language, seductive slogans from one of the flying advertising airships high up in the sky, the sound of a neon sign that is short-circuiting, etc. At many points in the sound space there are people talking to each other. Somewhere close by someone is playing on a recorder. The sound space is large; the individual sounds are sharply separated from each other and clearly positioned in the narrative space. The sound of the never-ending rain is incredibly differentiated: we can make out that there are many different types of rain falling at many different places in the space.

The music is part of this soundscape. Often it glides imperceptibly into the overall context and cannot be distinguished from all the other electronic sounds present in the story world. In other instances it clearly functions as a non-diegetic comment that comes from outside, singling out the individual scene and giving it an extra underscoring, for example, in the beginning, when Deckard flies in a spinner to the police headquarters. Here the diegetic sound suddenly disappears, and the trip gains an almost sacred feel to it, because it is accompanied by pealing 'organ' chords and the suggestion of a distant choir.

The music

Most of Vangelis's music is constructed in this way, of complex, 'fluid' sounds and musical effects. The music is interwoven with the total sound universe. It is an extra sound quality beneath an entire scene or during an event. Normally, it has the same functions as traditional film music: it marks transitions; it underlines the course of the action using well-known formulas and it occasionally breaks through and plays a more prominent role, especially in connection with crucial events and emotional climaxes in the relationship between Deckard and the beautiful Rachel (Sean Young).

Rachel works for the Tyrell Corporation. At one point Deckard carries out a test on her, which reveals – something she is unaware of – that she is a replicant. She later visits him at his flat and tries to convince him that he is wrong. As she realizes that he is in fact right, the music starts. Initially we hear isolated electronic sounds, which then gather to become an out-of-tune piano playing an introduction, accompanied by strings. And when Rachel leaves Deckard's flat in anger and despair, the piano plays the slow 'Memories of Green' from the Vangelis album *See You Later* (1980). This is not a melody in the traditional sense, rather a slow, melancholy meditation on a short motif that is played again and again while Deckard goes round his flat thinking about things (illus. 8.10).

8.10: *Blade Runner*: Memories of Green

The music has a similar function in a later scene. Rachel has saved Deckard's life. They are together in his flat. She asks him an important question, but discovers that he has fallen asleep on the sofa. As she looks at him, a blues-like phrase can be heard played by a saxophone above a string accompaniment (illus. 8.11). She sits down at his old grand piano, looks at some of his photographs, and when the melody is over, starts to play. After a while, her diegetic piano music glides imperceptibly over into the non-diegetic music, which starts up once more.

8.11: *Blade Runner*: Blues

Both these motifs, and those from the introduction, appear on a number of occasions during the sequence. We are not dealing with leit-motifs in a traditional sense here, rather with musical images that both characterize the total fictive universe and are used to underline the mood of particularly intense scenes.

Contrasts and fluid transitions

What came after the Golden Age and late Romantic orchestra music? It is difficult to give a clear answer to that question. The last 50 years of film music are a composite phenomenon that is hard to reduce to a single formula. But Ridley Scott's *Blade Runner* and Vangelis's eclectic music make an excellent point of departure if we wish to highlight certain main trends.

As discussed, Vangelis's music is seamlessly integrated into the soundscape in such a way that it is often difficult to determine precisely where it ought to be positioned in relation to the traditional boundary between non-diegetic and diegetic elements. Are we dealing with music coming from outside or simply with sound effects – music, noises – that are included as an integral part of the story world? An important part of the basis for this is the overall improvement of sound in films from the mid-1970s onwards. From a broader perspective this development is probably the most important trend of all when it comes to the production of modern film sound and film music. The new technology has made it possible to shape sounds in new ways, which, among other things, has meant that film music has been relieved of some of its earlier functions. In many instances sound designers solve the tasks that previously would have been a part of the film composer's area of responsibility, while today's film music often takes a back seat and is used more sparingly, as a kind of special effect.

Vangelis's *Blade Runner* music is oriented towards popular music and produced with the aid of advanced electronic equipment. This too is a characteristic feature. From the 1980s onwards much film music has had an electronic orientation. Sometimes electronically generated sounds are the sole form of accompaniment, at other times they interact with traditional instruments; sometimes in experimental forms, at other times adapted to a pop-music idiom. The pop-music orientation has been a predominant tendency since the 1960s. A look at the last decade's films, however, demonstrates at once that this orientation has not resulted in the establishing of a uniform practice.

Popular music is used in many films, but in many different ways. In a film like *Blade Runner* most of the music is composed for this particular film. In other films the music is made up of older hits, or there is a combination of old, well-known songs and new songs written directly for the film. Popular songs also occur in films that are provided with more traditional scored music. This last feature is common practice in modern romantic comedies. A film like *You've Got Mail* (Nora Ephron, 1998), for example, has relatively traditional music written by George Fenton, but during the film one also hears various songs by Carole King, Sinéad O'Connor and others. A number of films exploit the nostalgia factor, and the release of soundtrack CDs for popular films often gives old hits a new lease of life. When the male protagonist in *Notting Hill* (Roger Michell, 1999) has been abandoned by the woman he loves, he walks about the city in melancholic mood while we hear the old soul classic 'Ain't No Sunshine When She's Gone' from Bill Withers's debut album *Just As I Am* (1971). In this case the old song clearly functions as a representation of the main character's thoughts; in many other cases the lyrics – or possibly just the song titles – are used as a relatively loose, non-diegetic comment on the action as, for example, when one hears in the same film various versions of 'She', Charles Aznavour's romantic hit from 1974.

The *Blade Runner* music has a pop-music orientation, but in some cases it also points back to older musical genres and is used to perform relatively traditional functions. This too is a characteristic feature: modern film music is functionally speaking a composite phenomenon. It often functions as traditional film music did, but is also used to give a scene or event a particular colouring, as an effect on a par with scenography and editing; sometimes it comes into the foreground and 'carries' the whole action, especially in emotionally charged situations or in situations where the visual aspects of the narrative are presented as a 'spectacle'.

Popular music predominates, but since John Williams's success with the music for *Star Wars* in the late-1970s many mainstream films, especially blockbuster productions, have been provided with symphonic orchestral music. In a sense the music of the Golden Age has been revived, but here too there are fluid transitions. The non-diegetic orchestral music often functions in the same way as in the old films, but the actual musical idiom is far more composite than in the 1930s and 1940s. In John Williams's scores from the 1970s there are already large sections that point in different directions from the typical, heavy late Romantic orchestral sound, and in present-day orchestral scores one does not find only one but many musical idioms. And, as mentioned above, there is a considerable use of popular songs, even in films equipped with traditional symphonic music.

On the whole the music of present-day mainstream films is characterized by large contrasts and fluid transitions between formerly separate genres. The traditional sharp division of labour between symphonic, non-diegetic music and diegetic popular music has virtually disappeared. The entire musical spectrum from folk music, pop, rock, electronica and jazz to traditional and modernistic orchestral music is represented, often in unexpected combinations and effective mixes.

In an introduction to the films of the past 40 years, Geoffrey Nowell-Smith emphasizes this great diversity. He writes that even though, artistically and politically speaking, the most exciting developments have perhaps taken place elsewhere, mainstream films have at least blazed a trail when it comes to the innovative use of sound – and especially music. He concludes by saying that in this respect Hollywood films can be 'as artistically daring as the more openly modernist "art films" emerging from Europe and Japan'.[27] On the other hand there are film artists who feel that film music indicates the exact opposite of boldness and a willingness to experiment. The Danish 'Dogma' directors, for example, who struggle against 'the film of illusion', insist that shooting should take place on location, and that music should not be used unless music occurs in the location where the action takes place.

In the history of sound films there are a number of similar examples of experimental directors banning the use of non-diegetic music, normally in an attempt to increase cinematic realism. There have also been periods when non-diegetic music has been absent from certain mainstream films. But these are exceptions rather than the rule, ripples on the surface. The overwhelming tendency, from the silent films to the present day, is for fictive films to be accompanied by non-diegetic music. Why this is the case is a question that has been debated through the history of film theory. In the next chapter I will deal with some of the answers.

9
Necessity or Possibility?
The Psychology of Film Music

'By itself the screen is a pretty cold proposition. Music is like a small flame put under the screen to help warm it,' the composer Aaron Copland wrote.[1] His remark is one of two mottoes that introduce Charles Hofmann's book on the music of the silent films. The other is by the composer Kurt Weill, who writes: 'The fact remains that the silent movie needed music as a dry cereal needs cream.'[2]

Both Copland and Weill believe, then, that films *need* music, and both resort to the use of metaphor in order to explain the need. Copland's metaphor says that the music adds emotional warmth to the cold film experience. For Weill, on the other hand, the music is a kind of bait that will lure the spectators to accept the dry film, a luxury item, something that is added and turns a prosaic experience into a pleasurable one. The difference between the two metaphors suggests two slightly different attitudes towards film music, two slightly different views of what a film needs and of how music functions in the cinema. For Copland music is a necessity: it counterbalances a *lack* in the film. For Weill music is more a possibility, an aesthetic effect, an added bonus.

Both attitudes can be found in the literature, with reference to both silent films and sound films, and often within one and the same text as, for example, when Ernest Lindgren writes that one of the most important functions of music for the silent film was to add musical expression to the action and intensify it 'by arousing through the ear the same feelings as were being stirred through the eye', but that this, on the other hand, 'is not sufficient to explain the clearly deep-seated and instinctive demand for music with the silent film, which film audiences have always felt'.[3]

The origin myth

Films need music, and film music needs an explanation. Kurt London
has one. He imagines the situation when 'films' were small strips that
lasted only a couple of minutes in an out-of-the-way hall with a screen
at one end, a projector at the other and rows of chairs in between. 'The
projector made a terrible noise.' The commentator, who was to explain
what the pictures were showing, had to shout to make himself heard.
And young couples would be sitting cuddling in the dark. In places like
these film music was born: 'It began, not as a result of any artistic urge,
but from the dire need of something which would drown the noise
made by the projector.'[4]

That is the origin myth of film music: initially the music was the
solution to a practical problem. The noise of the projector disturbed
the film experience; the cinema owners neutralized an unpleasant sound
with pleasant music.[5] In the subsequent literature London's explanation
is found repeatedly.[6] If it is tenable is open to question, however. Much
would seem to indicate that he has simply projected a modern ideal
back onto the 1890s. The eager spectator who wants to get engrossed
in the film and who is irritated by the noise in the hall is someone who,
it would seem, does not emerge until around 1910. Before that time
there was noise and bustle in the cinema no matter whether music was
played or not; the spectators talked to each other, they commented on
and discussed what was taking place on the screen, they clapped at
spectacular scenes.[7]

No matter how much reality there might be in the story of the noisy
projector, it does at least lose its explanatory force as soon as we move a
couple of years after 1895. For, as most of the authors hurry to point out,
it did not take long before the projectors were removed from the cinema
halls and placed in soundproof rooms. And even if the noise of the
machinery disappeared, the music did not. 'There must have been a more
compelling reason for its rise', Kracauer concludes in *Theory of Film*.[8]

The power of tradition

Is it really necessary to find a compelling reason? As is known, the very
first films were presented in varieties, music halls and other popular
entertainment establishments, and there was a close connection
between the first film narratives and the spectacular melodrama. The

film, then, emerged from environments where music was already being played, and there is, in addition, a centuries-old tradition of accompanying plays with music.[9]

Since the nineteenth century there has admittedly been a tendency to identify music with instrumental music. 'Proper' music is 'pure' music, that of the concert hall: piano sonatas, string quartets, symphonies. We often tend to forget that instrumental music, historically speaking, is an exception. Throughout most of its history music has been connected with singing and acting. Music has been used as an *accompaniment* – to the psalms and hymns of the church, to religious oratorios, to the ballets of the court. And music has been an integral part of *mixed performances* – operas, operettas, pantomimes, melodramas, variety shows, etc. Films can be regarded as the latest in a long line of performative genres where music is used as an aesthetic device.

The film historian Martin Miller Marks places special emphasis on the connection between theatre and film. He writes about the theatre musicians who, like their successors in the cinemas, 'continually had to compose, arrange, conduct, or improvise functional bits and pieces'. In most respects theatre music was reminiscent of the music that was later indexed in the anthologies of the silent film period. Seen from this perspective, film music is a continuation of an established practice: The film composers took over an already existing repertoire, a series of stylistic prototypes and certain basic working methods.[10]

Are these actual historical circumstances and connections not sufficient explanation in themselves? Does the music of the silent film need a more 'compelling reason' than this? Yes, answers Claudia Gorbman. She admits that accounts of historical developments that underline the connection between film and earlier dramatic traditions 'go a long way toward explaining the presence of musical accompaniment in early cinema'.[11] But she adds in the same breath that such accounts cannot stand alone: there is always a risk that the reference to the power of tradition will conceal deeper causes for a tradition continuing. A tradition for scenic music that spans several centuries is not necessarily a justification for the tradition to continue under changed historical circumstances. Technologically speaking film was a new medium, and the first other combination of audiovisual means', writes Gorbman.[12] But films were actually shown with a musical accompaniment. The tradition of scenic music was not broken. What can the reason for this be?

Ghosts and apparitions

This is not life, but shadows of life. This is not movement, but the silent shadows of movement',[13] writes Maxim Gorky in 1896. He has been to Aumont's restaurant in Nizny Novgorod and seen a Lumière performance. He is overwhelmed. Not by the moving pictures but by the stillness, the silence. On the screen 'a grey, soundless, oppressed, unhappy and in some way deprived life' is portrayed, he writes. He continues:

> One cannot hear the wheels clattering against the cobblestones, no trip of footsteps, no voice, nothing – not a single note of the complex symphony that always accompanies human movement. Soundlessly, the ashen leaves of the trees rock in the wind; soundlessly, the grey, shadowy figures of people glide over the grey earth as if struck by some curse that has condemned them to silence and cruelly punished them – figures from whom every trace of colour has been taken away. Their smiles are dead – even though their movements are full of lively energy – and so quick that one can scarcely manage to perceive them. Their laughter is toneless – even though one can see how the muscles in their grey faces contract.[14]

In another article about the same performance he writes about the 'ghostly life' of the pictures, concluding that it is frightful to see 'this grey movement of grey shadows'.[15]

'Why is music always played during film performances?', asks Bela Balázs 30 years later in *Der sichtbare Mensch* (1924). 'Why does a film without a musical accompaniment seem embarrassing?'[16] Completely soundless movements on the screen are eerie, he continues, and it would be even more eerie if several hundred people were to sit together in a cinema in absolute silence and not say a word for hours. In a contemporary article he writes that the movements of nature are organically connected to noise; therefore, it seems unnatural when we suddenly 'hear that we hear nothing'. If music were not to be played, the film's speaking characters in particular, with their moving, mute lips, would seem 'eerie or comical'.[17]

There are many such formulations in the literature about early films, especially in writers who have experienced the period themselves. 'We see people speaking, and no sound is heard', Kurt London writes in 1936, 'life is enacted in a world of almost ghostly silence.'[18] The ghostly nature of the silent film is still a major theme when Kracauer writes 25 years later that 'life and sound are inseparable'. When the sound disappears, the world is transformed into a limbo. It is therefore a frightening experience to see unaccompanied silent films: 'shadows aspire to corporeal life, and life dissolves into intangible shadows'. Even though we know that the images of the silent film are photographs, imprints of reality, they seem so discomfiting; we involuntarily perceive them as 'pale apparitions'; they haunt places where real phenomena and real human beings ought to have been. The images of the film strike us as being 'a ghost-like replica of the world we live in'. It is here that music comes in: it prevents the apparitions from dissolving, it 'lights up the pale silent images on the screen so that they will stay with us'.[19]

Kracauer's formulation about music that 'lights up' the images of the film is reminiscent of Copland's description of the flame of music that warms the cold screen. In the same vein Ernest Lindgren says that a silent film without music has a 'curiously shadowy and flat effect'; when people in the past saw a silent film without music, they used to say that they saw it 'in the cold'.[20] The music adds life to the deathly cold of the silent film, one could say. Or, as Kurt London writes, it was the music 'which gave the silent film its life-blood, its soul, and its meaning'.[21]

Kracauer, however, is making a slightly different point. He does not feel that the silent scenes become more alive and real by the addition of some sound. The function of the music is 'to remove the need for sound, not to satisfy it'.[22] A similar point of view can be found in Bela Balázs, who writes in 1924 that the function of the music is to *conceal* the silence of the film.[23] And it reappears later in Theodor W. Adorno – the writer who more than any other has underlined the ghostly nature of the film. In *Composing for the Films*, the book he co-authored with composer Hanns Eisler, he writes that pure film must have had 'a ghostly effect like that of the shadow play – shadows and ghosts have always been associated'.[24] Music saves us from the discomfort of having depictions shown of living, acting and even speaking persons who are nevertheless unable to produce a sound. 'The fact that they are living and nonliving at the same time is what constitutes their ghostly character.' It is not the music's function to give the images life but to pacify our unconscious experience of the evil spirits. 'Motion-picture music corresponds to the whistling or singing child in the dark.' For Adorno the music functions as 'a kind of antidote against the picture'. But he adds that the intertitles also helped to pacify the silent images, and he concludes by saying that what is really menacing about the silent film is ultimately not the mute, ghostly figures, but that the spectators become conscious of the fact that they themselves are 'creatures of the very same kind' as those gesticulating masks on the screen, and that they thereby become 'strangers to themselves'.

Living photographs

The flat image is cold; the speechless film is eerie; the mute beings on the screen are ghostly and remind spectators of their own mortality. All the formulations I have quoted above clearly derive from the writers' own, personal experiences of the early film. Naturally, it is difficult to make use of such formulations as a basis for functional descriptions of the music of silent films. Subjective experiences are difficult to check empirically. Of necessity, they seem to be postulates, and therefore invite contradiction. As, for example, when Noël Carroll pays Adorno and Eisler a brief visit in his book *Mystifying Movies* and claims that they are simply mistaken.[25]

> They claim that film spectators experience it as discomforting to watch film images, because we find them ghostly . . . Informal evidence of this could be that spectators are often restive during silent films that are not accompanied by music, and that they often complain about the silence which strikes them, and not some presumed fear of ghosts. Perhaps, though, we ought to take them at their word; perhaps it is the silence that strikes them and not some putative fear of ghosts.[26]

Carroll is actually criticizing a modern interpretation of Adorno and Eisler.[27] His book, as the subtitle indicates, is a reaction to 'Fads and Fallacies in Contemporary Film Theory'. Which is perhaps why his reasoning at this point seems strangely insensitive to film history. It is doubtless correct that modern spectators who are used to seeing sound films find unaccompanied silent films strange and irritating. But this reaction can hardly be used as evidence as to how spectators reacted when films were a new, surprising medium.

The fact that the ghostly nature of silent films is a theme discussed in so many contemporary accounts probably has to do with the film being 'living pictures', or rather living *photographs* – and thereby containing the same time-paradox as the photograph itself: there is always a fundamental conflict between the *here and now* of the photograph and the *then and there* of the motif.[28] What is shown in the image is not only a depiction but also an imprint of a past event, a piece of reality that once existed, then and there, but that has been retained by physical and chemical means and is being shown here and now. There is thus always something melancholy about old photographs; one looks at them with the knowledge that this time will never return again. The living pictures of the film maximize this conflict. While the persons in a photograph have stiffened, been trapped in a kind of eternal present, the persons on the film screen move in their own past. This is probably what Adorno meant with his remark about the persons being 'living and nonliving at the same time'.

Lack of sound is an important part of the paradoxical experience of time that is connected to photographs. Similarly, the lack of sound in the silent film emphasizes its photographic character: what one sees on the screen is a recording of something that once was. So the task is to resolve this experiential conflict, to get film spectators to accept the picture of the past as being present in time and space, or at least to get them to ignore the past of the shooting and to accept that the pictures portray a fiction, that the action takes place in a parallel universe, in *another kind of* time.

The music strengthens the experience of *fictive time*. But, according to Kathryn Kalinak, it also functions more generally as a kind of 'bridge' between the reality of the spectator and the world of the fiction.[29] Contemporary sources often emphasize, for example, the 'social' nature of the live music: it brought the pictures closer to the situation of the spectators. It was as if the sight of the musicians 'transferred to the silent images a sense of here and now', Kalinak writes.[30] She also feels that a kind of transfer or glide took place between sound and image, with the spatial nature of the music being transferred to the flat image. This can at first glance seem rather speculative, but this point of view is supported by Kurt London who, in his retrospective account of the silent film period, writes that the music 'had a profound effect on this dimensionless character of the film image'.[31]

The rhythm of movement

Kurt London's most important explanation of the need for music is that film is an 'art of movement', and that the music articulates the movement, lends it structure: 'It was the task of the musical accompaniment to give it auditory accentuation and profundity.'[32] For him the articulatory and formative functions of the music are a necessity, although he also believes that the music ought not follow the narrative too closely. The quick changes of scene in the film will make it impossible to write an accompaniment that makes musical sense. The silent film called for the opposite, he writes. And he italicizes the requirement: *'Musical simplification of the mosaic of film images into one long line.'*[33] He stresses that one must not break off 'the even flow of the music', except in special, individual cases where dramatic considerations call for it. It is a question of 'avoiding too quick and jerky changes in the music, without destroying the significant line of the film'. The conclusion is: 'Variety in the film images and uniformity in the music.'[34]

It is easy to overlook these formulations in London's text. They are made almost in passing, in a section that has to do with constructing effective compilations of 'illustrative' pieces of music. But here he actually provides one of the most important psychological justifications for silent films normally having been accompanied by continuous music. The music was not to *repeat* or *reflect* the form of the visual sequence; it was to *give it* form, compel the non-uniform, fragmentary shots to coalesce under its own rhythm. Music is 'a meaningful continuity in time', Kracauer writes. As soon as there is music, 'we perceive structured patterns where there were none before'. Confusing changes of position become comprehensible. Fragmented images coalesce and follow a definite course. 'Music makes the silent images partake of its continuity.'[35]

New conditions: the music of the sound film

The music of the silent film was determined by two kinds of necessity: on the one hand it was to do away with the time paradox of the living pictures and get the spectator to accept the time of the fiction; on the other it was to lend form and structure to the fragmentary sequence of shots. The introduction of sound films has consequences for both functions. The possibility of working with synchronized sound weakens the time paradox of the film. The images lose their ghostly nature and are no longer experienced as eerie and frightening. Nevertheless, Adorno persists in claiming that the music continues to have the same function as in the days of the silent film. It is still necessary in order to calm the spectator's fear of the image. For the characters on the screen are not talking individuals but talking pictures. 'Their bodiless mouths utter words in a way that must seem disquieting to any unbiased person.'[36]

The 'unbiased' person who is disturbed by the images of the sound film must surely be Adorno himself, who was not known to be an avid cinema-goer. It is of course possible that the very first talking films had the effect he mentions here, but there is nothing to indicate that the ordinary film audience of the late 1940s, when he wrote these lines, reacted in that manner. In this instance it is easier to follow Noël Carroll when he criticizes Adorno and Eisler for postulating a way of reacting that does not correspond to anything in reality.[37]

Carroll himself suspects that talking films without music are not in any way a problem, assuming that the dialogue is sufficiently interesting. And if the spectators should actually become disturbed, it could well be because the dialogue was simply boring.[38] In this case one does not have to rely on suspicions and impressions, one can simply refer to film history. The first sound films were either musicals or talkies. In musicals music was the central attraction, and it usually had a diegetic justification. In the talkies it was the dialogue that was the attraction. The early talkies were film versions of popular theatrical plays; they had almost non-stop dialogue and only a little music during the opening and closing credits. As I mentioned in chapter Five, this practice continued until the mid-1930s. And even after the classical system had been established it was still common practice to give dialogue a higher priority than music. In mainstream films there are usually long stretches without music, and many of the classical screwball comedies are more or less devoid of music: when the entire film is based on lightning-speed, intelligent and high-tension dialogue, there is simply not any room for music. If spectators feel disturbed by Howard Hawks's comedy *Bringing Up Baby* (1938), it is hardly because they are scared by Katherine Hepburn's two-dimensional mouth on the screen, but because she speaks at such a furious tempo that one hardly has the time to pick up all the wisecracks.

In sound films the music no longer has to be the antidote that neutralizes the discomfort of the flat image and, gradually, even the formative and structuring functions of the music become less necessary. The sequence of images in the film admittedly become even more composite and fragmentary, but the diegetic sound supports the images and gives them a cohesion that was formerly created by the music. In addition, 'continuity editing' – the cinematic code developed during the second phase of the silent film – helps to stabilize the sequence, smooth out transitions, create connections through series of shots, etc. And in the same process the audience gradually learns how to 'watch films', which means that they learn to ignore the cuts and breaks between individual shots, to disregard the fragmentary mode of expression, to 'see' only the narrative.

With the sound film the role of the music in the totality of the film changes. It is no longer a necessity. It is an offer, a possibility, an effect that the film-makers can use to solve many diverse aesthetic and narrative tasks, and this ought to mean that the ghosts of the silent film had been laid to rest. But over the last few decades they have reappeared – not in cinematic practice but in the world of film theory, where they have haunted discussions about the functions of film music. What particularly attracts them is the idea that film music is not heard.

Unheard music

It is a recurring theme in the literature that people rarely notice the music while watching a film and afterwards can seldom recall what they actually heard. As with all other recurrent themes, this is first given a theoretical formulation by Kurt London. The music of the silent film was only remembered if it in some way deviated from the image and thus disturbed the spectator's concentration, he writes. 'Thus we reach the conclusion that good film music remained "unnoticed".'[39] This does not, however, mean that it was unimportant: film music is listened to unconsciously, and it is therefore heard with the greatest intensity, 'because everything that is apprehended by the subconscious self is much more deeply impressed on a man than conscious experience'.[40]

Film composers, understandably enough, react to this. 'There is a tired old bromide in this business to the effect that a good film score is one you don't hear,' Max Steiner writes and sullenly asks: 'What good is it if you don't notice it?'[41] And Miklós Rózsa says: 'I don't know who originated the idea that good film music is the kind that isn't heard, but I disagree entirely with this silly theory.'[42] It is easy to understand their irritation at what they must experience as a bagatellization of their work. And they are of course right: one does actually hear the film music, but in a different way from when one listens to music in a concert hall. In fact, it is not all that far from Kurt London's remarks about unconscious listening to Steiner's and Rózsa's own experiences from their practice as composers. Steiner writes, for example, that one should not use well-known pieces that people will recognize 'because it may detract from concentrating on the film'.[43] He concludes that 'the music should be heard and not seen. The danger is that the music can be so bad, or so good, it distracts and takes away from the action.'[44] And Rózsa writes in similar vein: 'Music should be heard, even if it is heard subconsciously, and it should join the drama and the acting, with everything together creating a work of art.'[45]

One could add that this is not merely the personal opinion of two well-known film composers. It was actually the very foundation of Golden Age music. It was to work in the background of the film narrative. It was to support the actions on the screen, match the mood of a scene, colour the dialogue, but not call attention to itself. Music would, for example, start at the beginning of a scene and be used to mark a change in time and space. If, however, it was to start up in the middle of a scene, one would often use *sneaking*, i.e. sneak the music in by beginning at very low volume, so that people did not discover it.

Wounds and stitches

It was Claudia Gorbman's book *Unheard Melodies* (1987) that put 'unheard' music on the agenda of modern film theory. She addresses many other issues as well, but the fact that the discussion of the unconscious functions of the music made such an impact was due to her interpreting them in the light of the so-called suture theory, which was a predominant paradigm of film theory at the time. The word *suture* comes from medicine, where it means 'the stitching together of wounds'. In connection with film theory it is used to refer to all the techniques that cause a film to cohere and form an aesthetic whole. Seen from the perspective of suture theory, a mainstream film is initially full of open 'wounds' that, with the aid of many different techniques, are 'stitched together' to form a smooth surface. The underlying idea is that films are, on the one hand, semantic constructions made up of many different elements, of fragmentary images, of sound and music, but that the spectator, on the other hand, seldom experiences them in this way – not at any rate if we are talking about classical Hollywood films, or more generally about international mainstream films.

The suture theory was first and foremost a critique of the 'deceptive' mainstream film. The classical film appears to be 'realistic', but the realism is an ideological construction. The fictive world is an illusion, which only succeeds because the wounds have been stitched. The reason why the classical film is so effective is that it removes all traces of the construction and 'masquerades as story', the psycho-semiotician Christian Metz writes.[46] The traditional film is like the traditional writing of history, where the narrator never draws attention to himself, where 'the events seem to relate themselves', as the linguist Émile Benveniste once put it.[47] The opposite of the cinematic illusion of reality is modernistic or avant-garde films that display their own construction, films that 'reveal' themselves as a fiction by pointing to the 'stitches'.[48]

Musical hypnosis

If the illusion of reality in the mainstream film is to succeed, the wounds must be stitched together in an ongoing process. This calls for spectator cooperation. Spectators must identify themselves with the fiction; they must let themselves be 'stitched into' the film. Gorbman's point is that music is helpful here. It removes the conscious barriers of the spectator and 'it bonds spectator to spectacle, it envelops spectator and spectacle in a harmonious space'. Film music is like a hypnotist: it silences the censor of the spectator – 'if it's working right, it makes us a little less critical and a little more prone to dream.'[49] This is the recurrent argument: film music is like supermarket music; the aim is to soothe spectators, to make them less troublesome, less critical, less on guard.[50] It is in this connection that one gets the feeling that the ghosts of the silent film have risen from the grave. For, according to Gorbman, the prime task of the music is still to ward off the spectator's *displeasure* at the film. The problem is no longer the ghostly, flat images, but 'the spectator's potential recognition of the technological basis of filmic articulation'. The music smoothes out things, it erases 'any reminders of cinema's materiality' that could threaten 'the process whereby the viewer identifies as subject of filmic discourse'.[51] According to this point of view the film is in constant danger of being

revealed as a construction. The same elements that present the narrative are a threat to its credibility.

Music is particularly effective as an adhesive because it is believed
to have a direct link with the unconscious, a point of view Gorbman
supports with references to various kinds of psychoanalytical literature, for example to Didier Anzieu, who is of the opinion that the
child, both before and after birth, is 'bathed in sound', swathed in a
'sonorous envelope'. Gorbman sees a link between this 'melodic bath'
and 'the oft-cited oceanic feeling' that adults experience when listening
to music.[52] Pleasure in music also has something to do with the fact
that music is 'free from linguistic signification and from representation
of any kind'. This makes it more pleasurable, less uncomfortable than
other forms of discourse. Music is a 'safe' language that 'circumvents
defenses and provides easier access to the unconscious'.[53] At the same
time music is subject to the same threat as the other techniques of
film-making. It can weaken our vigilance, but if we become aware of
it, the game is up.

Music's prime task is, then, to get the spectator to identify with the
fiction of the film, but Gorbman also mentions another function.
There are situations in the film where the music 'lends an epic quality
to the diegetic events', where instead of involving us in the narrative,
it causes us to observe it and thereby underlines the nature of the film
as a *spectacle*.[54]

The conclusion is that the music 'greases the wheels of the cinematic pleasure machine by easing the spectator's passage into subjec-
tivity'. Generally speaking, music acts 'as the hypnotic voice bidding
the spectator to believe, focus, behold, identify, consume'.[55]

Out of the hypnosis

It is not difficult to understand why Gorbman's points of view were so
popular in the 1980s. Her explanation of the need for film music was
completely in line with the predominant theoretical paradigm of the
time and, at the same time, she made music a privileged element of this
paradigm. Among all the cinematic effects and technical tricks of the
trade, music is the most effective hypnotic element, because it has
direct access to the unconscious. At the same time, this also explains
why we fail to hear it. This type of reasoning, however, raises far more
problems than it solves.[56] The underlying foundation for suture theory

is that the filmic fiction rests on a 'technological basis', and that spectators who become aware of this basis will experience discomfort, a 'loss of pleasure' that will prevent them from identifying with the fiction. 'Gaps, cuts, the frame itself, silences in the soundtrack' – all are 'reminders of cinema's materiality' and endanger the identification of the spectator with the film. Music removes this displeasure, smoothes out, closes all such openings.[57]

But if that is actually so, one can ask how spectators experienced the many talkies in the first phase of sound films. There are many explanations as to why music was not – or was very rarely – used in the talkies of the time. Basic technical problems made it difficult to mix dialogue and music, for instance. I do not intend to discuss these explanations here, but merely point out that if one follows Gorbman's line of reasoning, the spectators must have felt considerable displeasure when watching these films – a displeasure that did not disappear until Max Steiner and his colleagues started to write non-diegetic music around 1934. However, there is nothing to suggest that spectators from 1926 to the mid-1930s experienced a constant lack of pleasure every time they went to the cinema and saw a talking film. On the contrary there is much to suggest that they experienced film music as unpleasant. During this period non-diegetic music was not 'unheard'; it was perceived as being an extremely audible, unrealistic interruption of the world of fiction. Remember that Max Steiner's first attempts to use non-diegetic music were *heard* to a maximum extent and thought of as being an aesthetic device, a spectacularly different way of using music.

Similar objections can, of course, be raised when we are dealing with sound films after 1934. Hawks's almost musicless *Bringing Up Baby* (1938) was – and still is – an incredibly popular comedy. There is nothing to suggest that spectators then or now would be unable to identify with the film. On the contrary it is part of its continuing fascination that as a spectator one enters the fiction and experiences the events as almost intolerably embarrassing, while at the same time observing them 'from the outside' and experiencing them as comical. In many other classical Hollywood films there is considerably more music on the soundtrack, but there are always long sequences without any music. Do the spectators suddenly become aware of the technological basis of the fiction and experience a loss of pleasure when Marlowe at the beginning of *The Big Sleep* enters the general's conservatory and there are ten minutes of dialogue without any music? If the music is a hypnotic voice that draws the spectators into the film and causes them to overlook holes, why did Hitchcock not ask for 136 minutes of music for *North by Northwest* instead of the 40 minutes that Bernard Herrmann composed?

According to Gorbman the music causes the spectator to 'bond' with the film and forget its technological basis. But the music also creates another kind of bond, she writes, a bonding between the individual spectator and the other spectators in the cinema. It is this function she is referring to when she writes about music that serves to underline the *spectacle* character of a film. One of her examples is the grandiose orchestral music that is heard when the spaceships hurtle through the galaxies in *Star Wars*. The point about the first kind of musical bonding is that the spectator is to avoid the displeasure of experiencing the construction of the film, but when the spaceships slide across the screen, the music points to the film itself, and demonstratively underlines the fact that what we are watching is a film, a spectacle – a construction. So the question is: what happens when the identification between the spectator and the film is broken? Shouldn't one expect an experience of displeasure when the music switches to another mode?

Indirectly, Gorbman indicates an answer to such questions when she writes immediately afterwards that a mainstream film audience 'can (and does) slip in and out of "spectacle" and "narrative identification" music fairly readily'.[58] There are a number of similar formulations in the text; at one point she writes, for example, that the spectator's belief in the fiction 'ebbs and flows' in the course of a film. In this connection she cites Christian Metz with a remark that belief in the fiction is inversely proportional to the spectator's degree of wakefulness. The music 'lessens the spectator's degree of wakefulness,' Gorbman writes, 'at least in some cases.'[59]

At this and many other corresponding points in the text Gorbman undermines her own first, clear-cut formulation of the musical suture theory: the frightened spectator who has to be hypnotized in order to withstand the displeasure of the film is gradually replaced by a considerably more active spectator who slides in and out of the film from various positions in relation to the fiction, and the conception of the music alters correspondingly. The music is initially 'the hypnotic voice' that has to be there in order to calm the spectator and get him or her to lose conscious awareness. Later on, it becomes more of a technical narrative aid that is used to grease 'the wheels of the cinematic pleasure machine' and that can be used in certain contexts and omitted in others.

With the implicit shift from 'necessity' to 'possibility', Gorbman brings herself in agreement with more traditional accounts of the function of music in sound films. But what about the question that was her starting point? What about the title of her book? How is one to explain the 'unheard melodies' of the film?

Hearing what is unheard

Part of the foundation of Golden Age music was that it was to stay in the background, but when composers like Steiner and Rózsa comment on their own practice, they emphasize that of course the music is there to be heard. This is the 'fundamental paradox', Jeff Smith comments, the 'unheard' must be 'heard'; the music must – in some way or other – be experienced and registered by the spectator if it is to have a narrative function. The question, therefore, is not *whether* spectators hear the music but *how* they hear it.[60]

Take, for example, the scene from the nightclub in *The Big Sleep*, where Vivian sings alongside Stan Kenton's musicians. In this instance, of course, we hear the music very clearly. The whole scene has been constructed precisely so as to emphasize Vivian/Bacall's performance and to place the song centre-stage. Much diegetic film music functions in this way: the music is presented as an important event in the narrative, a 'number' that characters in the film also stop and listen to. But in other instances diegetic music is only a background factor, 'part of the scenery'. When Marlowe is standing at the parking lot in *The Big Sleep*, we can hear jazz coming from the nightclub, but neither he nor we who are sitting there in the cinema pay this much attention. The music is in the story world, not as an actual number but as 'nightclub music', 'music that is played at venues like these'. The scene with Vivian's song can also be used to illustrate how we glide from one kind of attention to another when watching films. When Vivian starts to sing, our – and Marlowe's – attention is focused solely on her and the music, but as soon as Marlowe begins to do something else, as soon as the action 'moves on', the narrative – and we – lose interest in the song, even though Vivian continues to sing in the background for a while.

The narrative context also determines how we hear non-diegetic music. There are times when we are extremely attentive and hear the music very clearly as, for example, in John Ford's *Stagecoach* (1939), when the cavalry ride into Monument Valley, accompanied by Max Steiner's characteristic Western music, or when the great spaceships in *Star Wars* hurtle across the sky to music by John Williams. In such cases the music is used to underline the spectacle character of the film. But we hear music just as clearly in many other contexts, when, for example, a leitmotif heralds the arrival of a character in the narrative arena, or when 'spooky' dissonant chords tells us that something sinister is about to happen.

Watching a film is an activity, an interpretative act. We are constantly interpreting the information presented to us. We classify it, we assess it in relation to other information, we scan it against our own background knowledge, and we contemplate how it is to be understood and positioned in relation to the narrative and its narrators. This is also what we do with musical information. Sometimes the music is in the foreground of our attention; at other times it slides into the background. When the diegetic music is not at the centre of the narrative, but only functions as part of the narrative setting, it glides out of our focus of attention. This is also what happens with the non-diegetic music.

Non-diegetic music is part of the narrative 'apparatus' of the film, and it does not function any differently from most of the other parts of this apparatus. While we are watching a film we seldom pay attention to the colour of the images or to the lighting, camera angles, editing, unless the purpose is for us to notice such things. Similarly, when we afterwards try to recall the film, we remember stories as relatively abstract information stated as utterances, interpretations and summaries, but we seldom recall how the stories were actually presented. As Edward Branigan writes: 'It requires great effort to recall the exact words used in a novel or the exact sequence of shots, angles, lighting, etc. used in a film.' Or, as he continues: 'When we say we remember a film, we do not normally mean that we remember the angle from which it was viewed in the movie theater, or the exact angles assumed by the camera in a scene.'[61]

When we are at the cinema, we do not experience a collection of images, lighting, camera angles, sounds, music; we experience a totality, a narrative, an organized collection of expressive elements that convey a story, and afterwards we remember this story as a series of events we can reproduce in a summary. In certain cases we recall snatches of dialogue, certain striking expressions, individual lines. Perhaps we also remember certain particularly interesting images that gradually come to represent the film in our memory.[62] Sometimes we remember some music. What and how we remember depends on the context and the importance of the information for the narrative. We remember the content of the narrative, but can only recall how it was expressed – including the music – if the effects are atypical, deviate from our expectations or step out of their context in some way and command special attention.[63] This happens relatively seldom. Normally film music is 'unheard' in the same way as camera angles, colours, lighting, are normally 'unseen'.

10

Musical Functions

Music was played in the cinemas of the silent film. Music is played on the soundtracks of sound films. What is the role of music in the history of film-making – in films in general? This question does not have one answer but many. The analyses and accounts of the previous chapters have provided most of them. But it might be a good idea to summarize those answers and to try to set up a more systematic overview of the main functions of non-diegetic film music, and to discuss some of the theoretical issues linked to them.

Music that 'fits'

The ideal music for silent films was continuous; there was a correspondence between music and image, the movement was based on leitmotifs.[1] In the reality of the cinema the concrete realization could often fall fairly short of the ideal. When the accompaniment had to be made up of whatever happened to be available, it could be difficult to fulfil all demands concerning musical correspondence and leitmotifs.

With the introduction of sound films continuous music quickly disappeared from the cinemas, and during the following decades the leitmotif requirement also became less insistent. Much film music in the 1950s was characterized by mono-thematic theme scores, and a composer like Bernard Herrmann mainly wrote music made up of 'numbers'. But there still had to be a correspondence between music and narrative. That is how it was in the era of the silent film, and how it was in the Golden Age and the period of transition in the 1950s. And that is still how it is today. The music has to 'fit' the narrative of the film.

During the age of the silent film some viewers reacted to the fact that images of a grieving widower were accompanied by the happy bachelor song 'No Wedding Bells for Me'.[2] The music did not 'fit', it contradicted what the images were saying. It makes one think of Kracauer's anecdote of the intoxicated pianist who accompanied a domestic row with cheerful melodies and played a funeral march during the ensuing reconciliation.[3] As far as Kracauer was concerned, this music was by no means unsuitable – it was the perfect accompaniment for, as he writes, the music made him experience the story in a new way. Which raises the question: what does it really mean to say that the music 'fits'? Are there really any cases where it does *not* fit? Isn't it always possible to find a 'fitting' connection between music and image? Indeed, couldn't those watching the film about the grieving widower have made the music fit the narrative if they had wanted to?

When we sit in the cinema we expect there to be an intention and a meaning with the music. Sometimes it is simple: on the screen we see people in old-fashioned clothes; they are walking around in some city or other; we hear a Strauss waltz on the soundtrack. The city, we realize, is 'Vienna in the nineteenth century'. We are at the cinema watching Hitchcock's *Waltzes from Vienna* (1933). At other times, it can be more complicated as, for example, when the Strauss waltz 'An der schönen blauen Donau' suddenly turns up in Stanley Kubrick's science-fiction film *2001: A Space Odyssey* (1968), where it accompanies a long sequence about a spaceship landing on the moon. When the waltz starts, there are presumably some viewers who experience it as referring to 'Vienna', but they quickly realize that this association is irrelevant in the present context, that the connotation 'Vienna' does not 'fit' the images, and even viewers who lack the necessary knowledge of the history of music will presumably register that this is 'strange' music. The discrepancy between 'old-fashioned', elegant waltz music and the futuristic hi-tech of the images produces a special effect: initially the sequence is of a slightly absurd, almost ironic nature but, as it proceeds, one feels the calm, sweeping waltz rhythm almost 'making its impact' on the images. It is as if the spaceships are following the music, as if they are dancing, and the result is that the whole sequence has a strangely cheerful, festive feel to it.

When we hear the Blue Danube Waltz in Kubrick's film, we deselect, then, the referential connotation – we push it into the background, at any rate – because it does not seem to be relevant, because the concrete reference to 'Vienna' does not 'correspond' to anything in the images. Instead we discover a connection at a far more abstract level. We experience that the movement of the spaceship in the images 'corresponds to' something in the music.

Synaesthetic equivalents and structural 'matching'

Occasionally one experiences a sound corresponding to a colour, a painting corresponding to a piece of music. The connection between music and images in a film such as *2001* is a similar type of phenomenon. Perception psychologists say that in such situations we discover or construct *synaesthetic equivalents*. I wrote above that the images in the *2001* sequence 'correspond to' something in the music. By this formulation I was referring to precisely the form of *matching* we undertake when we experience synaesthetic equivalents, and that many artists and filmmakers consciously try to evoke by combining heterogeneous material.

In his book *Art and Illusion* E. H. Gombrich uses a painting by Mondrian, *Broadway Boogie-Woogie*, as an example of a matching between music and image.[4] When we as spectators note that the title of the painting seems 'striking', 'apt', this does not mean that the painting and boogie-woogie music 'represent' the same or 'express' the same semantic content, but rather that the title encourages us to undertake a structural matching. One normally connects Mondrian with strict, formal pictures – straight lines, rectangles, bright colours. Against this background the boogie-woogie picture has a cheerful and laid-back effect. 'It is so much less severe than the alternative we have in mind that we have no hesitation in matching it in our mind with this style of popular music,' Gombrich writes.[5]

In other words Mondrian's pictures relate to the rest of his production in a way that is reminiscent of the relation between boogie-woogie and other forms of music or, to use Gombrich's more general formulation: 'Synaesthesia concerns relationships.'[6] The matching consists of our constructing an analogy between structural relations in two dissimilar materials. And if we change the relations, if, for example, we had Mondrian's work presented alongside a work by the Italian Severini 'who is known for his futuristic paintings that try to capture the rhythm of dance music in works of brilliant chaos', it would be considerably more difficult to experience the boogie-woogie title as adequate, while at the same time this new context would make it easier for us to accept that the Mondrian picture was matched with, for example, Bach's first Brandenburg Concerto.[7]

Synaesthetic equivalents are, then, not inevitably a one-to-one relationship. It all depends on the given context and the possible potential relations on offer. On the face of it, it would seem surprising to hear the Strauss waltz turn up in a science-fiction film such as *2001*, but we accept the rules of the game and, as soon as the context has been established, we attempt to get the music and the images to match. If Kubrick had chosen to use some completely different music, wouldn't we also have wholeheartedly tried to match music and images, i.e. to discover the implied analogy?[8] And, conversely, if he had chosen completely different images to the same music, we would also have found a hidden meaning in this, just as the author Ivor Montague once did when he was sitting in a hotel room watching TV. On screen were images of 'the burning of the Reichstag, the capture of Van der Lubbe, the trial of the accused and a football match' – these were accompanied by excerpts from a Vienna operetta. Montague, however, was not aware that he had accidentally turned on the radio. So he was listening to the 'wrong' soundtrack, yet was amazed at 'how well the music seemed to capture a particular meaning of the visuals'. George Burt, in retelling the anecdote, adds, 'The overblown pompousness and seriocomic tone of the Viennese waltzes apparently said something curiously revealing about each of the sequences, and, strangely enough, the sequences seemed to be bound together, sharing a common point of view.'[9]

The Montague story is amusing; whether it is true or not is hard to ascertain. At least it illustrates a more general point: when music, images and dialogue are coordinated and appear as a perceptual whole, we automatically expect there to be an underlying intention. We search for a meaning, and we find it – no matter whether the coordination was actually intentional or not.

The waltz examples also illustrate something else: that the correspondence between music and narrative can be established at many different levels. In Kubrick's *2001* the Strauss waltz matches and brings out a formal structure in the images. In Hitchcock's *Waltzes from Vienna* it underlines the time and place of the action and also plays an important role in the narrative as the film has to do with Strauss's own life. In the Montague anecdote, the music emphasizes and comments on a mood in the TV images.

Kubrick's use of 'old-fashioned' music for his science-fiction film was a surprising effect that added a new dimension to the images of the spaceship. Mainstream films are normally a lot less experimental. The music is basically to support and structure the narrative. So here it is a question of creating effective correspondences by exploiting well-known formulas and musical stereotypes.

Music and narrative

It is possible to tell stories with the aid of words or images. One can mime stories, possibly even dance them as a ballet. But one cannot tell stories with the aid of music. It is the ballet dancers who tell or 'present' the story of *Swan Lake*, not Tchaikovsky's music. There is no 'Lustiges Zusammensein der Landsleute' in Beethoven's 'Pastoral' symphony, only the title of a movement which via language refers to peasants spending a happy time together. A piece of music is not in itself a narrative, for music is a non-representative art form.[10]

On the other hand, music possesses certain formal characteristics that are reminiscent of the structures to be found in narrative texts. Music is sound in motion – sound that is formed in time. When it comes to Western tonal music, this movement is always based on arcs of tension being built up, restricted and then released. 'The two principal sources of musical energy are dissonance and sequence – the first because it demands resolution, the second because it implies continuation,' Charles Rosen once wrote.[11] The structuring of the sound material with the aid of formal repetitions and variations creates an expectation of a 'continuation' that drives the music forwards, while the dissonances, with their establishing of harmonic tension and their promise of later dissolution and resolution, give the forward movement a direction, a goal.

From a history of music perspective it is the second part of the duality, the goal-orientedness, that is accentuated and stands out as the central, characteristic feature of Western music from the classical period onwards. To quote Rosen again: 'The classical style immeasurably increased the power of dissonance, raising it from an unresolved interval to an unresolved chord and then to an unresolved key.'[12] What was originally series of local frictions around dissonant intervals becomes more and more dominant and ends up creating large, far-reaching tensions at the macro-level of the musical material. From the late eighteenth century onwards it is the goal-orientedness, 'the power of dissonance' that is the central formal principle of music.

Structured movement in time, drive, goal-orientedness, etc.: these are features that also characterize the narrative, which has caused some modern musicologists to claim that Western music is simply narrative.[13] Taken absolutely literally this point of view is absurd. Music is not turned into narratives just because the musical material is structured in a way that is reminiscent of the organisation of the content of narrative discourses. The connections between music and narrative are to be found at a different level.

The music psychologist John Sloboda, who is normally very cautious about ascribing referential qualities to music, and who emphasizes that musical behaviour can best be described as 'a closed sub-system with no essential links to other cognitive domains', believes that we have to accept that there is a kind of 'leakage' between the various areas, that the musical *experience* is in fact often translated into other modes of representation.[14] The narrative is one of these modes. Music itself does not relate anything, but under certain circumstances we can hear certain types of music *as* a narrative, which can cause us to tell stories *about* music – as when, for example, musicologists describe the sonata form as a 'drama', as a 'conflict that is resolved', as a 'Bildungsroman', etc.

At one point Sloboda refers to stories that begin in a state of balance: the balance is disturbed; the disturbance leads to problems and tensions, but these are finally resolved, and a new balance is established. What he is thinking of is clearly what narratologists usually call 'the canonical story'. He imagines that 'the mental substrate of music is something like that which underlies [this type] of story', and that the basic pattern in much music can be understood as 'a highly abstracted blueprint for such stories, retaining only the features they all have in common'.[15] The crux of the matter is of course the phrase 'something like'. A piece of music is not a narrative, but 'something like' a narrative, or rather 'something like' the underlying structure of a narrative – a sounding forward movement, a series of indefinite moments and arcs of tension that are built up and released. As concrete sequences in time, as formed sound sequences, music has certain formal characteristics that are reminiscent of the structures that generate narrative texts. It is this homology at the very basic, formal level that is the reason for it seeming natural to describe the experience of music in narrative categories. The Canadian music-semiotician Jean-Jacques Nattiez formulates a similar point of view: for the listener, a piece of music is 'not *in itself* a narrative, but *the structural analysis in music of an absent narrative*'.[16]

This is the basis for some of the most important functions of film music. When music is integrated into the context of a film, it functions as a structural analysis, not of an absent narrative but of the present cinematic narrative.

Formal functions

Music makes films 'hang together' in many different ways. At the broadest level music lends the individual film a feeling of wholeness that helps distinguish it from other films. The music for *North by Northwest* tells us that this is a different type of film to, for example, *Star Wars*, but the special instrumentation, the recurring motifs and themes, also give it a different feel to the other Hitchcock films for which Herrmann wrote the music.

The music creates a sound universe round the narrative and at the same time is one of the expressive elements that creates the narrative. By its presence the music can lend form to a sequence of shots. Bernard Herrmann says that one can edit a section of a film in many different ways, 'but once you put music to it, that becomes the absolutely final way'; the music gives the section 'an inevitable beginning and end'.[17] The forward-looking musical progression sets boundaries, it measures out and rounds off the individual narrative event, but music's own, internal arcs of tension are also used more generally to 'scan' the course of events. With the aid of its own structure, the music structures the events on the screen, separates them from each other or links them, points out connections and transitions, closes sections off and opens new ones.

At the level of the scene, continuous music marks the fact that there is a connection between the individual shots. Such a marking is not always necessary. When, for example, place, time, characters and other important parameters have first been established, the spectators are well able to understand what is going on, and the music can fade out and stop as, for example, happens in *The Big Sleep* when Marlowe begins to talk with the old general in the conservatory. On the other hand there will normally be music throughout montage sequences, where fairly long sequences of events are summarized and where there are leaps in time and space between the shots.

In transitions between scenes, the music sometimes marks both discontinuity and continuity. When in the introduction to *Star Wars* there is a cut from the imperial spaceship to the droids in the desert, the music changes from large, melodic orchestral sounds to floating, indeterminate notes played on flutes. The difference between the two types of music matches and underlines a discontinuity in the narrative. But at the same time the music marks continuity, for there is not a real musical break here; it is still the same orchestra that is playing and telling us that we are in the same narrative as before, that what we can now see on the screen is linked to what we have just seen. In other instances, it is the marking of continuity in the transition between two scenes that is the main point as, for example, in *The Big Sleep*, when Marlowe leaves the general's house and there is a cut to the public library. Here the music starts up once more after a long pause as he walks through the hall towards the door, and it continues past the cut so as to mark the fact that this is still Marlowe's story, even though he cannot be seen in the next picture.

Narrative functions

Most of the functions I have mentioned so far have to do with formal considerations, the marking of the passages of time, transitions between scenes, etc. The music, though, usually also has a number of more 'content-related' functions as regards the narrative of the film. Narrative theorists have told us that a narrative is a special type of discourse that is defined via its content. The narrative discourse deals with *events* that take place in *time and space*, with the *causes* of these events and the *persons* or human-like entities that act and carry out the events or are influenced by them. The film music is used to underscore most of these elements.

Time and space

The time and space of the film narrative can be marked musically, often with the aid of stereotypes. In John Ford's *Stagecoach* we see the stagecoach pulling in at a rest stop. Just in case we do not happen to notice that the people at the gate are wearing characteristic headgear, Max Steiner's music tells us that these are Mexicans.

In some cases the music of an entire film can be constructed on the basis of this function. Steiner's music for *Stagecoach*, for example, mainly consists of musical clichés: 'Western music', 'Red Indian music', 'Mexican music', 'cavalry music', etc. In other cases this function is used mainly at the beginning of a film to establish the narrative environment, or in transitions between scenes when the action is moved in time and space.

Events

In *Stagecoach* Steiner uses musical clichés to mark the time and space of the action, but also to underline and anticipate actual events on the screen, for example, 'Red Indian music' is played before Geronimo's men come into view and attack the stagecoach. This is an example of the more general function that music is used for: to emphasize, anticipate and 'interpret' crucial individual narrative events.

At the same time the music is often used to mark the tempo of the events, typically by its own rhythm matching the movements on the screen. Sometimes there may be mickey mousing – total coordination of image and music. At others the synchronization may be less close, but the music will always influence the experiencing of the tempo and rhythm of the action as, for example, in the introduction to *The Big Sleep*, where a change of rhythm anticipates the shot of Carmen and makes it seem as if she is moving in time with the music when she appears on the screen.

There are also cases where the music is used to intensify the events. It creates its own arcs of tension that underline those of the narrative. Sometimes the music creates an experiencing of a dynamics and drive for which there is no basis in the images. Bernard Herrmann says that music can 'propel narrative swiftly forward, or slow it down'.[18] As discussed, his own 'hurry music' in *North by Northwest* is an excellent example of this.

Agents

Music is used to characterize the agents in the narrative with the aid of leitmotifs that are not only connected to the characters as formal signals but can also sometimes be understood as statements about them, their personal qualities, their role in the plot, etc.

When film composers talk about their own practice, they often point to the fact that the music does not only underline structures and meanings that are already present in the images and dialogue, but that it also adds meaning, especially that it can grant the spectators access to the characters' subjective feelings. In the previous chapters I have used the term focalization for the general narrative technique that makes the spectators experience the events filtered through the consciousness of one of the characters. Such subjective experiences can be presented visually, for example with the aid of point-of-view shots; or they can be presented auditively, for example with the aid of voice-over or by our hearing diegetic music from the 'point of hearing' of one of the characters. Non-diegetic music is, however, also able under certain circumstances to be 'linked to' the focalizer in such a way that in certain sections of the film it is not used to shape and structure the narrative as a whole, but functions instead in relation to one particular character's experiences and actions. When Marlowe early on in *The Big Sleep* tells Carmen that his name is 'Doghouse Reilly', his leitmotif is played on cor anglais and clarinets in a mocking, cackling way that pokes fun at the name. In this case the music does not provide the point of view of the 'film' about the scene; it expresses Marlowe's attitude to Carmen at this particular point in the narrative.

Narrators

When analysing film music we must distinguish between the diegetic music that occurs in the universe of the narrative and the non-diegetic music that functions as an external comment on the events. But, as I mentioned in connection with the analysis of *American Graffiti*, there is also a third category, music that not only comes from a position outside the diegesis but that is also outside the universe of the fiction itself: *extra-fictional music*.

The music played during the opening and closing credits of a film normally belongs to this last category. It forms a musical frame round the fiction and the narrative, and it functions as a musical guide. At the end of the overture we are led into the fiction; when the closing credits begin to scroll, we are led out once more. This music also often functions as a guiding commentary that prepares us for what kind of fiction we are about to see. But, as mentioned in the analysis of *American Graffiti*, the music we hear while we are 'inside' the universe of the narrative can in some cases have extra-fictional functions. In *Metropolis* the distorted, 'skewed' quotation from the 'Marseillaise' works in this way: an extra-fictional narrator uses the music to indicate that the revolt of the workers is 'skewed' or 'wrong'.

Emotional functions

Music structures the course of the film and supports key sections of the narrative. The third main function of the music is to shape 'emotions' and 'moods' in the narrative as a whole or within individual sections. The basis for this function is the basic musical expressions of emotions and moods that were established during the Baroque period and that came to play a central role in the stage music of the nineteenth century. Along with the musicians from the varieties and vaudeville theatres, such musical formulas moved over into the cinemas of the silent films, being eventually codified in cue sheets and anthologies of mood music. In a film music context the most important of these formulas have to do with emotional tension. In Erdmann and Becce's *Handbuch* (1927), most of the examples under the heading 'Dramatic expression' are variations on 'Tension' and 'Climax'; in the sound film, a whole arsenal of musical techniques are developed that indicate tension and excitement, plus conventions as to how one concludes and tones down.[19]

The most important emotional function of the music in mainstream films is to intensify or articulate moods already indicated with the aid of other effects: images, dialogue, camera angle, etc. When Marlowe and Vivian flee from Realito in *The Big Sleep* the music underlines the speed of the car and the nervousness of the characters; when Vivian declares her love to Marlowe the music changes character and becomes soulful and romantic. When Thornhill at the end of *North by Northwest* fights to save Eve Kendall, who is hanging out over an abyss, the music underlines what we see – that the situation is menacing.

In certain situations, however, the music can actively shape the mood of the narrative or, more precisely, indicate to the spectator how a particular scene is to be understood and experienced: in the final scene from *North by Northwest*, there is an almost imperceptible cut from the situation at the abyss to a shot of Thornhill lifting Eve into the upper bunk of a sleeping car. But before we discover the cut, a change in the nature of the music has already told us that the danger is over and that a happy ending is on its way.

A particular emotional function is the one that Claudia Gorbman refers to when she writes about music that underlines the spectacular nature of a scene, creating a feeling that what we are witnessing on the screen is 'larger than life'.

Leitmotifs and perceptual unity

In connection with the analysis of *American Graffiti* in chapter Eight I used the term *chameleon music* to describe the fact that a piece of music can have many different functions in the course of a film, and that one and the same piece of music at a particular point in the film can be described in a number of different ways.

A final discussion of the role of leitmotifs may clarify the tension between these various functions and descriptions. The use of leitmotifs was one of the most important musical effects in the silent film era and the Hollywood Golden Age. Their role was reduced in the period from the 1960s onwards but they have never completely disappeared. Even today it is extremely rare to hear film music that does not use leitmotifs in one form or other. The technique is well known in nineteenth-century music, especially from Richard Wagner's music drama *Das Ring des Niebelungen*. In his treatise *Oper und Drama*, published in 1852 when he had just begun to compose *Das Ring*, he writes that musical themes can be made to represent emotions and thoughts in a music-drama context, assuming that they become associated with them in an earlier phase of the narrative. The associations are established by the orchestra presenting the motif the first time its referent appears on the stage or is named in the libretto.[20]

In other words leitmotifs are based on recognition. At some point or other in the course of a performance we recognize a melodic phrase; we understand that it is a repetition of something we have heard previously and, because of the repetition, the phrase is transformed: it is no longer merely an *element* in an unfolding musical progression; it has become a *motif*, a compositional element that links the musical present to the past. But a leitmotif is more than a repeated musical formal element; it is a *sign* and can be used for representational purposes. As a motif it refers to earlier musical events; as a sign it refers to extra-musical relations. How a motif is transformed into a sign is the vital question in all discussions concerning the semantic and emotional functions of leitmotifs.

The filmic leitmotif

Most current conceptions of the leitmotif and its semantic and emotional functions in nineteenth-century music drama recur in the literature about film music. Here, writers have been much preoccupied by
the question of *semantic expansion*. It is usually claimed that each new
marking of the leitmotif will articulate and consolidate the meanings
that have been established earlier, but that the motif will furthermore
accumulate new meanings from the new contexts.

It is, however, often problematic to use the concept in connection
with film music. For example, Claudia Gorbman believes on the one
hand that the leitmotif technique is the answer to the eternal question
of music and representation: 'although music in itself is nonrepresen-
tational, the repeated occurrence of a musical motif in conjunction
with representational elements in a film (images, speech) can cause the
music to carry representational meaning as well,' she writes.[21] On the
other hand, she emphasizes that it can be difficult to state the precise
meaning of an actual motif. After a brief discussion of a classical
Hollywood composition – Alfred Newman's music for *All About Eve*
(Joseph L. Mankiewicz, 1950) – she writes: 'In many cases, the theme's
designation is so diffused that to call it a leitmotif contradicts Wagner's
intention.'[22] And this is in fact a common observation in both older and
more recent literature on the subject. Even though most writers stress
the key role of leitmotifs in film music, they normally tend to express
doubt about the use of the concept in general or in particular contexts.

Gorbman's remarks about the unclear theme from *All About Eve*
suggests indirectly that Wagner's intention was for the leitmotif to be
semantically narrow and precise. Hanns Eisler and Theodor W. Adorno
adopt the diametrically opposite position. It is normally assumed that
leitmotifs are easy to grasp, and that they can therefore serve the expli-
cation of the narrative, they write in *Composing for the Films*. This, however, is an illusion, for there are obvious differences between the
mythological universe of Wagner's dramas and the more modest, realistic ambitions of an average Hollywood film.[23] In Wagner the leitmotifs
not only characterize people, emotions or things; their purpose is 'the
endowment of the dramatic events with metaphysical significance'.[24]
Since mainstream films do not have room for metaphysical symbolics
of this type, there is, according to Eisler and Adorno, no reason at all
to use leitmotifs. In their opinion the leitmotifs are not only reduced to

musical signals in the context of the film, the signals themselves are superfluous. Claude Debussy once called the Wagnerian leitmotif a musical 'visiting card'. There is an echo of this in Eisler and Adorno's remark that the leitmotif in Hollywood is 'reduced to the level of a musical lackey, who announces his master with an important air even though the eminent personage is clearly recognizable to everyone'[25] – a formulation that can be read as an ironic reply to Max Steiner's remark that 'every character should have a theme'.[26]

Music and representation

Are the 'Marlowe' motif in *The Big Sleep*, the 'Luke Skywalker' motif in *Star Wars* and all the other recurring motifs that are used in film music leitmotifs in the original sense? No, Eisler and Adorno reply. Other authors have given less rigorous, more pragmatic answers. Most of them willingly admit that it is doubtful if the concept can really be used in connection with film music; even so, they usually end up claiming that one form of leitmotif technique or other is actually used in film music. The problem with such discussions is that the focus is always on the semantic, representational aspects of the leitmotif. The basic question is: what does this motif mean? Does it mean 'Marlowe'? Does it mean 'tension'? The more interesting question as to how musical themes are able to mean anything at all is normally answered by repeating the traditional point of view that the meaning of the leitmotifs is established by their being associated with a text or a dramatic situation in such a way that the musical phrase at a certain point in time becomes able to represent a given referent, even in situations where this referent is absent.

This simple musical semiotics may perhaps work for Wagner's vast dramas, but even there it is normally fairly difficult to determine the precise meaning of the leitmotifs. There is no agreement in the literature as to what his themes represent, and the terms used to identify them often vary considerably from writer to writer. It can be claimed that this ambiguity has to do with the way in which the motifs are used in the drama: since they occur in ever new contexts, they will gradually accumulate new strata of meaning and become ever more complex. But, as Carolyn Abbate has pointed out, it seems as if the exact opposite happens, i.e. that the motifs gradually lose their meaning. The motifs often 'tend to have specific associations on their first occurrences', but these associations 'cannot be held by the music, and become imprecise'. Wagner's motifs can at exceptional, solemn moments absorb meaning, 'but unless they are maintained in this semiotic state, they shed their meaning and become musical thoughts'.[27]

It would seem as if this is exactly what happens, although on a lesser scale, in the mainstream film. Take, for example, *The Big Sleep*: the motif that is so emphatically associated with Marlowe the first time it occurs does not remain in this 'semiotic state'. As the plot unfolds the 'Marlowe' meaning fades, and finally there is nothing left except a musical form – a simple, recognizable theme.

An alternative interpretation

When Max Steiner spoke of the Gypo leitmotif in *The Informer*, he said: 'A blind man could have sat in a theatre and known when Gypo was on the screen.' He added: 'Music aids audiences in keeping characters straight in their minds.' And he is of course right: musical motifs and themes can be used as semiotic signals and thereby help the blind man and untrained spectators to keep track of the characters in a film. Or they can assume the role of Eisler and Adorno's valet and announce, and in certain cases pave the way for, basic changes in the plot, etc. But leitmotifs are something else and more than such simple semantic labels. Their musical functions are just as important as, and in most cases more important than, semantic functions, which was actually what Wagner believed, too.

The literature about the use of leitmotifs in mainstream film music is normally based on Wagner's statements in *Oper und Drama*, which he wrote in 1850–1, but the fact is overlooked that he actually arrived at a considerably subtler understanding of the technique after having worked on *Das Ring* for more than 20 years. His most direct statement on the subject is *Über die Anwendung der Musik auf das Drama*, a text he wrote in 1879. Here he criticizes people for being so preoccupied with the 'dramatic significance and effect' of leitmotifs.[28] Instead, they ought to concentrate on 'how they are employed in the musical construction'.[29] His basic aim is to create *musical unity* in the music drama with the aid of 'main themes' that, in the same way as the themes in a symphonic work, are to 'confront each other, supplement each other, reform themselves, separate and be connected once more'.[30]

The main point that Wagner is making in the text from 1879 is, then, that leitmotifs have a *musical function*; they establish and maintain the inner-musical coherence of the work. Compared to the presentation in *Oper und Drama*, the question of musical representation is pushed far into the background, which does not mean that Wagner now conceives the leitmotif as being an ordinary 'motif'. At many points in the text he emphasizes that the music follows the development of the drama; it is determined by the action but at the same time is a coherent composition that is held together with the aid of 'a network of main themes that flow through the entire work'.[31] In short, the Wagnerian leitmotif is also, perhaps first and foremost, the solution to a formal problem, a way in which he articulates his never-ending melody with the aid of inner-musical structures. Repetitions and gradual transformations of short themes are an effective means of structuring and guaranteeing musical and perceptual unity in his large-scale work.

A construction of unity is also the main task of the music in the mainstream film, and it would seem that Wagner's own structural interpretation of the leitmotif is actually far better suited than the representational one if we are to describe how the recurring themes function in a filmic context. The task of film music is to transform a stream of fragmentary, visual and auditive information into a cohesive whole, into a perceptual *Gestalt*. Naturally, the music does not play the same predominant role in films as it does in Wagner's operas – in addition to which, film music is designed to be listened to in a different way than music in a Wagnerian opera house. But to be able to contribute to establishing perceptual unity, the music itself must be a unity, and to be able to function as an integral part of a film narrative, it must neither be ear-catchingly good or bad nor uninteresting or monotonous.[32] It must be formally flexible and at the same time easy to follow. In order to make narrative sense, it must make musical sense.

The leitmotif technique is an important solution to these requirements. Virtually all leitmotifs in film music have semantic functions; they refer to and characterize persons and relationships in the diegesis but, as the previous analyses of music for *Metropolis*, *The Big Sleep*, *North by Northwest* and *Star Wars* indicate, in most cases their 'content' is quite simple and, narratively speaking, pretty superfluous, except perhaps for Steiner's blind man at the cinema. In a musical composition that has been synchronized with the dialogue and the dramatic happenings on the screen, the leitmotifs function first and foremost as formal, inner-musical markers. They are recognizable pieces of music that are used to articulate the composition, to distinguish musical events from the musical background and to link series of musical cues to form an integrated whole, and thus divide and link the segments of the narrative.

Another type of ingredient

At the beginning of the previous chapter I cited Kurt Weill, who was of the opinion that music functions like cream on the dry cereal of the film. Miklós Rózsa uses a similar culinary metaphor: 'Music is still considered as the salt that makes cinema meat taste better, but not as an equal ingredient which could be used with maximum efficiency in the kitchens of cinema cooks.'[33] It is the film composer who is talking here; one can detect a certain bitterness at a lack of recognition. It is probably correct that internally in the film industry it has been common practice to consider music as something extra, as a taste supplement that can enhance the 'real' product. But, it must be objected, in practice music has been used throughout the entire history of the film on a par with lighting, camera work, editing, etc.

Music is not something that is added from the outside after 'the film' is complete. Music is an integral part of the film – an 'equal ingredient', but another type of ingredient: music is something other than lighting, camera work, editing. Music 'says' something other than the actors' dialogue and gestures. It is precisely this that is the point. The reason why music has been – and still is – used in films is of course that music is *something other than* language and gestures and narrative. It is because music is *music*.

References

Introduction

1 See, for example, Ernest Lindgren's discussion of the music of sound films in his *The Art of the Film: An Introduction to Film Appreciation* (London, 1948). A more recent example is Jan G. Swynnoe's book *The Best Years of British Film Music, 1936–1958* (Woodbridge, Suffolk, and Rochester, NY, 2002), which deals exclusively with this type of film music.

2 See, for example, the subtitle of Roy Prendergast's *Film Music: A Neglected Art* (New York, 1977). A quarter of a century after Prendergast's formulation of neglected film music, one can still come across this point of view; see the introduction to J. Buhler et al., eds, *Music and Cinema, Music/Culture* (Hanover, NH, 2000), p. 2; or the introduction to K. J. Donnelly, ed., *Film Music: Critical Approaches* (New York, 2001), p. 1.

3 Claudia Gorbman, *Unheard Melodies: Narrative Film Music* (London and Bloomington, IN, 1987), pp. 177–86.

4 Gorbman's bibliography covers the literature up to the mid-1980s. The survey in the first chapter of Martin Miller Marks's *Music and the Silent Film: Contexts and Case Studies, 1895–1924* (New York, 1997), takes one as far as 1990 ('The Literature: A Survey to 1990'), but is based on an article from 1979 and is fairly sketchy when it comes to the 1980s. On the other hand, Marks's account of the literature of the first decades is very thorough. Since the mid-1980s, Gillian B. Anderson has worked on several bibliographical projects; one of the most recent of these is G. B. Anderson and H. S. Wright, *Film Music Bibliography* (Hollywood, LA, 1995).

5 Academic publications from 1970 to 2002 are registered in Gillian B. Anderson and Ronald H. Sadoff's unpublished 'Music and Image Bibliography', accessible at http://www.filmint.nu/eng.html.

6 See, for example, the introductions to Buhler et al., *Music and Cinema*, and K. J. Donnelly, *Film Music*.

7 A single example may suffice: the composer Aaron Copland wrote a newspaper article in 1946 in which he briefly summarized his practical experiences in film music in five points ('Tip to Moviegoers: Take off Those Ear-Muffs', *New York Times*, 6 November 1949. The article is reprinted in Copland's book *What to Listen for in Music* (New York, 1957)). In Roy Prendergast's *Film Music*, from 1977, the entire chapter on the aesthetics of film music is a paraphrase of these five points (pp. 213–26). They re-emerge in 1988 as the framework of Noël Carroll's discussion of the emotional potential of film music in *Mystifying Movies: Fads and Fallacies in Contemporary Film Theory* (New York, 1988), p. 216, and Jeff Smith uses them in 1996 as a point of departure for a cognitivist critique of Gorbman's *Unheard Melodies* ('Unheard Melodies? A Critique of Psychoanalytic Theories of Film Music', in D. Bordwell and N. Carroll, eds, *Post-Theory: Reconstructing Film Studies* (Madison, WI, 1996), p. 231). During the journey from Copland to Smith, the theoretical framework gets considerably modified, while the description of the basic musical functions remains unchanged.

8 Béla Balázs, *Der sichtbare Mensch* (1924), quoted from Balázs, *Schriften zum Film*, vol. 1, *Der sichtbare Mensch, Kritiken und Aufsätze 1922–1926* (Munich, 1982).

1 Silent Films, Talking Music

1 'Accustomed though we are to speak of the films made before 1927 as "silent", the film has never been, in the full sense of the word, silent. From the very beginning, music was regarded as an indispensable accompaniment' (Ernest Lindgren, *The Art of the Film: An Introduction to Film Appreciation* (London, 1948), p. 141). 'Even in the primitive days sustained efforts were made to redeem the cinema from its inherent silence' (Siegfried Kracauer, *Theory of Film: The Redemption of Physical Reality* (New York, 1960), p. 133). 'The silents were never silent' (Kevin Brownlow, *The Parade's Gone By* (New York, 1968), p. 337). 'Since the earliest days of the movies there has really been no such thing as a "silent film". Music was always an integral part of the showing of moving pictures, inseparable from the visual, indispensable as accompaniment to films' (Charles Hofmann, *Sounds for Silents* (New York, 1970, p. [2]). 'Almost all "silent" films had some sort of sound accompaniment' (Geoffrey Nowell-Smith, ed., *The Oxford History of World Cinema* (Oxford and New York, 1996), p. 10). 'Although cinema before the introduction of synchronised sound in the late 1920s is called silent cinema, most people are aware that it was never fully silent. The dominant mode for music in the cinema from 1896 until the late 1920s involved the production of live music as an accompaniment to the film's projection'

(K. J. Donnelly, 'Introduction: The Hidden Heritage of Film Music: History and Scholarship', in K. J. Donnelly, ed., *Film Music: Critical Approaches* (New York, 2001), p. 6). Many more examples are quoted in Rick Altman, 'The Silence of the Silents', *Musical Quarterly*, LXXX/4 (1997), pp. 657f.

2 Martin Miller Marks, *Music and the Silent Film: Contexts and Case Studies, 1895–1924* (New York, 1997), p. 31.

3 Roger Manvell and John Huntley, *The Technique of Film Music* (London and New York, 1957), p. 17.

4 René Jeanne, *Cinéma 1900* (Paris, 1965), p. 8. Unless otherwise stated, quotations from non-English sources are translated by the author.

5 Ibid., p. 13.

6 Martin Miller Marks is still hawking this rumour around as late as 1997: Marks, *Music and the Silent Film*, p. 249, n. 31.

7 Gianni Rondolino, *Cinema e musica* (Torino, 1991), p. 14.

8 Manvell and Huntley, *The Technique of Film Music*, p. 17.

9 Ibid.

10 Rondolino, *Cinema e musica*, p. 15.

11 Marks, *Music and the Silent Film*, p. 31. See also the discussion in Altman, 'The Silence of the Silents', p. 659.

12 Rune Waldekranz, *Så föddes filmen. Ett massmediums uppkomst och genombrott* (Stockholm, 1976).

13 Ibid., p. 5.

14 Ibid., p. 290.

15 Ibid., p. 330.

16 Cecil M. Hepworth, *Came the Dawn: Memoirs of a Film Pioneer* (London, 1951), pp. 31f.

17 See Rick Altman, 'Nickelodeons and Popular Song', in Philip Brophy, ed., *Cinesonic: The World of Sound in Film* (North Ryde, New South Wales, 1999).

18 See Rick Altman, 'The Sound of Sound: A Brief History of the Reproduction of Sound in Movie Theaters', *Cineaste*, XXI/1–2 (1995).

19 Douglas Gomery, *The Hollywood Studio System* (Basingstoke, 1986), p. 19f.

20 Erno Rapée, *Encyclopaedia of Music for Pictures* (New York, 1925). The book was reprinted in 1970, and is quoted here from http://www.cinemaweb.com/silentfilm/bookshelf.

21 Hugo Riesenfeld, 'Music and Moving Pictures', *Annals of the American Academy of Political and Social Science* (November 1926), special issue on 'The Motion Picture in Its Economic and Social Aspects', quoted here from http://www.cinemaweb.com/silentfilm/bookshelf.

22 Siegfried Kracauer, 'Kult der Zerstreuung. Über die Berliner Lichtspielhäuser' (1926), in *Das Ornament der Masse* (Frankfurt, 1963), p. 312.

23 Rudolf Arnheim, *Film als Kunst* (Berlin, 1932), p. 304.

24 Kurt London, *Film Music: A Summary of the Characteristic Features of its History, Aesthetics, Technique, and Possible Developments* (London, 1936), p. 28.

25 See Altman, 'The Sound of Sound'.

26 English: *lecturer*; Spanish: *explicador*; French: *bonimenteur*; German: *Rezitator*.

27 See Nowell-Smith, *The Oxford History*, pp. 5 and 177.

28 Rapée, *Encyclopaedia*.

29 Rainer Fabich, *Musik für den Stummfilm. Analysierende Beschreibung originaler Filmkompositionen* (Frankfurt and New York, 1993), p. 17.

30 Rapée, *Encyclopaedia*.

31 It was the introduction of the sound film that precipitated the discussion about the various functions of sound. As far as music is concerned, a distinction was initially made between *source music* and *background music*, i.e. between music that has a visible 'source' on the screen, and music that accompanies the film and forms a kind of 'background' for the action. The distinction is imprecise: if there is a cut from a pianist to a picture of the audience, the sound of the piano naturally does not suddenly change into background music. Later, the terms *realistic/non-realistic* were used, for example, or *naturalistic/non-naturalistic*, in order to distinguish between music that is experienced as a 'natural' part of the reality the film is trying to construct and music that functions as an outside commentary or effect. In the early 1980s Hansjörg Pauli summarized these points of view and proposed as a simple rule of thumb that a distinction be made between 'picture-sound', i.e. sounds that the *characters in the film* themselves can hear, and 'alien sound', i.e. sounds that can only be heard by the *viewers* (Pauli, *Filmmusik. Stummfilm* (Stuttgart, 1981), pp. 14f.). This distinction is not very appropriate, either. It seems illogical for the sound of dripping taps in an empty house to be categorized as 'alien sounds' because none of the characters in the film hear it.

32 Kracauer, *Theory of Film*, p. 137.

33 A few examples: the pianist 'played anything he liked, and there was little or no connection between music and the film it accompanied' (London, *Film Music*, p. 40). 'At first, the music played bore no special relationship to the films; an accompaniment of any kind was sufficient' (Lindgren, *The Art of the Film*, p. 141). 'In those earliest days, the music bore little relationship to what people saw on the screen. Any type of music seemed appropriate and sufficient . . . More often the same music was heard for every picture and there was little differentiation between one film and another. It was as if the musicians never watched the screen!' (Hofmann, *Sounds for Silents*, p. [3]).

34 Marks, *Music and the Silent Film*, pp. 30–61.

35 See Waldekranz, *Så föddes filmen*, pp. 362f.

36 Marks, *Music and the Silent Film*, p. 61.

37 9 October 1909, see Hofmann, *Sounds for Silents*, p. [8].

38 Hofmann, *Sounds for Silents*, p. [9f]

39 Ibid., p. [8].

40 Altman, 'The Silence of the Silents', p. 690.

41 Quoted from Fabich, *Musik für den Stummfilm*, p. 20. It ought to be added that not everybody was equally enthusiastic about combining music and images. For an avant-garde oriented film writer such as Béla Balázs, it seemed almost comical or embarrassing when the cinema orchestra played a funeral march at a funeral scene: 'For the music arouses different conceptions that those of the film only disturb when they get too close to each other.' (Béla Balázs, *Der sichtbare Mensch* [1924], in Balázs, *Schriften zum Film*, vol. 1 (Munich, 1982), p. 130).

42 Marks, *Music and the Silent Film*, p. 29.

43 That Saint-Saëns' film music has this more complex nature is expressed by the fact that he converted it into an orchestral suite that was included among his works as *L'Assassinat du Duc de Guise*, op. 128.

44 Tom Gunning, 'The Cinema of Attraction: Early Film, Its Spectator and the Avant-Garde', *Wide Angle*, VIII/3–4 (1986).

45 Arnheim, *Film als Kunst*, p. 304.

46 Emilie Altenloh, *Zur Soziologie des Kino; Die Kino-Unternehmung und die Sozialen Schichten ihrer Besucher, Schriften zur Soziologie der Kultur*, vol. 3 (Jena, 1914), p. 62.

47 See Kracauer, *Theory of Film*, p. 134.

48 Altenloh, *Zur Soziologie des Kino*, p. 20.

49 Marks, *Music and the Silent Film*, p. 10.

50 Rapée, *Encyclopaedia*.

51 Hofmann, *Sounds for Silents*, p. [14].

52 Reprinted in Hofmann, *Sounds for Silents*, p. [15f.].

53 Ibid., p. [15].

54 Martin Miller Marks, 'Music and the Silent Film', in Nowell-Smith, *The Oxford History*, p. 186.

55 See Kevin Brownlow, 'Silent Films – What Was the Right Speed?', *Sight & Sound* (Summer 1980).

56 John Stepan Zamecnik, *Sam Fox Moving Picture Music* (Cleveland, 1913). A copy of the booklet, plus versions of the individual numbers played by the pianist Rodney Sauer are accessible at: www.mont-alto.com. Here too is full biographical information about Zamecnik.

57 Erno Rapée, *Motion Picture Moods for Pianists and Organists. A Rapid-Reference Collection of Selected Pieces. Arranged by Erno Rapée. Adapted to Fifty-Two Moods and Situations* (New York, 1924).

58 Rapée, *Encyclopaedia.*

59 Hans Erdmann and Guiseppe Becce, *Allgemeines Handbuch der Film-Musik I–II* (Berlin and Leipzig, 1927).

60 For a thorough account of Erdmann and Becce's *Handbuch*, see Pauli, *Filmmusik*, pp. 143ff.

61 See Riesenfeld, 'Music and Moving Pictures'.

62 Ibid.

63 London, *Film Music*, p. 69.

2 Analysing Film Music

1 David Bordwell and Kristin Thompson, *Film Art: An Introduction* (Boston, MA, 2004), p. 415.

2 Ibid., p. 61.

3 Ibid., p. 64.

4 Ibid., p. 51.

5 See Bordwell and Thompson's discussion of 'symptomatic meaning', ibid., p. 57.

6 Nicholas Cook, *A Guide to Musical Analysis* (Oxford, 1994), p. 2.

7 Ibid.

8 Ibid., p. 215.

9 Ibid., p. 219.

10 The same criticism could just as well be levelled against certain modern music analysts, ibid., p. 2.

11 Bordwell and Thompson, *Film Art*, p. 51.

12 The problem of continuation plays a central role both for Heinrich Schenker, founder of modern musical analysis, and a modern music theorist such as Leonard B. Meyer, as well as for the film analysts Bordwell and Thompson, whose discussion of film form is based partly on Meyer's book *Emotion and Meaning in Music* (1956) (Chicago, 1961).

13 The example comes from Peter Kivy, who is referring to the American musicologist David P. Schroeder, in Kivy, *Introduction to a Philosophy of Music* (Oxford, 2002), p. 147.

14 Alan Walker, *A Study in Musical Analysis* (London, 1962), p. 23, here quoted from Cook, *Guide to Musical Analysis*, p. 230.

15 Ibid.

16 Ibid.

17 Siegfried Kracauer, *Theory of Film; the Redemption of Physical Reality* (New York, 1960), p. 139.

18 Ibid.

19 Bordwell and Thompson, *Film Art*, p. 416.

20 Ibid., p. 61.

21 William Drabkin, 'Motif', in John Tyrell and Stanley Sadie, eds, *The New Grove Dictionary of Music and Musicians* (London and New York, 2001).

The following presentation is based on Drabkin's articles on 'motif',
'theme', 'melody' and 'sequence' in that work.
22 Drabkin, 'Motif'.
23 Ibid.
24 See William Drabkin, 'Sequence', in John Tyrell and Stanley Sadie, eds,
The New Grove Dictionary of Music and Musicians (London and New York,
2001).

3 Back to the Future: *Metropolis*, 1927

1 See Willy Haas: 'Metropolis', *Film-Kurier*, 9 (11 January 1927), reprinted
in Anton Kaes, Martin Jay and Edward Dimendberg, eds, *The Weimar
Republic Sourcebook* (Berkeley, CA, 1994).
2 Initially, three negatives were produced consisting of virtually identical
versions. The first was used to produce the distribution copies to the
German-language market; the second was sent to Paramount, which at
that time had the American rights to UFA films; the distribution copies
to other countries were produced by UFA's export department and were
taken from the third negative. For a detailed account of the entire story
of *Metropolis*, see Enno Patalas, *Metropolis in / aus Trümmern. Eine
Filmgeschichte* (Berlin, 2001) and Martin Koerber, 'Notizen zur Überlieferung des Films Metropolis', in Wolfgang Jacobsen and Werner
Sudendorf, eds, *Metropolis. Ein filmisches Laboratorium der modernen
Architektur* (Stuttgart, 2000).
3 Koerber, 'Notizen zur Überlieferung des Films Metropolis', p. 214.
4 Patalas, *Metropolis in / aus Trümmern*, p. 10.
5 The most debated example in recent times is the tinted *Metropolis* version
from 1984 with music by Georgio Moroder performed by various
pop- and rock-singers, including Freddie Mercury, Pat Benatar and
Bonnie Tyler.
6 Huppertz's manuscripts are kept at Filmmuseum Berlin – Deutsche
Kinematek. Copies of the printed piano selections can be found at
Staatsbibliothek zu Berlin – Preussischer Kulturbesitz and Deutsches
Filminstitut in Frankfurt am Main, see Koerber, 'Notizen zur Überlieferung des Films Metropolis', p. 221.
7 See Rainer Fabich: 'Fallbeispiel: Metropolis. Anmerkungen zu Gottfried
Huppertz's Stummfilmkomposition (1927)', *Musikforum*, 94 (2001).
8 Fritz Lang, *Metropolis* (Munich, 2003).
9 I am relying here on Enno Patalas's account of the reconstruction in
Metropolis in / aus Trümmern. Patalas's text is the result of a collaboration
with Rainer Fabich, who wrote a number of useful comments about
the music. There are certain discrepancies between the DVD version of
the film and the reconstruction described by Patalas. A second problem is that the reconstruction is of course considerably shorter than

the film Huppertz once wrote music for. In other words, the music has had to be adapted and shortened in order to fit the reconstruction. But it is not evident from the DVD notes how this was done, or who actually did it.

10　In the following I am referring to Gottfried Huppertz, *Metropolis. Musik zum Gleichnamigen Ufa-Film. Op. 29*, Berlin: Universum-Film A.G., i.e. the printed piano part in Staatsbibliothek zu Berlin.

11　Contemporary machine music was, ironically, inspired by Stravinsky's *Le Sacre du Printemps*, which alludes to a primitive heathen ritual.

12　The waltz and the foxtrot were recorded in 1927 on two gramophone records (VOX 8386/7) along with a couple of the most important themes of the film and an introduction, read by Fritz Lang, see Fabich, 'Fallbeispiel'.

13　On the DVD Huppertz's music has been considerably shortened in relation to the original score, which reveals that large sections of the scene at the stadium have been lost.

14　When one now sees silent films on video or DVD, the boundary between the two spaces is erased. The music is no longer in an 'external' relation to the film, it has become an integral part of the projection and does not differ, technically speaking, from normal sound film music.

15　See the discussion of narrative *focalization* in chapter Eight.

16　Arnold Whittall, 'Leitmotif', in John Tyrell and Stanley Sadie, eds, *The New Grove Dictionary of Music and Musicians* (London and New York, 2001).

17　See Fabich, 'Fallbeispiel'.

18　See Kathryn Kalinak, *Settling the Score: Music and the Classical Hollywood Film* (Madison, WI, 1992), pp. 48f.

19　Ibid., p. 54.

20　Erno Rapée, *Encyclopaedia of Music for Pictures* (New York, 1925), quoted from http://www.cinemaweb.com/silentfilm/bookshelf.

21　Ibid.

22　Bert Vipond in *Moving Picture News* (19 March 1910), quoted from Kalinak, *Settling the Score*, p. 64.

23　Edith Lang and George West, *Musical Accompaniment of Moving Pictures* (Boston, MA, 1910), quoted from Kalinak, *Settling the Score*, p. 64.

24　Rapée, *Encyclopaedia*.

4　Musical Meanings

1　Antonio Vivaldi, *Concerto for violin and orchestra*, RV 335.

2　It is, in particular, Roland Barthes who has set his stamp on the modern semiotic understanding of the phenomenon, see his 'Éléments de sémiologie', *Communications*, 4 (1964). The point of departure for this understanding is a work by the Danish linguist Louis Hjelmslev, *Omkring*

Sprogteoriens Grundlæggelse [Prolegomena to a Theory of Language] (Copenhagen, 1943). Concerning Barthes' reading of Hjelmslev, see Peter Larsen, 'Barthes hos frisøren. Billedbeskrivelsens problem. Eller: Den forsvundne signifiant' [Barthes at the Barber's. The Problem of Image Description. Or: The Vanished Signifier], *Livstegn*, 8 (1991).

3   The American music theorist Leonard B. Meyer uses the concept 'connotation' in a more comprehensive way. He defines it as 'associations which are shared in common by a group of individuals within the culture'. Musical connotations in this sense are any result of associations between 'some aspect of the musical organisation and extramusical experience', see Meyer, *Emotion and Meaning in Music* (1956) (Chicago, 1961), p. 258.

4   Enno Patalas and Rainer Fabich, *Metropolis in/aus Trümmern. Eine Filmgeschichte* (Berlin, 2001), p. 27.

5   One example is Stravinsky's famous remark that 'music is, by its very nature, essentially powerless to *express* anything at all, whether a feeling, an attitude of mind, a psychological mood, a phenomenon of nature, etc.', *An Autobiography* (New York, 1958), p. 53.

6   Peter Kivy, *Introduction to a Philosophy of Music* (Oxford, 2002), p. 31.

7   Jean-Jacques Nattiez, *Music and Discourse: Toward a Semiology of Music* (Princeton, NJ, 1990), p. 123.

8   John Sloboda, *The Musical Mind: The Cognitive Psychology of Music* (Oxford, 1985), pp. 60f. Sloboda is writing about Deryck Cooke's book *The Language of Music* (New York and London, 1959).

9   Sloboda, *The Musical Mind*, p. 61.

10   Meyer, *Emotion and Meaning in Music*, pp. 267f.

11   Sloboda, *The Musical Mind*, p. 62.

12   Kivy, *Introduction to a Philosophy of Music*, p. 40.

13   Ibid., p. 47.

14   Ibid., p. 48.

5   Enter the Sound Film

1   Kurt London, *Film Music: A Summary of the Characteristic Features of Its History, Aesthetics, Technique, and Possible Developments* (London, 1936), p. 29.

2   Early in the century American Lee De Forest developed an amplifier based on vacuum tubes. This came into common use in the early 1920s and played an important role in the transition from acoustic to electronic sound recording and playing.

3   Hugo Riesenfeld, 'Music and Moving Pictures', *Annals of the American Academy of Political and Social Science* (November 1926), special issue on 'The Motion Picture in its Economic and Social Aspects', quoted here from http://www.cinemaweb.com/silentfilm/bookshelf.

4 See Rick Altman: 'The Sound of Sound: A Brief History of the Reproduction of Sound in Movie Theaters', *Cineaste*, XXI/1–2 (1995).

5 Sergei Eisenstein et al., 'A Statement' (5 August 1928, Leningrad), in Eisenstein, *Film Form* (New York, 1949), p. 258.

6 Ibid.

7 Ibid.

8 Rudolf Arnheim, *Film als Kunst* (Berlin, 1932), p. 282. Arnheim's argument anticipates Roland Barthes' remarks concerning the phenomenon *relais* – that the dialogue and pictures of the film convey different information by working 'in relay', see Barthes, 'Rhétorique de l'image', *Communications*, 4 (1964).

9 Arnheim, *Film als Kunst*, p. 286.

10 Vsevolod Pudovkin, *Film Technique and Film Acting* (New York, 1960), pp. 310f.

11 Ibid., p. 310.

12 Ibid., p. 311.

13 Ibid., p. 313.

14 Siegfried Kracauer, *Theory of Film; the Redemption of Physical Reality* (New York, 1960), p. 142.

15 Ibid., p. 137.

16 Ibid., p. 138.

17 Todd Berliner and Philip Furia, 'The Sounds of Silence: Songs in Hollywood Films since the 1960s', *Style*, 36 (2002), p. 20.

18 See Kathryn Kalinak, *Settling the Score: Music and the Classical Hollywood Film* (Madison, WI, 1992), p. 69.

19 Ibid.

20 Douglas Gomery, *The Hollywood Studio System* (Basingstoke, 1986).

21 Ibid., p. 8.

22 David Bordwell, Kristin Thompson and Janet Staiger, *The Classical Hollywood Cinema: Film Style and Mode of Production to 1960* (New York, 1986).

23 See Steiner's autobiographical sketch in Tony Thomas, *Film Score: The View from the Podium* (South Brunswick, NJ, 1979), pp. 75ff.

24 Kalinak, *Settling the Score*, p. 70f.

25 Quoted in Thomas, *Film Score. The View from the Podium*, p. 77.

26 Kalinak, *Settling the Score*, p. 71.

27 Thomas, *Film Score: The View from the Podium*, p. 77.

28 Kalinak, *Settling the Score*, p. 71.

29 See Kracauer's discussion in *Theory of Film*, pp. 139ff.

30 This is in a note for internal use at Warner Brothers, dated 11 March 1940, cited here from David Neumeyer, 'Introduction', in James Buhler, Caryl Flinn and David Neumeyer, *Music and Cinema* (Hanover, NH, 2000), p. 15.

31 Thomas, *Film Score: The View from the Podium*, p. 78.

32 See Steiner's account of the technique, cited in Thomas, *Film Score: The View from the Podium*, pp. 70f. Other conductors used visual markers to control the tempo during recording.

33 See Hugo Riesenfeld, 'Music and Moving Pictures'.

34 See Aaron Copland, *What to Listen for in Music* (New York, 1957), p. 261.

35 Bernard Herrmann, 'Score for a Film: Composer Tells of Problems Solved in Music for "Citizen Kane"', *New York Times* (25 May 1941).

36 Quoted from Thomas, *Film Score. The View from the Podium*, p. 88. The statement derives from an article Korngold wrote for José Rodríguez, ed., *Music and Dance in California* (Hollywood, 1940).

37 Initially some of the more low-budget productions were equipped with music composed for earlier films. This practice was forbidden in 1944.

38 Jan G. Swynnoe, *The Best Years of British Film Music, 1936–1958* (Woodbridge, Suffolk, and Rochester, NY, 2002), p. 21.

39 Ibid., p. 24.

40 Christopher Palmer, 'Film Music', in Stanley Sadie, ed., *The New Grove Dictionary of Music and Musicians* (London, 1980).

41 Royal S. Brown, *Overtones and Undertones: Reading Film Music* (Berkeley, CA, 1994), p. 96.

42 Kalinak, *Settling the Score*, p. 100.

43 Graham Bruce, *Bernard Herrmann, Film Music and Narrative* (Ann Arbor, MI, 1985), p. 7.

44 Brown, *Overtones and Undertones*, p. 96.

45 Roy M. Prendergast, *Film Music: A Neglected Art: A Critical Study of Music in Films* (New York, 1977), pp. 39f.

46 Kalinak, *Settling the Score*, p. 101.

6 Film Music from the Golden Age: *The Big Sleep*, 1946

1 Concerning Chandler's novel, see Peter Larsen, *Det private Øje. Et essay om billeder og blikke* [The Private Eye. An Essay on Images and Gazes] (Copenhagen, 1991).

2 The story of how the script evolved can be read in, for example, Al Clark, *Raymond Chandler in Hollywood* (London and New York, 1983).

3 A popular anecdote relates that Hawks himself lost the overall view and was unable to work out who the perpetrator of one of the many murders in the film was. He sent a telegram to Chandler, who replied that he didn't have the faintest idea.

4 The following analysis of the opening of the film is based on my article 'Betydningsstrømme. Musik og moderne billedfiktioner' [Currents of Meaning. Music and Modern Visual Fictions], *Studia Musicologica Norvegica* (1988).

5 Quotations in the following are from Steiner's conductor's score, in the

USC Warner Brothers Archives, School of Cinema-Television, University of Southern California, Los Angeles.

6 Stan Kenton plays the piano in this scene.

7 This is also reflected in the fact that from quite early on, two categories of music were introduced at the Oscar awards, one for 'Best Music, Original Score' and one for 'Best Music, Original Song'.

8 See the discussion about 'narrators' and narrative information in chapter Eight.

9 For a closer analysis of the role of leitmotifs in films of the Golden Age, see Peter Larsen, 'From Bayreuth to Los Angeles: Classical Hollywood Music and the Leitmotif Technique', in Dominique Nasta and Didier Huvelle, eds, *Le son en perspective. Nouvelles recherches / New Perspectives in Sound Studies* (Brussels, 2004). The topic is also discussed in the present book in chapter Ten.

10 K. J. Donnelly, 'Introduction. The Hidden Heritage of Film Music: History and Scholarship', in K. J. Donnelly, ed., *Film Music: Critical Approaches* (New York, 2001), pp. 9f.

11 Steiner in the *New York Times* (29 September 1935), quoted here from Roy M. Prendergast, *Film Music: A Neglected Art: A Critical Study of Music in Films* (New York, 1977), p. 42.

12 Ibid.

13 The following analysis is based on my article 'The Sound of Images: Classical Hollywood and Music', in Ib Bondebjerg, ed., *Moving Image, Culture, And the Mind* (Luton, 2000).

14 Raymond Bellour, 'L'Évidence et le code' (1973), quoted from his collection of articles *L'Analyse du film* (Paris, 1980). An English translation, 'The Obvious and the Code', is in *Screen*, xv/4 (Winter 1974–5).

15 Ibid., p. 123.

16 Ibid.

17 Ibid., p. 130.

18 David Bordwell, *Narration in the Fiction Film* (London, 1985), p. 158.

19 Bellour, 'L'Évidence et le code', p. 130.

20 Edward Branigan, *Narrative Comprehension and Film* (London, 1992), p. 140.

21 Ibid., p. 141.

22 This correction would probably have appealed to Bellour, considering his sense of repetitions and symmetries. In the analysis, he places special emphasis, for various reasons, on shot 7, which he considers the turning point of the segment. When shot 13 is added, shot 7 becomes the numerical centre of the segment. In addition, the first and last shot of the segment now mirror each other both formally and in terms of content. The segment starts with an overview of a car driving to the right, and ends with a car driving to the left and stopping. The first

image is one of departure, the last one of arrival.

7 Other Ways: *North by Northwest*, 1959

1 Robert Wise's *Executive Suite* (1954) is an example of this.
2 See Graham Bruce, *Bernard Herrmann: Film Music and Narrative* (Ann Arbor, MI, 1985), p. 29.
3 For details of Herrmann's biography, see Bruce, *Bernard Herrmann*. This book gives a solid, broad introduction into Herrmann's musical universe, written from a musicologist's point of view and with many analytical examples. There is also a fairly large section on Herrmann, in particular on his music for Hitchcock's films, in Royal S. Brown, *Overtones and Undertones: Reading Film Music* (Berkeley, CA, 1994). David Cooper has written an interesting, highly detailed account of one of Herrmann's scores in *Bernard Herrmann's* Vertigo: *A Film Score Handbook* (Westport, CT, 2001).
4 Herrmann in Ted Gilling, 'The Colour of Music', *Sight and Sound* (Winter, 1971–2), p. 36.
5 Quotations in the following are from Herrmann's unpaged score of *North by Northwest*. The manuscript is in the Department of Special Collections, Donald C. Davidson Library, University of California, Santa Barbara.
6 Brown, *Overtones and Undertones*, p. 158.
7 It can be seen from the score than Herrmann had originally planned the overture to merge into a new piece of music, *The Street*, which was to accompany the introductory presentation of Thornhill. *The Street* is used several times later in the film as 'hurry' music.
8 *It's a Most Unusual Day* was written by Harold Adamson and Jimmy McHugh for one of MGM's earlier productions (*A Date With Judy*, directed by Richard Thorpe, 1948).
9 Brown, *Overtones and Undertones*, pp. 291f.
10 Bernard Herrmann, 'Score for a Film: Composer Tells of Problems Solved in Music for "Citizen Kane"', *New York Times* (25 May 1941).
11 Gilling, 'The Colour of Music', p. 37.
12 Herrmann, 'Score for a Film'.
13 Gilling, 'The Colour of Music', p. 37.
14 According to Brown, *Overtones and Undertones*, p. 69, the 'muzak' is in fact a piece of film music written by André Previn for the MGM comedy *Designing Woman* (Vincente Minnelli, 1957).
15 Bruce, *Bernard Herrmann*, p. 120.
16 Herrmann, 'Score for a Film'.
17 Bernard Herrmann, 'Music in Films – a Rebuttal', *New York Times* (24 June 1945). The article is a polemical answer to one about film music by the conductor Erich Leinsdorf.

18 Ibid.

19 Gilling, 'The Colour of Music', p. 37. In expressing this view Herrmann was completely in agreement with Alfred Hitchcock, who as far back as the first years of sound films stated that music makes it possible 'to express the unspoken'. Hitchcock named as an example a scene between two characters talking politely and quietly to each other while an emotional crisis is in the offing. Neither by means of gestures nor dialogue do they betray the atmosphere of this situation. 'But I think you could get at the underlying idea with the right background music.' See Stephen Watts, 'Alfred Hitchcock on Music in Films', *Cinema Quarterly*, 2 (1933–4), p. 82.

20 *Focalization* means that the narrative universe is conveyed via one of the fictive character's subjective experiences, see Edward Branigan, *Narrative Comprehension and Film* (London and New York, 1992), p. 100f.

21 See Branigan, *Narrative Comprehension and Film*, p. 103. Internal focalizations can vary in depth. A *point of view* shot is relatively 'superficial', but a shot that portrays subjective hallucinations is an example of *deep* internal focalization. An example of deep internal focalization occurs later in the film when Thornhill drives a car while drunk. The blurred, double-exposed pictures of oncoming traffic show not only *what* he sees through the windscreen but also *how* he subjectively sees and experiences it.

22 Cooper, *Bernard Herrmann's* Vertigo, p. 30.

23 Bruce, *Bernard Herrmann*, p. 215.

8 Striking a New Note: Film Music after the Golden Age

1   The story of the conflict is related in Donald Spoto, *The Dark Side of Genius: The Life of Alfred Hitchcock* (Boston, MA, 1983), p. 491.

2   See Kathryn Kalinak, *Settling the Score: Music and the Classical Hollywood Film* (Madison, WI, 1992), pp. 179ff. See also Jon Burlingame, 'Scores to Swoon Over', *Variety* (6 March 2001).

3   The following presentation is based on Roy M. Prendergast, *Film Music: A Neglected Art: A Critical Study of Music in Films* (New York, 1977), pp. 98 ff., and Royal S. Brown, 'Modern Film Music', in Geoffrey Nowell-Smith, *The Oxford History of World Cinema* (Oxford and New York, 1996).

4   Kalinak, *Settling the Score*, p. 185ff.

5   Prendergast, *Film Music: A Neglected Art*, p. 102.

6   This account of Simon's work on the music for *The Graduate* is based on Patrick Humphries, *The Boy in the Bubble: A Biography of Paul Simon* (London, 1988).

7   At a point early on in the film, where Ben, very much against his will, has to demonstrate his new diving equipment for some friends of his

parents, we see the world as he sees it, through the swimming mask, and the only thing we hear on the soundtrack is his heavy breathing. We not only see the world from his *point of view*; we also hear it from his *point of hearing*.

8　Todd Berliner and Philip Furia, 'The Sounds of Silence: Songs in Hollywood Films Since the 1960s', *Style*, 36 (2002), pp. 24ff.

9　Edward Branigan, *Narrative Comprehension and Film* (London and New York, 1992), p. 103.

10　Berliner and Furia, 'The Sounds of Silence', p. 25.

11　Ibid., pp. 25f.

12　Ibid., p. 26.

13　The film takes place in the late 1960s but has no reference to the Vietnam War or to the widespread student protests of the time at Berkeley.

14　Berliner and Furia, 'The Sounds of Silence', p. 25.

15　On the relationship between *syuzhet* and *fabula*, see David Bordwell, *Narration in the Fiction Film* (London, 1985), pp. 48ff.

16　There are many examples of ingenious use of first person narrators in the history of film. In Billy Wilder's *Sunset Boulevard* (1950), for example, the whole story is told as a flashback by a dead man.

17　Branigan, *Narrative Comprehension and Film*, p. 95.

18　See Rick Altman, 'Nickelodeons and Popular Song', in Philip Brophy, ed., *Cinesonic: The World of Sound in Film* (North Ryde, New South Wales, 1999).

19　Branigan, *Narrative Comprehension and Film*, p. 166.

20　Subjective sound also appears elsewhere in the film. For example, one hears Terry's violently beating heart when he suddenly discovers that Debby has left him and he is alone in a deserted area outside town.

21　For information about the music, see Michael Matessino's notes for the CD release *Star Wars: Episode IV – A New Hope (1977)*, special edition reissue of the complete score, RCA Victor (1997).

22　*Twentieth Century Fox*'s logo is accompanied by Alfred Newman's fanfare, composed in the 1930s and later re-recorded in stereophonic sound in 1954 for use in the company's Cinemascope films. The fanfare had more or less been consigned to oblivion until Lucas reintroduced it in *Star Wars* to underline the link back to an age when films were 'larger than life'.

23　John Williams, *John Williams Anthology* (Secaucus, NJ, 1991).

24　See the interview at http://www.filmscoremonthly.com/features/williams.asp.

25　Claudia Gorbman, *Unheard Melodies: Narrative Film Music* (London and Bloomington, IN, 1987), p. 68.

26　Paul M. Sammon presents facts and anecdotes about the shooting of

Blade Runner in *Future Noir:The Making of Blade Runner* (London, 1996). The book has, however, only sparse information about Vangelis's work on the music.

27 Nowell-Smith, *Oxford History*, p. 464.

9 Necessity or Possibility? The Psychology of Film Music

1 Charles Hofmann, *Sounds for Silents* (New York, 1970), unpaged. The quotation originally comes from the periodical *Modern Music* (1940).

2 Ibid. The quotation comes from *Harper's Bazaar* (1946).

3 Ernest Lindgren, *The Art of the Film: An Introduction to Film Appreciation* (London, 1948), p. 144.

4 Kurt London, *Film Music* (London, 1936), p. 27.

5 Ibid., pp. 27f.

6 See Rick Altman, 'The Silence of the Silents', *Musical Quarterly*, LXXX/4 (1997), pp. 669f. and the references in note 73 of the article.

7 See, for example, Jean Châteauvert and André Gaudreault, 'The Noise of Spectators, or the Spectator as Additive to the Spectacle', in Richard Abel and Rick Altman, eds, *The Sounds of Early Cinema* (Bloomington, IN, 2001).

8 Siegfried Kracauer, *Theory of Film: The Redemption of Physical Reality* (New York, 1960), p. 133.

9 Plays have always been accompanied by sounds, Leonid Sabaneev writes in one of the first theoretical texts about film music, *Music for the Films* (1935) (New York, 1978), p. 18. Ernst Lindgren develops this argument, and says that 'music has been a servant art throughout greater part of its history', *The Art of the Film*, p. 147.

10 Martin Miller Marks, 'Music and the Silent Film', in Geoffrey Nowell-Smith, ed., *The Oxford History of World Cinema* (Oxford and New York, 1996), p. 183. See also Marks, *Music and the Silent Film: Contexts and Case Studies, 1895–1924* (New York, 1997), p. 28.

11 Claudia Gorbman, *Unheard Melodies: Narrative Film Music* (Bloomington, IN, 1987), p. 36.

12 Ibid.

13 Maxim Gorky, 'Drei Texte über den Cinématographe Lumière' (1896), *Kintop*, 4 (1995), p. 13.

14 Ibid., pp. 13f.

15 Ibid., p. 18.

16 *Der sichtbare Mensch* (1924), in Béla Balázs, *Schriften zum Film*, vol. 1 (Munich, 1982), p. 130.

17 Béla Balázs, 'Kinomusik', *Der Tag* (30 May 1924), cited from *Schriften zum Film*, vol. 1, p. 294.

18 London, *Film Music*, p. 33.

19 Kracauer, *Theory of Film*, pp. 134f.

20 Lindgren, *The Art of the Film*, p. 144.

21 London, *Film Music*, p. 35

22 Kracauer, *Theory of Film*, p. 135.

23 Béla Balázs, 'Kinomusik', cited from *Schriften zum Film*, vol. 1, p. 294.

24 Hanns Eisler and Theodor W. Adorno, *Composing for the Films* (London, 1947), p. 75. This and the following quotations from the book are checked against the German version: Theodor W. Adorno's *Komposition für den Film*, published in his *Gesammelte Schriften*, vol. 15 (Frankfurt, 1997), pp. 74–6. The American version is normally registered under Hanns Eisler's name, but most of the text was written by Adorno, including the section quoted from here and in the following, see the editorial remark in *Gesammelte Schriften*, p. 406.

25 Noël Carroll, *Mystifying Movies: Fads and Fallacies in Contemporary Film Theory* (New York, 1988), pp. 214ff.

26 Ibid., p. 215.

27 Carroll's target is Philip Rosen's article 'Adorno and Film Music: Theoretical Notes on Composing for the Films', *Yale French Studies*, 60 (1980).

28 The time paradox is the central theme in Roland Barthes' discussion of the photograph in his early article 'Rhétorique de l'image', *Communications*, 4 (1964), as well as in the book *La chambre claire. Note sur la photographie* (Paris, 1980).

29 Kathryn Kalinak, *Settling the Score: Music and the Classical Hollywood Film* (Madison, WI, 1992), p. 44.

30 Ibid. Bernard Herrmann believes that the conserved music of the sound film can also give similar experiences of togetherness. Music is 'the communicating link between the screen and the audience, reaching out and enveloping all into one single experience', 'Music in Films – A Rebuttal', *New York Times* (24 June 1945).

31 London, *Film Music*, p. 34.

32 Ibid., p. 35.

33 Ibid., pp. 59f.

34 Ibid., p. 60.

35 Kracauer, *Theory of Film*, p. 135.

36 Eisler and Adorno, *Composing for the Films*, p. 76; the translation is adjusted with reference to *Komposition*, pp. 75f.

37 Carroll, *Mystifying Movies*, p. 216.

38 Ibid.

39 London, *Film Music*, p. 37.

40 Ibid., pp. 37f.

41 Tony Thomas, *Film Score: The View from the Podium* (South Brunswick, NJ, 1979), p. 81. The remark comes from Max Steiner's uncompleted and unpublished autobiography.

42 Ibid., p. 35. The remark comes from one of Rózsa's lectures on film music.

43 Ibid., p. 81.

44 Ibid.

45 Ibid., p. 35.

46 Christian Metz, 'Histoire/discourse. Note sur deux voyeurismes', in Julia Kristeva et al., eds, *Langue, Discours, Société – Pour Émile Benveniste* (Paris, 1975), p. 301, English translation in Metz, *Psychoanalysis and Cinema: The Imaginary Signifier* (London, 1982), p. 91.

47 Émile Benveniste, 'Les relations de temps dans le verbe français', in his *Problèmes de linguistique générale* (Paris, 1966), pp. 237ff.

48 Bernard Herrmann would not have shared this enthusiasm for modernistic revealing of the illusion. In an interview in the early 1970s he said: 'Until recently, it was never considered a virtue for an audience to be aware of the cunning of the camera and the art of making seamless cuts. It was like a wonderful piece of tailoring; you didn't see the stitches. But today all that has changed, and any mechanical or technical failure or ineptitude is considered "with it".' See Ted Gilling, 'The Colour of Music', *Sight and Sound* (Winter, 1971–2), p. 37.

49 Gorbman, *Unheard Melodies*, p. 55.

50 Ibid., p. 58.

51 Ibid.

52 Ibid., p. 62.

53 Ibid., p. 63.

54 Ibid., p. 68.

55 Ibid., p. 69.

56 For a detailed cognitivist critique of Gorbman's book, see Jeff Smith, 'Unheard Melodies? A Critique of Psychoanalytic Theories of Film Music', in David Bordwell and Nöel Carroll, eds, *Post-Theory: Reconstructing Film Studies* (Madison, WI, 1996).

57 Gorbman, *Unheard Melodies*, p. 59.

58 Ibid., p. 68.

59 Ibid., p. 64.

60 Jeff Smith, 'Unheard Melodies? A Critique of Psychoanalytic Theories of Film Music', pp. 235f.

61 Edward Branigan, *Narrative Comprehension and Film* (London and New York, 1992), pp. 14f.

62 See Peter Larsen, 'Erindringsbilleder. Fra det indre filmmuseum', [Recollected images. From the inner film museum] in Eva Jørholt, ed., *Ind i Filmen* (Copenhagen, 1995).

63 Branigan, *Narrative Comprehension and Film*, p. 15.

10 Musical Functions

1 See chapter Three.
2 See chapter One.
3 Siegfried Kracauer, *Theory of Film: The Redemption of Physical Reality* (New York, 1960), p. 137.
4 Ernst H. Gombrich, *Art and Illusion: A Study in the Psychology of Pictorial Representation* (1960) (London, 1986), pp. 313f.
5 Ibid., p. 313.
6 Ibid., p. 314. Seen from this point of view, synaesthetic equivalents can be described as a result of a metaphorization, see George Lakoff and Mark Johnson, *Metaphors We Live By* (Chicago, 1980). The metaphor is the form of 'analogizing' understanding that is generated when experiences from one area are used to understand and describe another. The transfer process is based on analogies between structural relations in the two fields. If, for example, one says that 'time is money', one is apparently pointing at a simple similarity between the two elements, but the process also involves a further mapping of a whole series of relations from the time-field onto the money-field: if time is money, time must also be valuable, in short supply, etc.
7 Gombrich, *Art and Illusion*, p. 313.
8 Composer Alex North had actually written a completely different sort of music for this sequence and for the film as a whole, but Kubrick decided to use his temp track instead: Johann Strauss's 'An der schönen, blauen Donau' as well as works by Aram Khachaturian, György Ligeti (*Atmosphères*, *Lux Aeterna*, *Adventures* and *Requiem*) and Richard Strauss (the introduction to *Also sprach Zarathustra*).
9 Montague told the story in his book *Film World* (1964). It is cited here from George Burt, *The Art of Film Music: Special Emphasis on Hugo Friedhofer, Alex North, David Raksin, Leonard Rosenman* (Boston, 1994), p. 33.
10 For a more detailed discussion of the relationship between music and narrative, see Peter Larsen, 'Den fraværende fortælling' [The absent narrative], *Spring*, 21 (2003).
11 Charles Rosen, *The Classical Style: Haydn, Mozart, Beethoven*, 2nd edn (London and Boston, 1976), p. 120.
12 Ibid.
13 See *inter alia* sections of Susan McClary, *Feminine Endings: Music, Gender, and Sexuality* (Minneapolis, 1991), and sections of Lawrence Kramer, *Classical Music and Postmodern Knowledge* (Berkeley, CA, 1995). See also various critical objections in Jean-Jacques Nattiez, *Music and Discourse: Toward a Semiology of Music* (Princeton, NJ, 1990), in Nattiez, 'Can One Speak of Narrativity in Music?', *Journal of the Royal Musical Association*, CXV/2 (1990) and in Carolyn Abbate, *Unsung Voices: Opera and Musical*

Narrative in the Nineteenth Century (Princeton, NJ, 1991). I discuss a number of the main points of view in 'Den fraværende fortælling', using as my point of departure the article by Anthony Newcomb, 'Schumann and Late Eighteenth-Century Narrative Strategies', *Nineteenth-Century Music*, XI/2 (1987).

14 John A. Sloboda, *The Musical Mind: The Cognitive Psychology of Music* (Oxford, 1985), p. 59.

15 Ibid., p. 20.

16 Nattiez, 'Can One Speak of Narrativity in Music', p. 249.

17 See Ted Gilling, 'The Colour of Music', *Sight and Sound* (Winter 1971–2), p. 37.

18 Bernard Herrmann, 'Music in Films – a Rebuttal', *New York Times* (24 June 1945).

19 See Kathryn Kalinak, *Settling the Score: Music and the Classical Hollywood Film* (Madison WI, 1992), p. 93.

20 Richard Wagner, *Oper und Drama* (1851) (Berlin, 1914).

21 Claudia Gorbman, *Unheard Melodies: Narrative Film Music* (London and Bloomington, IN, 1987), p. 27.

22 Ibid., p. 29.

23 Hanns Eisler and Theodor W. Adorno, *Composing for the Films* (London, 1947), p. 5.

24 Ibid.

25 Ibid., p. 6.

26 *New York Times* (29 September 1935), cited here from Roy M. Prendergast, *Film Music: A Neglected Art; A Critical Study of Music in Films* (New York, 1977), p. 42.

27 Abbate, *Unsung Voices*, p. 168.

28 Richard Wagner, 'Über die Anwendung der Musik auf das Drama' (1879), in *Gesammelte Schriften und Dichtungen*, Bd. 10 (Berlin, 1913), p. 185.

29 Ibid., p. 186.

30 Ibid., p. 185.

31 Ibid.

32 This is what Max Steiner meant by his remark that 'the music can be so bad, or so good, it distracts and takes away from the action', see Tony Thomas, *Film Score: The View from the Podium* (South Brunswick, NJ, 1979), p. 81.

33 Ibid., p. 35.

Bibliography

Abbate, Carolyn, *Unsung Voices: Opera and Musical Narrative in the Nineteenth Century* (Princeton, NJ, 1991)

Abel, Richard and Rick Altman, eds, *The Sounds of Early Cinema* (Bloomington, IN, 2001)

Adorno, Theodor W., *Komposition für den Film. Gesammelte Schriften Vol. 15* (Frankfurt, 1997)

Altenloh, Emilie, *Zur Soziologie des Kino. Die Kino-Unternehmung und die sozialen Schichten ihrer Besucher* (Jena, 1914)

Altman, Rick, 'The Sound of Sound: A Brief History of the Reproduction of Sound in Movie Theaters', in *Cineaste* 21,1-2 (1995)

—, 'The Silence of the Silents', *Musical Quarterly*, LXXX/4 (1997)

—, 'Nickelodeons and Popular Song', in P. Brophy, ed., *Cinesonic: The World of Sound in Film* (North Ryde, New South Wales, 1999)

Anderson, Gillian B. and Ronald H. Sadoff, 'Music and Image Bibliography', http://www.filmint.nu/eng.html

Anderson, Gillian B. and H. Stephen Wright, *Film Music Bibliography* (Hollywood, 1995)

Arnheim, Rudolf, *Film als Kunst* (Berlin, 1932)

Balázs, Béla, *Schriften zum Film. Bd. 1. Der sichtbare Mensch. Kritiken und Aufsätze 1922-1926* (München, 1982)

Barthes, Roland, 'Rhétorique de l'image', *Communications*, 4 (1964)

—, 'Éléments de sémiologie', *Communications*, 4 (1964)

—, *La Chambre claire. Note sur la photographie* (Paris, 1980)

Bellour, Raymond, 'L'évidence et le code', in D. Noguez, ed., *Cinéma: Théorie, Lectures* (Paris, 1973)

—, 'The Obvious and the Code', *Screen*, XV/4 (1974)

Benveniste, Émile, *Problèmes de linguistique générale* (Paris, 1966)

Berliner, Todd and Philip Furia, 'The Sounds of Silence: Songs in Hollywood Films since the 1960s', *Style*, XXXVI/1 (2002)

Bordwell, David, *Narration in the Fiction Film* (London, 1985)

Bordwell, David and Noël Carroll, eds, *Post-Theory: Reconstructing Film Studies*

(Madison, WI, 1996)

Bordwell, David and Kristin Thompson, *Film Art: An Introduction* (Boston, 2004)

Bordwell, David, et al., *The Classical Hollywood Cinema: Film Style and Mode of Production to 1960* (New York, 1985)

Branigan, Edward, *Narrative Comprehension and Film* (London and New York, 1992)

Brophy, Philip, ed., *Cinesonic: The World of Sound in Film* (North Ryde, New South Wales, 1999)

Brown, Royal S., *Overtones and Undertones: Reading Film Music* (Berkeley, CA, 1994)

—, 'Modern Film Music', in G. Nowell-Smith, ed., *The Oxford History of World Cinema* (Oxford and New York, 1996)

Brownlow, Kevin, *The Parade's Gone By* (New York, 1968)

—, 'Silent Films. What Was the Right Speed?' *Sight & Sound* (Summer 1980)

Bruce, Graham, *Bernard Herrmann: Film Music and Narrative* (Ann Arbor, MI, 1985)

Buhler, James et al., eds, *Music and Cinema* (Hanover, NH, 2000)

Burlingame, Jon, 'Scores to Swoon Over', *Variety* (6 March 2001)

Burt, George, *The Art of Film Music: Special Emphasis on Hugo Friedhofer, Alex North, David Raksin, Leonard Rosenman* (Boston, 1994)

Carroll, Noël, *Mystifying Movies: Fads and Fallacies in Contemporary Film Theory* (New York, 1988)

Châteauvert, Jean and André Gaudreault, 'The Noise of Spectators, or the Spectator as Additive to the Spectacle', in R. Abel and R. Altman, eds, *The Sounds of Early Cinema* (Bloomington, IN, 2001)

Clark, Al, *Raymond Chandler in Hollywood* (London and New York, 1983)

Cook, Nicholas, *A Guide to Musical Analysis* (Oxford, 1994)

Cooke, Deryck, *The Language of Music* (London and New York, 1959)

Cooper, David, *Bernard Herrmann's* Vertigo: *A Film Score Handbook* (Westport, CT, 2001)

Copland, Aaron, *What to Listen for in Music* (New York, 1957)

Donnelly, K. J., 'Introduction: The Hidden Heritage of Film Music: History and Scholarship', in K. J. Donnelly, ed., *Film Music: Critical Approaches* (New York, 2001)

—, ed., *Film Music: Critical Approaches* (New York, 2001)

Drabkin, William, 'Motif', 'Theme', 'Melody' and 'Sequence', in J. Tyrell and S. Sadie, eds, *The New Grove Dictionary of Music and Musicians* (London and New York, 2001)

Eisenstein, Sergei, *Film Form* (New York, 1949)

Eisler, Hanns and Theodor W. Adorno, *Composing for the Films* (London, 1947)

Erdmann, Hans and Giuseppe Becce, *Allgemeines Handbuch der Film-Musik I–II* (Berlin and Leipzig, 1927)

Fabich, Rainer, *Musik für den Stummfilm. Analysierende Beschreibung originaler Filmkompositionen* (Frankfurt and New York, 1993)

—, 'Fallbeispiel: Metropolis, Anmerkungen Zu Gottfried Huppertz's Stummfilmkomposition (1927)', *Musikforum*, 94 (2001)

Gilling, Ted, 'The Colour of Music', *Sight and Sound* (Winter 1971)

Gombrich, E. H., *Art and Illusion: A Study in the Psychology of Pictorial Representation* (1960) (London, 1986)

Gomery, Douglas, *The Hollywood Studio System* (Basingstoke, 1986)

Gorbman, Claudia, *Unheard Melodies: Narrative Film Music* (London and Bloomington, IN, 1987)

Gorky, Maksim, 'Drei Texte über den Cinématographe Lumière (1896)', *Kintop*, 4 (1995)

Gunning, Tom, 'The Cinema of Attraction: Early Film, It's Spectator and the Avant-Garde', *Wide Angle*, VIII/3–4 (1986)

Hepworth, Cecil M., *Came the Dawn: Memoirs of a Film Pioneer* (London, 1951)

Herrmann, Bernard, 'Score for a Film: Composer Tells of Problems Solved in Music for "Citizen Kane"', *New York Times* (25 May 1941)

—, 'Music in Films: A Rebuttal', *New York Times* (24 June 1945)

Hjelmslev, Louis, *Omkring Sprogteoriens Grundlæggelse* (Copenhagen, 1943)

Hofmann, Charles, *Sounds for Silents* (New York, 1970)

Humphries, Patrick, *The Boy in the Bubble: A Biography of Paul Simon* (London, 1988)

Huppertz, Gottfried, *Metropolis: Musik zum Gleichnamigen Ufa-Film. Op. 29* (Berlin, [1927])

Jacobsen, Wolfgang and Werner Sudendorf, eds, *Metropolis. Ein filmisches Laboratorium der modernen Architektur [Metropolis: A Cinematic Laboratory for Modern Architecture]* (Stuttgart, 2000)

Jeanne, René, *Cinéma 1900* (Paris, 1965)

Kaes, Anton et al., eds, *The Weimar Republic Sourcebook* (Berkeley, CA, 1994)

Kalinak, Kathryn, *Settling the Score: Music and the Classical Hollywood Film* (Madison, WI, 1992)

Kivy, Peter, *Introduction to a Philosophy of Music* (Oxford, 2002)

Koerber, Martin, 'Notizen zur Überlieferung des Films Metropolis', in W. Jacobsen and W. Sudendorf, eds, *Metropolis. Ein Filmisches Laboratorium der modernen Architektur [Metropolis: A Cinematic Laboratory for Modern Architecture]* (Stuttgart, 2000)

Kracauer, Siegfried, 'Kult der Zerstreuung. Über die Berliner Lichtspielhäuser' (1926), reprinted in Kracauer, *Das Ornament der Masse* (Frankfurt, 1963)

—, *Theory of Film. The Redemption of Physical Reality* (New York, 1960)

Kramer, Lawrence, *Classical Music and Postmodern Knowledge* (Berkeley, CA, 1995)

Lakoff, George and Mark Johnson, *Metaphors We Live By* (Chicago, 1980)

Lang, Fritz, *Metropolis* (1927), Friedrich-Wilhelm-Murnau-Stiftung and Transit-Film, 2002

Larsen, Peter, 'Betydningsstrømme. Musik og moderne billedfiktioner' [Currents of Meaning: Music and Modern Visual Fictions], *Studia Musicologica Norvegica* (1988)

—, *Det private øje. Et essay om billeder og blikke [The Private Eye: An Essay on Images and Gazes]* (Copenhagen, 1991)

—, 'Barthes hos frisøren. Billedbeskrivelsens problem. Eller: Den forsvundne signifiant' [Barthes at the Barber's. The Problem of Image Description. Or: The Absent Signifier], *Livstegn*, VIII/1 (1991)

—, 'Erindringsbilleder. Fra det indre filmmuseum' [Recollected images. From the inner film museum], in E. Jørholt, ed., *Ind i filmen* (Copenhagen, 1995)

—, 'The Sound of Images: Classical Hollywood and Music', in I. Bondebjerg, ed., *Moving Images, Culture and the Mind* (Luton, 2000)

—, 'Den fraværende fortælling' [The Absent Narrative], *Spring*, 21 (2003)

—, 'From Bayreuth to Los Angeles: Classical Hollywood Music and the Leitmotif Technique', in D. Nasta and D. Huvelle, eds, *Le Son en perspective: Nouvelles recherches [New Perspectives in Sound Studies]* (Brussels, 2004)

Lindgren, Ernest, *The Art of the Film: An Introduction to Film Appreciation* (London, 1948)

London, Kurt, *Film Music: A Summary of the Characteristic Features of Its History, Aesthetics, Technique, and Possible Developments* (London, 1936)

Manvell, Roger and John Huntley, *The Technique of Film Music* (London and New York, 1957)

Marks, Martin Miller, 'Music and the Silent Film', in G. Nowell-Smith, ed., *The Oxford History of World Cinema* (Oxford and New York, 1996)

—, *Music and the Silent Film: Contexts and Case Studies, 1895–1924* (New York, 1997)

McClary, Susan, *Feminine Endings: Music, Gender, and Sexuality* (Minneapolis, 1991)

Metz, Christian, 'Histoire/Discourse. Note sur deux Voyeurismes', in N. Ruwet et al., eds, *Langue, Discours, Societé. Pour Émile Benveniste* (Paris, 1975)

—, *Psychoanalysis and Cinema: The Imaginary Signifier* (London, 1982)

Meyer, Leonard B., *Emotion and Meaning in Music* (1956) (Chicago, 1961)

Nattiez, Jean-Jacques, 'Can One Speak of Narrativity in Music?' *Journal of the Royal Musical Association*, CXV/2 (1990)

—, *Music and Discourse: Toward a Semiology of Music* (Princeton, NJ, 1990)

Neumeyer, David, 'Introduction', in J. Buhler et al., eds, *Music and Cinema, Music/Culture,* (Hanover, NH, 2000)

Newcomb, Anthony, 'Schumann and Late Eighteenth-Century Narrative

Strategies', *Nineteenth-Century Music*, XI/2 (1987)

Nowell-Smith, Geoffrey, ed., *The Oxford History of World Cinema* (Oxford and New York, 1996)

Palmer, Christopher, 'Film Music', in S. Sadie, ed., *The New Grove Dictionary of Music and Musicians* (London, 1980)

Patalas, Enno and Rainer Fabich, *Metropolis in/Aus Trümmern. Eine Filmgeschichte* (Berlin, 2001)

Pauli, Hansjörg, *Filmmusik: Stummfilm* (Stuttgart, 1981)

Prendergast, Roy M., *Film Music: A Neglected Art: A Critical Study of Music in Films* (New York, 1977)

Pudovkin, Vsevolod I., *Film Technique and Film Acting* (New York, 1960)

Rapée, Erno, *Motion Picture Moods for Pianists and Organists. A Rapid-Reference Collection of Selected Pieces. Arranged by Erno Rapée. Adapted to Fifty-Two Moods and Situations* (New York, 1924)

—, *Encyclopaedia of Music for Pictures* (New York, 1925)

Riesenfeld, Hugo, 'Music and Motion Pictures', *Annals of the American Academy of Political and Social Science* (November 1926)

Rodríguez, José, *Music and Dance in California* (Hollywood, 1940)

Rondolino, Gianni, *Cinema e musica. Breve storia della musica cinematografica* (Torino, 1991)

Rosen, Charles, *The Classical Style: Haydn, Mozart, Beethoven*, 2nd edn (London and Boston, 1976)

Rosen, Philip, 'Adorno and Film Music: Theoretical Notes on Composing for the Films', *Yale French Studies*, 60 (1980)

Sabaneev, Leonid L., *Music for the Films* (1935) (New York, 1978)

Sadie, Stanley, ed., *The New Grove Dictionary of Music and Musicians* (London, 1980)

Sammon, Paul M., *Future Noir: The Making of Blade Runner* (London, 1996)

Sloboda, John A., *The Musical Mind: The Cognitive Psychology of Music* (Oxford, 1985)

Smith, Jeff, 'Unheard Melodies? A Critique of Psychoanalytic Theories of Film Music', in D. Bordwell and N. Carroll, eds, *Post-Theory: Reconstructing Film Studies* (Madison, WI, 1996)

Spoto, Donald and Alfred Hitchcock, *The Dark Side of Genius: The Life of Alfred Hitchcock* (Boston, 1983)

Stravinsky, Igor, *An Autobiography* (New York, 1958)

Swynnoe, Jan G., *The Best Years of British Film Music, 1936–1958* (Woodbridge, Suffolk and Rochester, NY, 2002)

Thomas, Tony, *Film Score: The View from the Podium* (South Brunswick, NJ, 1979)

Tyrell, John and Stanley Sadie, eds, *The New Grove Dictionary of Music and Musicians* (London and New York, 2001)

Wagner, Richard, *Oper und Drama* (1851) (Berlin, 1914)

—, 'Über die Anwendung der Musikk auf das Drama' (1879), in W. Golther, ed., *Gesammelte Schriften und Dichtungen in zehn Bänden*, vol. 10 (Berlin, 1913)

Waldekranz, Rune, *Så föddes filmen. Ett massmediums uppkomst och genombrott* (Stockholm, 1976)

Watts, Stephen, 'Alfred Hitchcock on Music in Films', *Cinema Quarterly*, 2, (1933)

Whittall, Arnold, 'Leitmotif', in J. Tyrell and S. Sadie, eds, *The New Grove Dictionary of Music and Musicians* (London and New York, 2001)

Williams, John, *John Williams Anthology* (Secaucus, NJ, 1991)

Zamecnik, John Stepan, *Sam Fox Moving Picture Music* (Cleveland, 1913)

Acknowledgements

I started working on this book during a stay as visiting scholar at University of California, Santa Barbara (UCSB). I would like to thank Janet Walker for inviting me to UCSB, and my friends, Edward Branigan and Melinda Szaloky, for their hospitality and generous support during that memorable autumn of 2003. I also wish to acknowledge the Faculty of Social Sciences at the University of Bergen, the L. Meltzer Foundation, and the Norwegian Critics' Association for financial support and grants that made my stay at UCSB possible. Thanks also to the Department of Information Science and Media Studies at the University of Bergen for supporting the English translation of the book.

The staff at the Department of Special Collections, Donald C. Davidson Library, UCSB, helped me during my stay in Santa Barbara. When I returned to Norway I got invaluable professional assistance from Gertie Tjore at the Social Sciences Library at the University of Bergen. Gunnar Iversen at the Norwegian University of Science and Technology (NTNU) in Trondheim read the manuscript in its final stages and suggested several improvements, and Hege Gundersen at Universitetsforlaget was an inspiring and efficient editor. I thank them all for advice and assistance. Finally, very special thanks to Karin – as always.

Index